WE GOTTA GET OUT OF THIS PLACE

Also by Gerri Hirshey

Nowhere to Run: The Story of Soul Music

WE GOTTA GET OUT OF THIS PLACE

The True, Tough Story of Women in Rock

GERRI HIRSHEY

Atlantic Monthly Press
New York

Portions of this book have appeared in different form in *Rolling Stone*, *GQ*, *Vanity Fair*, *Mirabella*
and *Details*.

Due to limitations of space, permissions appear on page 278 and constitute a continuation of
the copyright page.

Published simultaneously in Canada
Printed in the United States of America

FIRST EDITION

Library of Congress Cataloging-in-Publication Data

Hirshey, Gerri.
    We gotta get out of this place : the true, tough story of women in rock/Gerri Hirshey.
        p. cm.
    ISBN 0-87113-788-7
    1. Rock music—History and criticism. 2. Rock musicians—biography. 3. Women
rock musicians—Biography. I. Title.
    ML3534 .H58 2000
    781.66'09—dc21   00-056923

DESIGN BY LAURA HAMMOND HOUGH

Atlantic Monthly Press
841 Broadway
New York, NY 10003

01 02 03 04   10 9 8 7 6 5 4 3 2 1

In memory of my father

- Dinah Washington "the Bessie Smith Songbook" '58
  Song: "What a difference a day makes"

- Sarah Vaughan & Earl Fatha Hines in 1944 w/
  Billy Eckstine

○ Ruth Brown "Wild, Wild Young Men" Atlantic 1955

Erykah Badu
Les Nubians
Me'shell Ndegeocello

CONTENTS

WE GOTTA
GET OUT OF
THIS PLACE

INTRODUCTION

L et's go deep, deep to the thudding heart of rock and roll with a peek into Janis Joplin's cavernous purse. She's groping far within it, grumbling that in this mad life of hers, things are always getting lost. Last week she left a wallet "with a grand in it" at a bar.

"Just can't seem to hold on to anything, man."

And now she can't find her lighter. She's at the outset of a summer tour in 1970, a few months before her death. The Beatles' "Let It Be" has gone gold, Woodstock is a newly minted legend and *The New York Times* has declared that rock music is "the most popular of creative arts today." For Janis, it's just another gig, another dash to the airport and Flight 729 to . . . where? Is it Louisville tonight? She's dumped her bag's contents on the limo floor, frantic for the lighter. Seated beside her is *Rolling Stone* reporter David Dalton, who will soon find himself documenting her short life in a book. "Awesome" is the best he can come up with to sum the funky efficiencies of Ms. Joplin's road kit:

. . . two movie stubs, a pack of cigarettes, an antique cigarette holder, several motel and hotel room keys, a box of Kleenex, a compact and various makeup cases (in addition to a bunch of eyebrow pencils held together with a rubber band), an address book, dozens of bits of paper, business cards, matchbox covers with phone numbers written in near-legible barroom scrawls, guitar picks, a bottle of Southern Comfort (empty), a hip flask, an opened package of complimentary macadamia nuts

from American Airlines, cassettes of Johnny Cash and Otis Redding, gum,
sunglasses, credit cards, aspirin, assorted pens and writing pad, a corkscrew, an
alarm clock, a copy of Time *and two hefty books—Nancy Milford's biography of*
Zelda Fitzgerald and Thomas Wolfe's Look Homeward, Angel.

That bag is its own blues, loosing a tumble of human need and inspired
effrontery onto the vibrating carpet. It's all there: the useless numbered keys
of a transient life, the momentary chemical balms, the scribbled missed connections, the uplifting doses of carry-on Art. Our Pearl can wrap herself in
Wolfe's lapidary prose or Otis's achy, gut-bucket soul—whatever it takes to
get her through this jet fuel–scented night and a string of sixty more.

Over half a century before Janis instructed her stylist to stitch up a
handbag "big enough for a book and a bottle," blueswoman Ma Rainey—
known in her day as "the ugliest woman in show business"—barnstormed
the south in a scrappy wooden trailer lashed to a car. Ma (born Gertrude
Pridgett) left home with the Rabbit Foot Minstrels in 1904 and stayed on
the road for thirty years. And she had her own essentials: frying pans and
feather boas. But with a few adjustments, I doubt she would have taken
issue with the breadth and efficacy of Janis's road kit.

I'd add Dramamine and my kids' photos; after nearly two decades
of writing about rock music, I've encountered plenty of turbulence—that
of the skies and highways, and of the soul. The road can be an especially
bumpy ride for a sex conditioned by human history to stay at home. As
a rheumy-throated bass player once scolded me when I flipped open a
notebook long past the midnight hour, "Honey, your line of work ain't
natural."

The life it occasions may yield strange moments, but I'd argue that the
compulsion to make and appreciate music—be it heaven-sent or hell-bent—
is surely natural to those anchored to the earth with a solid matched pair of
X chromosomes. The serious weirdness comes with taking it on the road.
Unlike artists and writers, most musicians have to haul their work—and themselves—directly to market. For women, this was long considered unseemly.
Or a temporary dementia. After all the miles Ma Rainey logged, despite her
well-earned billing as "Mother of the Blues" (and de facto matriarch of rock
and roll), her hometown obituary still listed her as "housekeeper."

That won't happen to the last decade's most famous cradle and stadium rocker, Madonna. Or Ani DiFranco, or Mary J. Blige. So much has

changed: Women own their own copyrights, record companies and destinies. They keep their publishing rights and run their own labels. And they are finding new ways to keep the domestic hearth burning—and stay on the move. Roadies lug amps and playpens; rock nannies gently fit waxen earplugs into the ears of toddlers who get to stay up late and watch Mama stomp, bop and wail in the pretty blue lights. But despite the social, economic and technical changes, there are constants as well, particularly if you're considering, as we are here, the strong and supple voices of women. Talk to them, immerse yourself in their biographies, memoirs, interviews and songs and you'll hear a couple of insistent refrains:

Gotta sing.
Gotta go.

Compulsion and propulsion have long powered the American mystery train. Popular music—that mongrel form—is nomadic by its nature, mindful of the old but always ravenous for the new. If you want to roll with it, you've got to get out there.

Rock biographies are teeming with truants, male and female. But it's surprising, if you're one to collect their stories, to measure the determination and difficulties of female escapees. Over and over in interviews, I've heard variants on the same mantra: I just had to get out of the house. Joan Jett's first all-girl band may have been messed up and misbegotten, but they got the name right: the Runaways. Writing in 1967, when an entire generation seemed bent on escape, Lennon and McCartney nicely caught the turmoil of a girl slipping out her bedroom door and on her way in "She's Leaving Home." The Animals, that macho Brit group, may have sung it best: "We Gotta Get Out of This Place."

The departures have brought everything from terror to triumph to relief: Here's Big Mama Thornton pulling out of sultry, segregated Montgomery—at last!—with Sonny Green's Hot Harlem Review. Dust rims the wide dark-lashed eyes of teenage Maybelle Carter, eight months pregnant with her first baby, as she jounces down a rough mountain road from the hamlet of Maces Spring, Virginia, in her brother-in-law's battered Model A Ford to the Carter Family's first studio session with the Victor Talking Machine Company. *Gotta go . . .*

Visit the tatty, funk-trapped-in-amber recording studio at the Motown museum and you can still trace the crescent punctures of enameled teen fingernails in the acoustic tiles. Picture Diana, Mary and Flo, nervous as fillies on Derby day, climbing into the cramped, wheezy bus that would take the Supremes and the very first Motortown Revue out of the Detroit projects and into pop/cult history. Consider the dark, uncertain L.A. nights of habitual runaway Rickie Lee Jones, camped out beneath the Hollywood sign. And another refugee in sunny San Diego: It's Jewel, cosseting a Tupperware container full of Alaskan dirt—a bit of home—as she bivouacs in her van and sings nights at the Innerchange coffeehouse, wondering aloud at 18, "Who will save your soul?"

Here are teenage Lauryn Hill and her two male co-conspirators, leaping off the bus outside Howard University, gleeful rap guerillas slapping every surface on their route backstage with stickers: THE FUGEES. That's for refugees—so breathless, so hungry to be heard that after a show, Lauryn sometimes faints with fatigue. Stumbling back to the bus, she is woozy with all this high-impact wandering. The driver swings open the big hissing bus door and says—again:

Come on now, baby—we got to go.

Whether you get yourself to the next gig by Concorde, bus or outstretched thumb, there is one reliable mode of transport for the soul. And it, too, is fired by a form of internal combustion. *Gotta sing.* The compulsion to do so is its own life force. I felt its astonishing power at close range one night when Aretha Franklin was "just foolin' around" in a cramped Manhattan rehearsal hall. I was a few feet away when Lady Soul let fly with a few idly scatted notes that all but pinned me to my chair; it was like some neural tsunami, a moment that left me with gooseflesh and an indelible flash of human connectedness.

Later, as Aretha talked about vocal transport in her soft, shy speaking voice, she explained rather matter-of-factly that singing "does get me out of myself. I guess you could say I do a lot of traveling with my voice."

Too often—and especially now—the industry tends to measure that journey in units sold, tickets bought and the frequency of website hits. And so it is that during the final two years of the twentieth century, headlines trumpeted the "news" that after all these long, strange trips, Women Have Arrived. Noted a *New York Times* story, "not since the glory days of Motown in the late sixties have so many female voices been at the top of the pop charts, forcing onetime giants like R.E.M., U2 and Aerosmith to sag far below them." "Galapalooza!" shrieked a *Time* cover in 1997 about that summer's all-female Lilith Fair. Since mood-swing muses like Fiona Apple and Alanis Morissette first glared miserably, haughtily from the MTV screen, platoons of A&R types have been deployed to comb college coffeehouses for the next singer/songwriter with a womb, a navel ring and a rucksack full of anorectic angst.

Please, please, please. As the following mystery tour will show, women have been at the heart of rock and roll all along. They were wailing loudest at rock's beginning—in its blues and gospel pre-history. At times, they've sung stalwart background, had their sounds and their looks arranged by the whims and marketing plans of men. And at other moments—like now—they've held forth in the boldest of spotlights. They've been worshipped and objectified, overdubbed and underpaid. Like their male counterparts, they can be deeply passionate or chillingly calculated. But they have never—ever—been quiet.

When it comes to defending my own life in rock and roll, things aren't quite as clear-cut. I am a small, quiet woman with a deep-seated aversion to public displays. Along the road, trying to suss the passions and compulsions that have impelled these artists' lives, I've had to look hard at my own motivations. Just what kept me out there in the dark with a laminated pass bouncing off my collarbone? The music, surely. The stories. But at bottom, it had to be a certain restlessness of my own. I liked accumulating the psychic sky miles; I enjoyed the bracing contrapunto between the minor blue notes of lone travel and the baroque conversational fugues that lay at journey's end. It has been, I realize now, my own modest adventure. I, too, had to get out of the house. And I have collected some swell yarns of my own:

"Mommy, tell us the story about you and Michael Jackson and the boa constrictor."

I suppose it's fun to have a dash of celebrity spice to toss into the family lore. But when our first child was born, I resolved to quit the rock

and roll life for good. By 1990, I had spent more than a decade enduring—
and enjoying—the rigors of that adjectivally overwrought ghetto, rock journalism. The logistics had become impossible—two A.M. feedings and
midnight-hour interviews are mutually exclusive work modes. Worse,
though I'd always written on other matters—even held a "straight" job at
the *Washington Post*—I was feeling uncomfortably typecast. Like the music
itself, rock journalism has long been considered a bastard form, patch-
worked, jerry-rigged, opinionated and occasionally brilliant. But somehow
not serious. Like sportswriting, it's a fan's genre and an indulgent one. It's
easy to get lazy.

It's easier still to burn out. The long-haul rock journalist must have
a high tolerance for absurd and unexpected dislocations of place, and of
mind. When the phone rang at three a.m. and it was James Brown, confid-
ing that he had just invented "nuclear soul," I could discuss it gravely
("Gerri, we got to get in touch with world leaders!"), roll over and go
straight back to sleep. Get in deep enough, and very strange days can seem
quite normal. I hadn't thought much about this until one night, accompanying the majestically turbaned Screamin' Jay Hawkins to a Manhattan
gig, I noticed people staring at me as I helped him tote a few of his essential stage props. Jay saw it, too, and began to giggle. "Baby, you just look at
yourself. Go on, look!"

I was walking down Fourteenth Street carrying Henry, Jay's human
skull-on-a-stick, part of a smoke machine—and a bottle of white shoe
polish. We both roared. Then Jay's booming query startled a couple of
passersby: "Your mama know what kind of work you do?"

It has been, as the Grateful Dead opined, a long strange trip. Working on a profile for *Rolling Stone*, I had indeed let Michael Jackson's pet
boa constrictor, Muscles, cakewalk around my legs during an exercise
in mutual trust between myself and the Gloved One. We taped two hours
of interview with Muscles's forked tongue flickering several inches from
my ear. I'd taken luxurious afternoon tea with a cashmered Tina Turner,
ridden blue highways in Dolly Parton's pink-lounged bus. I'd sat, enthralled and silent in a darkened NBC green room as James Brown and
a trembling Muhammad Ali privately compared the burdens of their
revolutions. Somewhere between Dallas and Tulsa, as beef cattle and
ammo shops flew past the open bus window, I heard B. B. King sunder

the hiss and honk of traffic with a field holler his uncle loosed at the end of a King Cotton workday:

If I feel like this tomorrow . . .
Feel like I'm gonna make my getaway . . .

There is an undeniable thrill to such ad hoc witnessing. Like Jerzy Kosinski's celebrated cipher Chauncey Gardner in *Being There*, I, too, like to watch. Hitching a ride during rockers' epic (and antic) journeys, bearing witness to the epiphanies, detonations and contagions that inform popular culture, can be its own unforeseen reward. Having sat with both Michael Jackson in a plush L.A. studio and Lauryn Hill in her New Jersey basement, as they tinkered with the records that would so alter their lives (*Thriller* and *The Miseducation of Lauryn Hill*), I am a confirmed process junkie.

I have watched in garages, studios, mansions and housing projects. More often than I'd like, I've seen brilliant improv calcified beneath press agentry and product endorsement. Two months before the millennium, I watched slack-jawed with the rest of America as a cackling Bob Dylan, along with the matchless guitarist/producer T-Bone Burnett, did wry "mystery guest" cameos on the ditzy, weren't-those-sixties-madcap sitcom *Dharma and Greg*. The Jokerman as complicit ABC ratings booster? Would Gandhi have done *Oprah*? Ah, but it's okay, Ma. If Bob survived the firestorm that greeted his going electric in 1965, he went network without blood, rage or tears; he was clearly having fun. And by now, nobody has to be a weatherman to map the corporate drift of rock.

Certainly, writing about the evolution of an art form that has gone from outlaw status to global colossus is not without its vexing conundrums and moral dilemmas. There's never been more crassness and crapola in the music industry than there is now. But I've rarely encountered an artist—with the obvious exceptions such as Vanilla Ice and Milli Vanilli—who, while short on content, didn't at least have some fairly intriguing context. Popular music performs so many essential functions, from heartfelt anthem to knee-jerk ad slogan, from the rapper's barked social chastisements to joyous Saturday-night release. Today's rock/commerce juggernaut commands a serious look just for the sheer amplitude of its siren song.

This may not be advanced metaphysics, yet it is an attempt to make sense of the world as we experience it. I cheerfully admit to being a dyed-in-the-dynel pop tart, but a thinking one. I had planned on what I thought would be a rigorous but safe academic career in what are still quaintly called the social sciences. Like so many leftie sixties idealists, I fell in thrall with the gleaming semiotic models of Roland Barthes and Claude Lévi-Strauss. I was attracted to the astringent simplicity of conjugating the unruly human condition into neatly opposing—and diagrammable!—constructs like the Raw and the Cooked. But ultimately, I turned my back on these suave Gallic reductionists for their failure to plumb the magnificent *différences* in human expression—the untidy stuff that makes life interesting. I left graduate school and ran away with the rock and roll circus. But I carried the social scientist's pesky nosiness with me.

I took a few object lessons along as well. Once, as an anthropology undergrad, I was lucky enough to have lunch with Margaret Mead. And in between grumping about the parking meters and the institutional food, the great lady tossed off a remark comparing her groundbreaking field-work to sifting the lint in life's pockets. Mingling with the strange tribes I have known, browsing for what's totemic in heavy-metal "supermarkets," in reeking punk pits, I never forgot that.

Rock music affords its own finger-poppin' ethnographies. It, too, is fashioned from an unmindful detritus—true gospel, cheap sentiment, gum wrappers and blood. And now, its poets and pranksters can go beyond shared myth and memory, enjoying digital access to all cultures, present and past. They are gleeful plunderers. Visit the sample vault of a hip-hop producer who customizes rhythm tracks for jabberwocky MCs and you will find tapes labeled with humankind's Babel: ballpark peanut vendors, sirens, babies' wails, five seconds of "David's Lamentation," a two hundred-year-old shape note hymn, Aunt Bee calling "Opie!" from a black-and-white dream.

I'm a sucker for the enlightened excavation, the well-considered juxtaposition. The artist—that habitual outsider—often does his or her best work by stepping out of the frame and rearranging the elements of the present. And broader cultural forces—call them trends, zeits or marketing plans—work their own mojo. In this way, popular music—folk, blues, rock—is a medium as fertile and unpredictable as alluvial Mississippi silt.

You never know what's going to wash up at its broad, voracious delta—or in what recombinant form. As folklorist Alan Lomax found, hauling his recording equipment to fly-blown tobacco barns and juke joints, there are a million answers to "Who put the bomp?" The anthropologist of true funk understands that even if your thoughts are in the clouds, you're going to have to get your feet dirty.

On the job or not, I have always gone to great lengths for the music itself. Standing in the wings, a few feet from the epicenter of one's passion—that sound—watching fragments of shattered drumstick streak through blue light, I have felt ecstatically, totally at home in the world. Sometimes, if only for the duration of a single, perfectly bent note, the fractured components of work and play, of low culture versus high, quit warring and dance.

Not long ago, I discussed those instants of wordless communion with B. B. King, who was celebrating a half century of laying folks out from the bandstand. We compared lists of who could elicit that neural frisson; Aretha does it for us both. B.B. went on: "Bobby Bland sings the blues to me like nobody can. Lonnie Johnson, Django Reinhardt, Blind Lemon Jefferson, each one of them had that certain something that would get to me. And I'm right there with them. Right there. I couldn't point it out exactly. If I had to go to jail, I wouldn't know. One of the things is phrasing. They seem to take time with a note. Whatever it is just goes through me like a sword."

Finally, we agreed that only a physical description could come close—and a cliché at that. But when the transmission is dead solid perfect, the hairs do stand on the back of your neck. When it happens, it thrills me completely; sometimes it makes me bawl. And it also reminds me of the limits of my journalistic objectivity. Clearly, this job is not for the dispassionate or blasé. Surrendering to the deep spinal hoodoo of a fatback bass line, I'd remind myself—honey, you're getting paid for this.

Of course, there is a lot of tedium between such ecstasies. And even when the conversations are priceless, the mileage takes its toll. If I carry any Proustian sensory imprint of the experience, it would be the smell of coffee-shop eggs and hash browns mingled with diesel fumes. Yo, the bus is leavin' . . . It's a sure path to indigestion, but it's also a singular, off-the-beaten-track way to see America. After all, this nation was founded on the unsettling premise of dislocation, willful and otherwise. Its indigenous forms—blues, jazz, rap, country—are all restless stirrings and loneliness cants. I'm hardly the first to point out that there would be no rock without the roll of the open road.

Unlike some of the gifted balladeers I've traipsed after, I'd never claim I wrote poetry out there. But I can credit my pithier prose effusions to meditations in the Gone Zone. I call them my airplane epiphanies. They come at the end of a good road trip, at 30,000 feet with solid interview tapes safe in the carry-on, highway-seamed prairies below and, with some luck, a non-talkative software rep snoozing in the next seat. Which is to say, when one feels totally alone, unmoored and free to just flat think.

I won't dispute the widely held notion that being such a rolling stone—a rock writer!—is still an adolescent boy's dream job. But though it remains a male-dominated field, I can say that being female was never a very troublesome issue. Most dressing rooms, like professional locker rooms, have managed to accommodate my ilk. And no matter what you look like, security guards' eyes will roll reflexively at the words "I'm with the band." I've always breezed along and taken the Temptations' advice: *Don't look back.*

Most unorthodox professions tend to have their unsettling moments. And I have been fortunate to have the support of my odd-duck colleagues who can appreciate the delectable tragicomedy of visiting backstage at a Queen concert with an impressionable Michael Jackson, who looked on, aghast, as the late Freddie Mercury's mondo jockstraps tumbled from a dressing-room trunk. For the most part, my peers are flexible professionals who have learned to go deep Zen when trapped for two hours in a hotel room with a half-dozen chain-smoking French journalists ("C'est dope!") while a hip-hop diva gets her nails lacquered to match her newest car.

I was also very lucky to find an older, wiser and compassionate travel guide to this illusory, day-for-night universe—my Obi Wan, if you will. Jerome "Doc" Pomus—who died in 1991—was a bona fide rock poet, having written (often with his partner Mort Shuman) classics from the Drifters' "Save the Last Dance for Me" to Ray Charles's "Lonely Avenue," Elvis's desolate, murderous "Suspicion" and that swell bit o' vinyl kitsch,

"Viva Las Vegas." Doc couldn't do too much traveling himself, being wheelchair-bound due to a bad fall and lingering effects of childhood polio. But no matter, everybody came to Doc. He held forth in his small, cluttered apartment not far from mine on Manhattan's Upper West Side. And always, Doc kept his phone listed.

He was the guy Elvis called in the middle of the night from a tough session (Doc thought he was just a cracker sideman and kept it short). He was the bard Bob Dylan consulted when he was hung up on the bridge of a song. John Lennon insisted on meeting Doc so he could tell him how his songs, one by one, changed his adolescent Liverpool life. Doc helped get Dr. John off heroin; grief over Doc's death nearly unmoored a devoted Lou Reed. Plan to drop by Doc's 72nd Street Batcave for ten minutes and you emerged two hours later reeling with stories, song riffs and funky homilies.

Doc's was a messy, forgiving gestalt. He was casual, but peerless at finding higher truths in so-called low art—he could knit you a parable worthy of Lao Tze from an obscure boxing card he saw in Brooklyn, circa '58. And he called a stinker a stinker—notably his own bit of treacle, "Sweets for My Sweet," perpetrated by The Drifters in 1961. Doc's terse explanation: "Sometimes you gotta send the superego on vacation, Babe." But foremost amid the Tao of Doc was his gift of perspective regarding my own wacky passions. As a master of the pop song, Doc knew how to edit. He told me one day: "The longer I live, the more I learn how much of life you can get into three and a half minutes."

Nobody else has better explained the appeal of popular music to me. When it's good, its economy is genius; its power to transport, if only for the duration of a red light, is, for millions of human beings, as nourishing as the greatest literature, as reassuring as prayer. Years past one's glory days, there is no more potent conjuring tool than a few bars of something which, at a dark, doubtful and hormonal nineteen, convinced you that life was indeed worth living.

Doc was a potent conjurer of all those existential and biological blues, in teen and adult versions. And he didn't quit dispensing antidotes when he closed his writing notebooks. He called one night as I approached the lumbering end of my first pregnancy to offer his van and driver for any midnight run to the hospital. I was whiny and unwieldy, walleyed with terror at what I was taking on, unsure about what I was leaving. And once again, Doc settled me: "What, you need a travel agent for adventure? You learned nothing about alternative modes of transport from a crabby old shut-in like me?"

Doc torqued it up into his favorite rant: The music business will kill you, buncha greedy, heartless bastards, whaddaya need it? The music, stick with that. "Put something worthy on the stereo and watch the baby dance. Now that's a trip."

So I hung it up, happily. And for several years, it was fine. I wrote about film, dance, politics, fashion, and most of that I did at home in Manhattan. I strapped Sam into his stroller and wheeled him over to see Doc, who fed him bagels and introduced him to the visiting Bonnie Raitt. Things were copacetic until an editor called with an intriguing proposition. Bob Dylan's youngest son, Jakob, and his band, the Wallflowers, seemed to finally have a hit after toiling for five years in determined obscurity. All that time, Jakob refused even to utter his father's name or discuss his upbringing. Did I want to see if I could change his mind? Jakob felt he might be ready to talk, but he was apprehensive: "Do I think people are curious about growing up with one of the most influential minds of the twentieth century? Of course I do. Am I confident I can get it right? Shit, no."

As a sworn member of the Professionally Curious, I figured I was bound to help him try. And I had to yield to my personal weakness for the Great American Tale. What were those family car trips like with five kids and Bob "Freewheelin'" Dylan at the helm of the station wagon? Does it help a child make sense of the world when his parents' breakup is laid out, as Jakob put it, like "family snapshots" in that jagged LP masterpiece, *Blood on the Tracks*? How did Jake—an L.A. garage-band kid—find his own sound? In short order, I found myself opening another Fed Ex envelope with crisp tickets and a shiny laminated pass. With the car service honking outside, I peered down at two small faces and announced, "Mommy's going on the road. Listen to Daddy. I'll call and say good night. Okay, gotta go."

I took a slow train north to Boston, where the Wallflowers were still campaigning in small clubs. 'Long about New Haven, as a tweedy clutch of Yale professors decamped, I realized that I'd been missing the purposeful dislocations. Certain senses did get keener. And disengagement from the expected (domestic or workaday) was actually relaxing. Many hours later that day, after a tentative first interview, a show, another gulped bar meal, I climbed onto the bus with Jakob and his lost boys. I watched the minstrel's son pitch himself onto a bunk, pull a quilt over his dark, curly head and fall asleep within seconds, perfectly at home. As we headed south, Jakob's father, a multimillionaire, was back out playing cramped college auditoriums—by choice. If there is a ramblin' man gene, these guys have the dominant strain. My own may be recessive, but I now recognize its tug on my sleeve. As the moon rose, Jakob's diesel chariot hauled us all toward Providence. I took it as a sign.

I returned to rock journalism in 1997, as the sub rosa death watch had begun on Old Blue Eyes and the stuffiest media pundits were getting lachrymose about the cultural contributions of a saloon singer. It was the year the august Kennedy Center Honors were conferred on that cranky reprobate Bob Dylan as "the most distinctive of poets." Hip-hop music—which began two decades earlier as the ultimate outsider music—was about to be recognized by the ultimate Establishment organ, *Time* magazine, for having "changed our lives" across America. Five bar-coded babes called the Spice Girls had emerged to remind us just how canned and co-opted our rebel music could become. But the most ballyhooed change was, as some of my grouchier male colleagues put it, "the woman thing."

The Lilith Fair, it was turning out, was a well-hyped signpost for a much larger shift. By millennium's end, women were everywhere: at the top of the charts, at televised podiums accepting every industry award there was. From folky singer/songwriters and feisty female MCs, their ascent was precipitous and loud and immensely profitable, and it wasn't going away. Divas, new and reincarnated, were so vocal, so dominant—and so saleable—that Mattel would market diva dolls that throw hissy fits via computer chip. Still, I wasn't too receptive in the spring of 1998 when the editors at *Rolling Stone* suggested we celebrate their achievements in a 30th-anniversary issue dedicated to "Women of Rock." As I've just argued, women have always been at the heart, if not the helm, of rock and roll. And like some of the female artists who declined to participate, I had reservations about further ghettoizing their contributions.

Those qualms diminished as I started to collate some of my own interviews with the names on the magazine's "must" list. I realized that my own work was rather gal-heavy, from Motown dream girls to Madonna, rap refugees to my own teen totem, Ronnie Spector. I reminded myself that I got into this line of work via that galvanizing encounter with Aretha Franklin, the woman who got me through—and out of—adolescence. Going back over the stacks of articles that followed, I saw that my own talky professional impulses were drawn again and again to conversations with a lot of extraordinary—and big-mouthed—women. The stories were always about the music first, but none could be written without addressing the profound changes in female lives—as well as the ageless frustrations. Often my subject and I would stumble on a shared flashback to girlish mortifications: bad jobs, bad hair, good bad boys, the first knowing good vibrations . . .

It's always been clear to me: These tend to be women of appetites. Early on, there was a wellspring of womanly hedonism that relieved the tedium of the road—and enlivened the music. Many pioneering blues and jazz women were feeling, thinking sorts for whom sex, food and drink—not to mention personal adornment—were aspects of life to be wholeheartedly enjoyed. But they were singing, eating and loving in a culture that still viewed appetite as a vice to be controlled. Things have changed considerably when a Foxy Brown can demand her just desserts in language that would transport Larry Flynt. But the shifting boundaries between appetite and its acceptance is still a torrid and hazardous zone. Janis Joplin may have died negotiating it; others, like Tina Turner, have learned to chant blissfully on the volcano's edge.

On vinyl and on the job, I have always loved these loud adventuresses. They are so much braver than I could ever be. Earthbound, I'd press them to describe the weightless thrills of performance. And for years, I have been collecting stories of their willful disengagements. No matter where their narrative first finds them, these girls are somehow luminous and different from the outset—rough, natural pearls growing in childhood rooms, amid troubled families, in neat tract homes and hellish urban coops. Suddenly they shoot out, streak across the pop horizon—but what's the volition? One of my warm-up interview questions, always guaranteed to elicit a biographical motherlode, was some variant on this: *Tell me, what do you remember about the day you actually left home to do this crazy thing?*

Some were hard-eyed opportunists at fourteen. But—at least in my experience—the majority of these girls on the brink are romantic, pliant, heartbreaking creatures. And many of their odysseys are epic, given the bumpy terrain. Taken as a whole, their narrative amounts to a sort of cultural travelogue, fraught with bandstand suffrage and pillow talk, gender wars and loving cease-fires. It documents the stunning trajectories, over the last half century, of women determined to rock their worlds—if only for a hit or two. It is full of stories about just what it took to get up and out. It is about the long struggle for ownership and entitlement, about earning the right and the desire to come back in off that road and claim a home of one's own.

It is also the confessional tale of our own infatuation with rock sirens, a thrumming codependency that is stronger than ever. As the later chapters illustrate, pop divas have long been cultural and emotional lightning rods for their times, from Jenny Lind in pre–Civil War America to the multi-selved Madonna of the Information Age. Yet only now do they have the sales puissance and the business savvy to amplify or modulate their beguilements. And if, as Aretha sang (with Annie Lennox), "sisters are doing it for themselves," they're pulling it off in what is still a very male-dominated industry. It's a feat worth measuring against the other seismic changes in women's lives over the last half century.

A few words about methodology. Too many rock and roll histories burden their subjects with a gravitas that would horrify its impulsive, lightning-thighed perpetrators. As I write this, earnest academics are deconstructing Madonna's bustier sequences with shadings of Barthes, Foucault, and, yes, Lévi-Strauss. That's fine if it gets your tenure-seeking ya-yas out. But I prefer an approach as fluid as the music: Get out there, listen to people—and above all, let them have their say. Faced with so many big-mouthed women, I'd be a fool to do otherwise.

I've tried to fit their voices, their memories and my own observations within a manageable chronology. It is divided into decades for the sake of organization, with the understanding that no pop/cult phenomenon, least of all rock, falls into tidy divisions of ten. And that no rock chronology is going to be entirely *manageable.* Following such headstrong music, we will encounter reverses, premature outbursts, retro efflorescences. Switching gears, and sometimes time frames, is the only way to stay on track.

Much like the artists' lives and careers, this narrative pivots and turns on *moments.* As an interviewer, I am an inveterate curator of moments—

the daily calamities and triumphs that flare up to illuminate a life. Sometimes summoning such wee nonces is useful in simply evoking a certain time or place. The longer forays into portraiture, I hope, serve to make a few points in more vivid *tableaux vivants*.

Over the years, and often in conjunction with rock journalism, I have done a good deal of reporting on fashion and style. There are few areas of the arts where presentation of self is so paramount—and so endlessly amusing. From the beginning, with Elvis's gold lamé suit, rock style was an outsider's brash imperative. Now it's a cultural and economic force of its own. Young people have had their own style only since the postwar years; rock and roll has been a huge influence on just how they walk and talk it.

Nine out of ten rockers—from the venerable B. B. King to Tina Turner—can tell you what they first wore onstage, and the permutations they went through to get that look just right. Now that sharkskin suit, that leopard-skin pillbox hat are also big business. The rock and fashion nexus is so powerful, so embedded, now, that you hear the damnedest things in couture's sacred temples. Sitting behind Karl Lagerfeld's desk with him in the Chanel atelier as he oversaw fittings of $30,000 couture gowns, I listened to him deconstruct "Achy Breaky Heart" ("Really, it's a lousy song"). Giorgio Armani giggled like a schoolboy in the office of his minimalist palazzo when he described going with his nephew to his first Madonna concert in Turin. Gianni Versace told me that he revered his rock star pals as he did Picassos—with an appreciation for their bold statements as well as those tiny idiosyncracies that speak volumes.

In giving some context to women's music, then, I'd be seriously remiss if I didn't take into account their alluring and well-considered visual mystique—and the reactions they elicited in the concert hall and the marketplace. My episodic sidetrips into rock style here don't aim to ignore musical substance. They simply recognize that, given today's primacy of image, the two are inseparable. And watching their mad dance is *so* much fun. . . .

For the most part, I've been fortunate enough to choose my interview subjects. That being the case, the women represented here do embody certain prejudices for which I make no apology. This book does not purport to be encyclopedic—it is less a definitive reference work than an evocative and affectionate insider's tour. In my travels, sheer exhaustion and too many superstar flashbacks may have led me to pass up encounters with the likes of mega-acts Fiona Apple, Britney Spears and Celine Dion. Smaller, more esoteric genres—say, the Pacific Northwest riot grrl scene—blossomed largely when I was nursing my own girl terrorist and forsook the mosh pits for the nursery. Trying to toss a net of analytic prose over such wild things after the fact can just leave all parties panting and unsatisfied. Worse, it can miss the essence of that scene: the compelling but evanescent vitality of a music that's more phenomenon than form.

I have, however, tried to look ahead and spend some time with women on the brink, smart anti-divas with undeniable impact and more varied bodies of work (as producers, songwriters and performers). Driving home from Lauryn Hill's house, playing four as-yet unfinished cuts from what would be her solo debut, it was clear I'd unwittingly caught a comet in my tape recorder. The stunning odyssey of Missy "Misdemeanor" Elliott is at once very old in its deprivations and entirely new in its digital triumphs. Learn to withstand the megawoof of Missy's automobile sound systems, and her quietly told *stories* transport.

Anyone can argue any of my choices and/or omissions; that is the democratic beauty of this non-pedigreed music. Though we are a nation of inveterate rock critics, I have never tried to be one in print; that I've gladly left to folks with stronger hides and stomachs than mine. Rock and roll heaven is a big, forgiving place with unlimited zip codes; I believe it has room for Big Mama Thornton and Lil' Kim. If the stories I've collected here make any case passionately, it's for the redemptive and nonsectarian powers of rock. What the music has done for people historically disenfranchised—women, and especially black women—is nothing short of miraculous.

Lastly, I have little patience with so-called rock "purists" who drone on about crassness and commercialism. "Be My Baby," by the Ronettes, was written and recorded with the basest motive—HIT!—in mind. But that does nothing to diminish its status as a nearly perfect pop record. Likewise, you can't argue for any kind of purity in a form that found its apotheosis—ELVIS!—in a southern white boy who dressed and sang black. Do I rue the ossified state of corporate rock? Certainly. Do I tire of seeing every fresh face tattooed with endorsements, every tour with a Sponsor?

You bet. But to all the gloomy prognosticators—usually well-informed children of the sixties who truly *did* hear and see some of the best—I say lighten up. In the words of the late Sonny Bono, who assessed his unlikely career for me as we sat in his very *un*rock and roll congressional office, "The beat does go on. You just don't know where the heck it's gonna take you."

Rock and roll didn't die when the Beatles broke up or Otis Redding's plane went down or Janis and Jimi OD'd. The music just moved on—as those artists would have. The twitchy, fitful sounds that we've grown up with have ambled along as well. There's no use bemoaning that fact—and nothing to be gained by making your kids' ears bleed with endless Motown or Dylan compilations. I thrill to the fact that our eight-year-old daughter loves Emmylou Harris's sublimely mordant "Deeper Well"; I sigh stoically—and out loud—when she cues up an icky Backstreet Boys tune. Still, I'm happy to dance with her. It's all rock and roll to me.

MOTHERS OF INVENTION

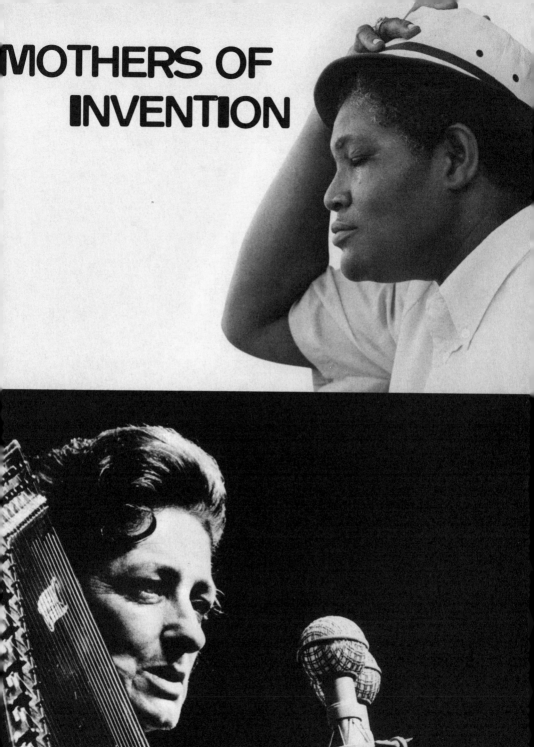

Blues is a good woman feeling bad.
—*Thomas Dorsey*

Women do *talk*; perhaps it's the intimacies and isolations of domestic life that have made them queens of the cut-to-the-bone colloquial. And before they dared press it in vinyl and send it to market, women had long told one another the unvarnished truth. If you think about it, the blues was the first serious *public* consciousness raising—frank, sexy and mercifully non-PC. Since the first blues recordings were made by and for African-Americans, it wasn't necessary to deeply encode the plain facts. There is no mistaking what Bessie Smith meant when she sang "I Need a Little Sugar in My Bowl."

America's very first rush of popular record buying was ignited in the twenties by the talents of black female blues artists telling it like it was, is and damn well ought to be. Folks just had to have it, at home and in dirt-floor juke joints. Call them the true Mothers of Invention—blues pioneers whose echos can be heard in the primmest, Orlon'd girl groups of the sixties as well as today's most avant female MCs.

Like the best of rock, theirs was not a studied sound. Largely recorded in the south, in makeshift studios, they were strong women singing hard truths in a twelve-bar blues format. That three-line stanza song form came across the Atlantic Ocean and north along the Mississippi delta; it is the root of nearly all pop, from rhythm and blues to acid rock to reggae to rap. And like the drums that first thrummed it across West African skies, it was *talking* music.

In the nineties, African-American women could swap truths in spirited, Oprah-inspired reading groups called Go On Girl. But listen to Ma
Rainey warn "Trust No Man," Mae Glover declare "I Ain't Givin' Nobody
None," or Ida Cox sing "Wild Women Don't Get the Blues," and it's clear
these women weren't waiting to exhale. They could blow a lyric and a feeling from Augusta to Kansas City under conditions that would make today's
divas bolt for cover under the massage table. Stylists? Maybe some crone
heating a hair iron in an alley behind those colored-only boardinghouses.
Security? A razor laced to the instep of a dainty boot.

I found the most vivid account of a traveling woman's trials and compulsions by chance at a used-book sale. I paid a quarter for my dusty copy
of *His Eye Is on the Sparrow*, the long out-of-print autobiography of Ethel
Waters. It was published in 1951, when she was fifty-one and an accomplished actress with Broadway credits like "A Member of the Wedding."
But Waters, whose Dickensian first line ("I never was a child.") unspools
into a harrowing but matter-of-fact narrative, began as a teenage blues
singer called Sweet Mama Stringbean.

From the outset, life had offered Waters little to sing about; she was
the result of the violent rape of her thirteen-year-old mother, who was understandably unfit to raise her. She spent much of her childhood in the
care of two alcoholic aunts. Waters wrote that her own compositions came
naturally, with such blues all around her: "I also believe that [my audi-
ences] were intrigued by my characterizations which I drew from real life.
I'd hear a couple in another flat arguing, for instance. Their voices would
come up the airshaft and I'd listen, making up stories about their spats and
their love life. I could hear such an argument in the afternoon and that night
sing a whole song about it."

Sweet Mama Stringbean delivered odes to joy as well. They came
with the help of the debonair Harlem enablers she called the "hot piano
boys"—men with knowing smiles and quicksilver fingers in the mold of
Jimmy Johnson: "Men like [Johnson], Willie (The Lion) Smith, and
Charlie Johnson could make you sing until your tonsils fell out. Because
you wanted to sing. They stirred you into joy and wild ecstasy. They
could make you cry. And you'd do anything and work until you dropped
for such musicians."

It stands to reason that on the rough and ready Theater Owners Booking Association (also known as Toby Time or Tough On Black Asses), a

black vaudeville circuit covering most southern cities, the best rose to the top on vocal firepower and strength of character. Ma Rainey was born to a pair of road-toughened minstrel troupers and at eighteen married William "Pa" Rainey, who took her on the road working levee camps, tent shows and cabarets. They were billed as "Rainey and Rainey, Assassinators of the Blues."

Ma's massacres are now credited as the crucial link between rural southern blues and the more sophisticated versions later sung by Bessie Smith and Ethel Waters. Ma's delivery was direct, down-home and folksy— pure country. But she was professional. And her presentation of self prefigured rock's most outrageous impulses for puttin' on the glitz. Starting at the top with stiff horsehair wigs framing her battered face, Ma accessorized with a brio that would make those Spice Girls gasp. Amid the floaty feather boas hung a chain weighted by $20 gold pieces. A contemporary described the vision: "Ma was loaded with diamonds, in her ears, round her neck, in a tiara on her head. Both hands were full of rocks, too: her hair was wild and she had gold teeth! What a sight!"

By all accounts, her generosity was also multi-karat. Debunking old myths that had Ma "kidnapping" the young Bessie Smith for a traveling show, Chris Albertson's landmark 1972 biography of Smith reveals that the older Rainey was, in fact, "more like a mother to her" when they both toured with the Rabbit Foot Minstrels.

Bessie Smith lived just forty-three years, from 1894 to 1937. Yet for the next half century, in legend, liner notes and an Albee play (*The Death of Bessie Smith*), she would be held up as the archetype of Woman Wronged. Even her death was shrouded in a myth that had her bleeding to death after a car crash when a white hospital refused her admission. With careful scholarship, including interviews with Dr. Hugh Smith, a Memphis orthopedic surgeon who came upon the accident and treated Bessie at the scene, and documentation from the black hospital where she died, Albertson set the record straight. The black ambulance driver never took her to a white facility; both Smith and the hospital confirmed that her right side was virtually crushed; several hours after the crash, she died of shock and multiple internal injuries. Smith was revealed as a woman with plenty of trouble in mind: a sizable drinking problem, a penchant for abusive men, ceaseless run-ins with unchecked racism. But she was never a passive victim; in her music and her life, Bessie Smith preferred dealing from strength.

For much of her career, she could command top rates. Despite the historic inequities of male and female salaries, blueswomen were initially paid *better* than men. The first black blues vocal recording, notes Greil Marcus in *Invisible Republic*, was Mamie Smith's "Crazy Blues," released in 1920. It sold over a million copies in its first year. In much the same way, "Fiddling" John Carson enthralled white "hillbilly" buyers with "The Little Old Log Cabin in the Lane" three years later. This was a populist explosion, a self-discovery of sorts for poor black and white southern audiences, according to Marcus, who writes, "Many copies of these records were bought by people without phonographs. They bought the discs as talismans of their own existence; they could hold these objects in their hands and feel their own lives dramatized." To his amazement, James Brown encountered a similar phenomenon traveling in Africa half a century later. Leon Austin, a member of his entourage in Zaire, described it for me: "They come out of mud shacks with James Brown albums, don't never play them, no electricity, for sure no Victrola. But they know who is *James Brown*."

Just as they knew *Bessie Smith*. Her voice and her renown could earn her as much as $200 a side—nearly fifteen times the average fee for a black male singer at the time. This is not to say she wasn't cheated, over and over. But if Bessie got wind of it, you'd do well to have your insurance paid up. Having found that her pianist, Clarence Williams, had appropriated $375 that was rightfully hers, Bessie—close to two hundred pounds of handsome, towering outrage—cornered Williams, pounded him to the floor and kept whaling at him until he tore up their lopsided contract.

Racism was no match for Bessie in a mood. Put on display in Manhattan by a patronizing white grande dame who demanded a kiss in front of her society pals, Bessie knocked Madame on her astonished keester. On a southern swing with her tent show, Bessie was informed that hooded Ku Klux Klan terrorists were at work outside, sabotaging the poles. "Some shit!" she snorted, and according to Albertson's sources, she ran outside and faced them down alone, bellowing, "What the fuck you think you're doin'? I'll get the whole damn tent out here if I have to. You just pick up them sheets and run." And they did.

Among her contemporaries, Bessie was a diva. When she met up with Mama Stringbean at 91 Decatur Street, a joint in Atlanta, she expected the younger woman to call her "Miss Bessie." And she had some instructions for the theater owners as well. Ethel Waters recalled: "Bessie's shouting brought worship wherever she worked. She was getting fifty to seventy-five dollars a week, big money for our kind of vaudeville. The money thrown to her [onstage] brought this to a couple of hundred dollars a week. Bessie, like an opera singer, carried her own claque with her. These plants in the audience were paid to throw up coins and bills to get the appreciation money going without delay the moment she finished her first number. And if Bessie ordered it, her followers would put the finger on you and run you right off the stage and out of sight, maybe forever.

"Bessie was in a pretty good position to dictate to the managers. She had me put on my act for her and said I was a long goody. But she also told the men who ran No. 91 that she didn't want anyone else to sing the blues."

Like some sixties performers now confined to oldies shows, Bessie Smith suffered a dimming of her star when the Depression flattened box offices in the early thirties and restless, sophisticated black audiences cast off the blues as hopelessly old-fashioned. She sold the beloved private railroad car that had spared her some of the discomforts and humiliations of segregated travel, and took gigs in the lowest gin mills again. But when Bessie died in 1937, her career had been back on the rise. She had no reservations about joining the Swing Era. Producer John Hammond had plans to record her with Basie on piano; Lionel Hampton wanted to work with her; and she had a new film contract. The hysteria at her Philadelphia funeral—not unlike that which surrounded the rites for Supreme Florence Ballard in 1976—was the grief of a community belatedly acknowledging the immensity of her achievement against ridiculous odds.

If Rainey and Smith were the Mother and the Empress, respectively, there was no shortage of titled blueswomen—Little and Big Mamas, Canaries and Queens. For the most part, they were self-ordained. Theirs was a genre where modesty gets you nowhere—mighty Chicago blueswoman Koko Taylor still bills herself, justifiably, as the Earthshaker. Among the more regal originals were Ida Cox, Sippie Wallace, Alberta Hunter, Ethel Waters, Victoria Spivey. Of course, there were scores more; some of their ghostly, piney-woods voices have been respectfully disinterred in archival collections. There's a lot more desolation than deliverance in Shanachie Records' two-volume collection, *I Can't Be Satisfied*. Listening to it all at once can send you headfirst toward the kitchen oven—or out to kneecap the first man you see. It's a raucous, ghostly symposium on Women's Issues in the rural south—everything from Victoria Spivey's "Dirty T. B.

Blues" to Sara Martin's determined "He's Never Gonna Throw Me Down."
More lost women—Bertha "Chippie" Hill, Lucille Bogan, Ivy Smith,
Madlyn Davis, Rosie Mae Moore, Geeshie Wiley, Ruby Glaze—swoop,
soar and moan from the musky retrieved tracks. But just as many fervent
shouters remain nameless. The blues may have been about endurance, but
the popular music marketplace has always been about change.

Nobody knows that better than B. B. King. When I shipped out on
tour with him in 1998, he was celebrating a half century on the road in a
tour jacket that proclaimed him "King of the Blues Worldwide." Making
his way as a blues singer had afforded B.B. some less than regal moments—
many of which he recounted as his big custom bus rolled on those long
hauls between the two-hundred-fifty-plus one-nighters a year he still does,
at age seventy-five. One muggy evening, amid an almost biblical plague
of crickets in North Texas, I asked B.B. what he'd seen of the lives of
blueswomen over his five decades on the move. He shook his head.

"They've had a harder time than most men. A lot of the places we
could go, they could not. The juke joints, the start-up places. It wasn't
comfortable for them. There have been many times I've had to change
clothes behind a sheet 'cause there's no dressing room. And that's hard
for ladies."

And sometimes it didn't matter how well their records sold if they
didn't measure up to other standards. Audiences *looked* harder at a woman.
"Yeah, they were the hitmakers," said B.B. "But there was another thing
you have to think about. Men had more money. They did the work like
laboring. So if it was a beautiful woman that could sing, she got a good
crowd of men. They would usually bring the ladies with them. But a lot of
these women wasn't pretty women. If they were not, like Big Mama
[Thornton], they had to sing good. *Very* good. Big Mama, if she didn't have
a hit record, she caught H-E-double L."

He says the chitlin circuit had its own variants on the casting couch:
"Most of the promoters, or the people that were in power to give her a
push, didn't. Because *they* [the promoters] didn't *want* them [the women]
personally. "

Respect—onstage, in contracts and even in death—would prove
maddeningly elusive, even for the greatest of blueswomen. In 1970, a
housewife's letter to *The Philadelphia Inquirer* called attention to the fact
that Bessie Smith's grave in nearby Mount Lawn Cemetery had lain un-

marked for over three decades. The resulting publicity brought pledges from two women to share in the cost of erecting a marker: Juanita Green, a registered nurse who had scrubbed Smith's floors as a teenager and was by then president of the North Philadelphia NAACP, and Janis Joplin, the white rock singer who swore she owed her own success to Smith's well-spring blues. The marble headstone—secured at cost ($500) from a sympathetic monument company—was set in place in August of 1970, just two months before Joplin died. Albertson's account of the rather haphazard if earnest "unveiling" is mindful of its final irony: As no family members were present, Bessie's epitaph was composed by Columbia Records' publicity department. At least, he notes, the claim was true:

The Greatest Blues Singer in the World Will Never Stop Singing

It's no surprise that the echos of early blueswomen would reach contemporary audiences largely through the music of white rockers. Bonnie Raitt virtually apprenticed herself to Sippie Wallace, performing and recording with her. Theirs was a genial, respectful collaboration. But Willie Mae "Big Mama" Thornton, who lived and performed until 1984, did not conceal her irritation over the riches that came to Elvis Presley and Janis Joplin with their remakes of her records "Hound Dog" and "Ball and Chain," respectively.

Listen to the Solid Smoke live recording of Big Mama singing at the 1979 San Francisco Blues Festival—introducing her own version of "Ball and Chain" by noting that Joplin had had "the nerve to do it"— and you can hear old frustrations crackle through the tumultuous reception. It took several people to help the frail, shockingly thin Thornton to her chair on the stage. In photos of the concert, a man's pin-striped suit flaps loosely, and beneath her straw cowboy hat, her face is all angles. But the performance is 120-proof as she rocks back in her chair to talk to these little girls about . . . *men*. They are shouting with recognition; Big Mama has *been* there and sent back postcards. Some are weeping for her desiccated womanhood and her outright valor. Vocally, and on harmonica, she gets stronger throughout the set; the crowd is noisily worshipful. Finally, Big Mama roars at one groovy chick who keeps echoing her lines in a Joplinesque whine: "AW SHUDDUP!" She recovers her humor as a fan deposits a watermelon onstage: "I see you givin' me a San Francisco ham."

The Lieber & Stoller–penned hit "Hound Dog" made it to #1 on the R&B charts in 1953 for Thornton. But as she grumped to journalist Ralph Gleason: "That song sold over 2 million copies. I got one check for $500 and I never seen another." Though she wrote "Ball and Chain," the royalties were assigned to her record company. Big Mama died frail, alcohol-ravaged and poor in a Los Angeles boardinghouse. Other blues musicians did respect Thornton's considerable chops, including her ease on the hitherto unladylike harmonica and drums; the backup band for one of her later albums featured James Cotton and Muddy Waters.

Most serious blues guitarists also acknowledge the gifts of Memphis Minnie (born Lizzie Douglas), who began picking as a five-year-old in 1902 and, when her family moved to Mississippi in 1904, developed a regular habit of running off to Memphis to soak up the Beale Street flavor. At her peak, Minnie played as well or better than any man, once besting Big Bill Broonzy in a contest. She played in parks and streets as well as vaudeville houses, and saw plenty; her blues were full of streetwalkers, dope fiends and doomed consumptives. As Ethel Waters did, Minnie sketched from life; her "Outdoor Blues" is a window-rattling evocation of homelessness during the Depression. But much of her oeuvre consists of twelve-bar tone poems sharply observing domestic life, from making biscuits to making love.

White hillbilly girls knew the blues, too. Theirs were the hardscrabble trials of sharecroppers' wives and coal miners' daughters. But nearly four decades before Loretta Lynn warned "Don't Come Home A-Drinkin' (With Lovin' on Your Mind)," few of them dared to voice it aloud. Early country artists confined themselves to the rather polite conventions of traditional forms— the reels, jigs and laments of their Scottish and Irish antecedents.

The Carter Family—A. P. Carter, his wife, Sara, and their sister-in-law Maybelle Addington Carter—began their remarkable career with "old-timey" tunes. Theirs was a body of folk work so deep and wide that virtually every country star that followed declared they "grew up on the Carters." The folk revival of the late fifties and early sixties, as well as the stark, reedy strains of today's "alternative" country, "No Depression" music drew straight from the Carter well. (The name is from the Carter song "They'll Be No Depression in Heaven.")

In 1927, the Carters auditioned in Bristol, Tennessee, for a talent scout named Ralph Peer, who had traveled south for the Victor Talking Machine Company of New York City. That first day, A.P.'s car juddered into town with his wife and his brother's wife, the very pregnant Maybelle, it was a different sound they poured into Peer's portable equipment. The trio's voices dominated their instruments; they would usher an age of strong, idiosyncratic vocal performance in southern folk music. In 1928, one of their best-known tunes, the pluckily optimistic "Keep on the Sunny Side," was a huge hit in the mountains and valleys that had yet to see the bustling prosperity of the Roaring Twenties. But more surprising was the success, earlier in 1928, of their rewrite of a traditional song, "Single Girl, Married Girl." Sara resisted singing it in the family's first recording session the previous year; she said she didn't like the song. But the record man insisted. The lyrics limned the great divide in women's fates:

Single girl, single girl, she goes to the store and buys.
Married girl, married girl, she rocks the cradle and cries.
Single girl, single girl, she's going where she please.
Married girl, married girl, a baby on her knees.

Once the original trio disbanded, it was "Mother" Maybelle who kept the Carter name in country, enlisting her daughters Helen, Anita and June (who later married Johnny Cash). Though June would later inject a comic, flirty element, the quartet remained basic as biscuits and resolutely God-fearing. There is a piece of black-and-white TV footage of a young Cash and the Carter women, accompanied by just a mandolin and Maybelle's autoharp, singing what the slick-haired announcer calls "an old sacred song," "Were You There (When They Crucified My Lord)?" The performance is an Appalachian act of faith so solemn and chilling it all but vaporizes the hokey, rifle-hung fireplace that serves as a backdrop. The people's music was never so direct as when Cash's ragged baritone thunders: *Were you there?*

Cash and the women do not look at one another or the camera; when tall, beautiful Anita —the one Elvis was mad for—looses her piercing keen atop it all, every piney woods terror that ever ringed Clinch Mountain,

Virginia, rises up with it. Her voice is at once gorgeous and wounding; you can't tell if what she sees is salvation or devastation, if she is in a state of grace or mortal dread. It's a hillbilly righteousness torn straight from the strident shakers who washed up at Plymouth. As the other singers fall in, sequentially, in seamless harmony, on the word "tremble," the listener does just that.

There is no question, watching any of those preserved performances, that Mother Maybelle was the rock, and perhaps the seer. Through it all, on corny TV hoedowns and plain home-movie footage of family gatherings, Maybelle's gaze seems fixed on a point no one else can see. Like her sister-in-law Sara, she is almost expressionless in a sharp-planed, American Gothic way, rarely smiling until she seems to remember she probably should. But her right hand is never less than eloquent. Generations of spandexed ax-men (and women) owe much of the reverence now accorded to lead guitar to Maybelle's innovative playing. Modestly, she held her own amid guitar greats. Says Johnny Cash, "Maybelle was friendly with and admired Chet Atkins, Merle Travis and Django Reinhardt. Her Appalachian style, which she called Carter Scratch, is not easily imitated."

Nor was it easily learned. Mother Maybelle's "simple" technique combined melody and rhythm strumming on the same instrument. Study her performance legerdemain and you see a right thumb as busy as the forefingers but keeping its own beat. In his 1997 autobiography, *Cash*, Johnny explained it this way: "In purely musical, not cultural, terms, Maybelle was more influential than either Lennon or Dylan. She figured out a way to pick the melody on the lower strings of her guitar while she strummed chords on the higher strings, thereby creating the most influential guitar style in country and folk music."

Maybelle, as her old fishing buddy Cash describes her, was an "absurdly" humble person: "She never grasped how important she was to the music, how revered she was by everyone from Pete Seeger and Bob Dylan to Emmylou Harris and Michelle Shocked. We'd tell her time and time again, but she'd just say, 'Naw, that's just stuff I did a long time ago.'"

Maybelle prefered life's simple pleasures. She'd cook for all comers, and she loved to fish. Recalled Cash: "She was a worm baiter; she wasn't afraid to pick that worm up and get the hook through it the way so many people are." She could also look through your soul, according to those who knew her. Maybelle's eyes were huge and dark-lashed beneath long, expressive brows, but the centers were a striking light blue. Said her daughter Anita, "The first thing you saw about my mother were her eyes. Her eyes just jumped out at you. Liz Taylor had that, I've heard. Mama's eyes were so sweet. She never said much, though. When somebody would do something they shouldn't she'd just stare at them." According to Anita, country legend Hank Snow caught the effect best when he declared, "Mama just whips us to death with those eyes."

Maybelle and her quiet ways were a saving balm to the troubled men she encountered on the road, like the hard-drinking, tubercular Jimmie Rodgers, who sang and behaved with sure knowledge of his early doom. When he turned up nearly insensible for one recording session, Maybelle stepped up and played Rodgers's guitar parts for him. She later said she endured his wild behavior and volcanic temper because "he was dying and everybody knew it. He was taking drugs and drinking because of the pain, and it just made him a little bit crazy." As gentle confessor to other road-ravaged country boys like Hank Williams and Johnny Cash, Mother Maybelle did her best to live up to the name. She listened, she counseled— and she always forgave.

If the Carters virtually started the country-music industry, it was Kitty Wells, the young wife of another hillbilly singer, who finally, emphatically trashed Nashville's sexist bromide that solo girl singers couldn't sell records. Kitty's 1952 "It Wasn't God Who Made Honky Tonk Angels" laid into the devilment of two-timing married men with a double shot of hurt and sass. It flew to #1 on the country charts. As country's first bona fide female star, Wells blazed a ruffles-and-rhinestone path for a host of Lorettas, Tammys, Dollys and Rebas.

Rock's other great root is, of course, gospel. Listen to any group sound, from the Beatles' "It Won't Be Long" to Lauryn Hill's "Zion" and you can hear tech'd-up reverbs of the classic call-and-response format that rang between gospel choir and soloist, quartet leads and background singers. Gospel—spreading the good news—is by its nature a group sound. Where blues found its art in perfectly realized solitude, gospel's amazing grace flows from the succor of community.

Sometimes it's a mighty roar. The first "girl group" that left me truly thunderstruck was *not* all got up in moist puce lipstick and snug mohair.

And they were surely *not* spreading the 411 on m-e-n. When I saw the Clara
Ward Singers on TV, on some folkie show, they were singing about Jesus—
Jaaaaay-eeeeeee-zus! And they *flew*. I watched in envious thrall as these
ample women with thick ankles seemed to shoot *straight up*, weightless in
their transport, their glossy, sky-high wigs shaking like lopsided pyramids
of plum Jell-O. They whanged tambourines on pillowy hips, strained seams
and sound equipment with the strength of their convictions. These were
women who *had* to sing. And they moved people; I have never seen anyone—believer, agnostic, Asian or high WASP—fail to at least twitch when
I've filled a room with the ladies' live, funky organ testament "Something
Got a Hold of Me."

Years after that first snowy TV vision, I would learn that it was Miss
Ward, guardian angel to then-motherless child Aretha Franklin in Detroit,
who would hip the Queen of Soul to her magnificent destiny. It was Miss
Ward who demonstrated firsthand the glories of vocal transport. Aretha
described it to me as a true gospel moment: She was still a girl the day she
attended a funeral where Clara Ward got happy mid-song, crouched like
a discus thrower and hurled her hat toward the coffin. "That *did* it," Aretha
said.

From birth, Aretha had been steeped in gospel; her father was Reverend C. L. Franklin, known as the Man with the Million-Dollar Voice.
Chess Records sold freight cars full of his shake-down-the-thunder ser-
mons. The Reverend James Cleveland, another gospel luminary, lived with
the family for a time and taught C.L.'s three girls some Rock of Ages piano. "But the ladies," Aretha told me. "How I loved my gospel ladies." They
included Ward, her singers Marion Williams and Frances Steadman, and
the great Mahalia Jackson.

Later, Aretha would realize that even before she understood her gift,
the big generous women who used to come to her father's house had intu-
ited that this shy child was *the one*. That in fact she had little choice in the
matter. "Clara *knew*," Aretha explained. "She knew I had to sing."

Aretha sang at the funerals of both Ward and Jackson, sending those
great ladies home after hugely successful careers. If blues ruled the twenties and thirties, the gospel boom gathered hurricane strength over the turmoil of the forties. Majestic soloists like Marion Williams, Sallie Martin
and Willie Mae Ford Smith had large followings, but no one did more to
spread the good news than the queen, Mahalia Jackson.

Her voice could drop a sinner like a thunderbolt. And when Mahalia got happy, she would grab up her long skirt and run down a church aisle. To a war-wearied nation, to a long-suffering black populace, Mahalia was an ebony casting of Miss Liberty; her torch shone straight into heaven's gate. In 1946, her "Move On Up a Little Higher" sold two million copies. Her word was revered; her wit was wicked and her combination of talent and personality opened the door to showbiz gospel—the kind that landed Mahalia on the *Tonight Show* couch battling wits with Colonel Sanders and bounced the Clara Ward Singers from AME choir lofts to praising His name on the Vegas Strip.

As early as 1938, Sister Rosetta Tharpe, native of Cotton Plant, Arkansas, saw no problem with "singing both sides," taking her big, bold voice and blues-tinged guitar out of church and into the Cotton Club. Sister Rosetta could segue from "Jesus Is Here Today" to "I Want a Tall Skinny Papa" without changing her fretwork. Before anyone had heard of Ray Charles or James Brown, Sister Rosetta cut a version of "Jonah" that jumps like a netful of live minnows. She had enough command to serve as Cab Calloway's featured singer, recording a peppery "Pickin' the Cabbage" with his orchestra in 1940.

Sister Rosetta's album *Gospel Train*, assembled from recordings made in 1944 and '49, is an unmatchable stew of gospel, jazz and blues. I searched it out on the advice of Wilson "The Wicked" Pickett, a soul screamer who treasures his massive collection of gospel records. "If it don't kill you," Pickett said of Sister Rosetta's sound, "it just might save your life." The day I came upon *Gospel Train* in an East Village record shop, I played it over and over, spent that rainy afternoon in some sort of trance, especially when the needle hit "Strange Things Happening Every Day," and you could hear the devil himself trying to slip through a breath in Sister Rosetta's phrasing. It is a sound the French jazz writer Hugues Panassie described as "the extraordinarily mordent." Nat Hentoff has called Sister Rosetta a gifted tragedienne. For me she is an ageless oracle in a church-lady hat. Like the Carters, she seems to have seen what the rest of us can only guess at; her voice and her playing are genuinely possessed.

If the gospel ladies communed with the Almighty, jazz women had to please lesser, but just as demanding, gods. Musical innovation throughout the Jazz Age and swing era was largely the province of men: Armstrongs and Basies, Ellingtons and Hamptons. Fronting those classy combos and orchestras were female vocalists who could play fiery intellectual chess with the greatest instrumentalists. Generations of women rockers would take their cues—visual and musical—from a brace of sophisticated ladies who set the standard for ballads, upscale blues and jazz.

They were as original and unpredictable as the music itself. For Billie Holiday—the legendary Lady Day—life was a short and rather desperate improv. She was singing in speakeasies and turning tricks as a teenager to overcome the crushing poverty of her birth to a pair of unwed teens in 1915. She cleaned at a brothel so she could play Bessie Smith records on the bawdy house Victrola. Hard times, heroin and string of abusive men tempered Holiday's instrument to almost unbearable sensitivity. She had a flexibility, a hoodoo exactness of expression that moved millions. In 1939, her 200-proof cocktail of artistry and audacity caused a sensation when she began singing "Strange Fruit," an anti-lynching song (from a Lewis Allen poem) that could not have been more graphic in painting the landscape of southern racism. The aural picture was Hieronymus Bosch by way of hell itself: bloody trees hung with the corpses of lynched black men. Sometimes, Holiday cried when she sang it; unsuspecting clubgoers gasped, wept—or fled into the night. Over half a century later, David Margolick's vivid biography of the song (*Strange Fruit: Billie Holiday, Café Society and the Early Cry for Civil Rights*) made a strong case for its stunning—and lasting—social impact.

Despite the furor, Holiday remained a huge star. She was one of the highest-paid entertainers in America in the mid-forties, favorite of black connoisseurs and the white leftie intelligentsia. Lady Day headed for Hollywood, where she got to play . . . a maid. Entrenched racism, a longtime drug habit and the relentless hounding by narcotics agents resulted in a fatal dimming of the spirit. Heart and liver failure killed her in 1959. She was not spared the final indignity of being fingerprinted in her hospital bed.

Two years after Billie Holliday was born, a Brooklyn couple became the doting parents of pretty little Lena Horne, who began performing as a grade-schooler. She was sixteen when she joined the chorus line at the Cotton Club in Harlem; her trajectory was an ever-upward arc, from stints as a singer for Noble Sissle's orchestra, then with saxman Charlie Barnet's big, muscular band. If Lady Day was the era's tragic muse, Horne was Harlem's Barefoot Contessa—elegant, almost preternaturally soigné, yet unafraid to swing. Purists would not call her a jazz singer; her vocals were accommodating rather than improvisational. It didn't hurt that Horne was—and still is—astonishingly beautiful, a silken, light sepia dream acceptable to Hollywood, which beckoned in 1942 with an MGM contract. During the war years, her title song to the 1943 film *Stormy Weather* was a huge national hit; she has remained successful and beloved for the last half century, collecting a Lifetime Award Grammy, an honorary doctorate from Harvard and the icon's prerogative to appear—regally chinoed—in a Gap ad.

The same year that Billie Holiday died, another black club singer— an orphan who had also come up hard—was hitting her stride as the hardest-swinging jazz singer this musically misbegotten nation has ever produced. In the mid-fifties, Ella Fitzgerald tore through Cole Porter, Gershwin and Rogers and Hart standards, rearranged their very molecules with her nuclear scat, and joyfully, spookily put them back together with an air traffic controller's precision and sangfroid. You can never tell where Miss Ella is going until she makes a perfect one-point landing on a note that hollers *Yes! Of course!* Illness, age and the amputation of both legs halted her performing days, but as recently as 1988, she recorded for Quincy Jones's *Back on the Block* album along with other jazz greats— and the humbler company of Big Daddy Kane and Kool Moe Dee. She died in 1996 at the age of seventy-eight.

Quincy Jones also inveigled the nonpareil Sarah Vaughan to come out of semi-retirement for that record. Its cut, "Setembro (Brazilian Wedding Song)," was the last track she would record before she died in 1990. Jones's and Vaughan's collaborations in the sixties—among them, *Sassy Swings the Tivoli* and *You're Mine You*—were mutually satisfying, to say the least; Jones declared himself devastated at the death of "Sassy." Decades of cigarettes may have added a lived-in patina to her voice in later years, but lung cancer killed her.

Vaughan was an instinctive, protean artist whose jazz piano playing earned her as much respect as her urbane vocals. Certainly, coming up in an era so dominated by jazz*men*, she was that rare woman known for her sheer musicianship. Listening to her upend a standard like "All of Me"—recorded on Valentine's Day of 1957— you can hear both aspects of her gifts. The scat phrasing swings easily and impeccably; the lyrics drift into eddies of high notes, then settle into warm, controlled alto tones. Rarely could one woman travel so far in one note. What Aretha Franklin would do with her slurring, soaring melisma, Vaughan had achieved with a vibrato that seemed to come from the center of the earth and shimmer off toward Venus.

Like Aretha, seven-year-old Sarah began singing in church in Newark, New Jersey. By age eleven, she was church organist. The instrumental quality of her voice was doubtless linked to her talents and inventions as a jazz pianist; she got her start in 1942 when Billy Eckstine heard eighteen-year-old Sarah on the Apollo Theater's Amateur Hour. Eckstine persuaded his employer, band leader and keyboard sorcerer Earl "Fatha" Hines, to hire the girl as a vocalist *and* second pianist. Eckstine then added Vaughan to his new band in 1944, into the more experimental form that would become bebop. Apprenticing with the likes of trumpeter Dizzy Gillespie, saxophonists Dexter Gordon and Sonny Stitt and drummer Art Blakey, her destiny was sealed. Vaughan's experimentations and her career survived the heartaches and distractions of faithless husbands and managers—among them trumpeter George Treadwell. In the end, Ms. Sassy's most uplifting relationships were professional, with jazz men from Miles Davis to Oscar Peterson and Zoot Sims who respected, challenged and showcased her gifts.

If there is a paramount body of early evidence to support that seventies poster slogan "Sisterhood is powerful," it is Dinah Washington's 1958 LP tribute to the Empress, *The Bessie Smith Songbook*. Having come up through gospel, jazz and R&B, Washington (born Ruth Jones in 1924) was hardly a straight-up blues singer. But on that album, her interpretations of Smith standards—from the sublimely sophisticated "After You've Gone" to the gin-soaked "Jailhouse Blues"—reveal a keen harmony of spirit. It's a communication across time and death that outpaces even the digitally engineered duet between Natalie Cole and her late father that made a hit of "Unforgettable" in 1991.

Washington could sing anything; at nineteen, she held her own as a vocalist with Lionel Hampton's band in the mid-forties, sliding easily between jazz and the singular straight talk of "Salty Papa Blues"—("I got a man that treats me like a rat"). Her biggest hits were R&B songs cut on Mercury, mainly in the fifties. She breached the pop chart Top 10 only once, with her languid, knowing "What a Difference a Day Makes."

Washington was also one of the first big female stars to effectively mind her own business. She opened a Detroit restaurant and convinced the likes of Aretha Franklin, Muhammed Ali and Sammy Davis, Jr., to sign with her booking agency, Queen Attractions. Dinah was also queen of the Flame Show Bar and the Twenty Grand clubs in Detroit, where hopefuls like Marvin Gaye, Diana Ross and Aretha Franklin clamored to see her. The Queen was not reluctant to anoint her certain successor, either. Pointing out Aretha Franklin to Quincy Jones one night, she informed him, "That one—C.L.'s girl—*that's* the one to watch."

The next local black enterprise, Motown Records, was just gathering speed when Washington died in 1963, at 39. At the Detroit funeral, Aretha sang yet another of her idols home. A lifelong voluptuary, Washington downed the wrong casual mix of liquor and pills. It's still unknown whether she enjoyed seven or nine husbands during her short time on earth. But her live-fully-and-fiercely philosophy epitomizes that other legacy of women in rock—that willing embrace of appetites.

By the late forties and mid-fifties, women—more specifically, white middle-class women—were not supposed to have (or admit to) appetites of any kind. Sitcom couples slept in twin beds; bra cups and girdles were iron maidens, triple-stitched to contain the merest hint of flesh that rippled or moved. Even recipes were repressed; we had entered an age of cookery that would replace fresh with frozen and embrace artificial flavors, instant puddings, TV dinners. Raw appetite hadn't a prayer against the new pre-cooked efficiency. Family meals could be planned and flash-frozen once a week—about the accepted recipe for dutiful marital sex.

Such meager helpings were hardly satisfying to blues and jazz women whose very art was fueled by appetite. Things would loosen up a good deal by the nineties, when Madonna chose to explore her sexuality with a coolly conceived, limited-edition book (*Sex*), pricey bondage props and the co-conspiracy of a top fashion photographer. But when women were first tasting the freedoms of the road and the royalty check, things were a bit more ad hoc.

This is not to say that meticulous planning didn't go into the stadium wedding thrown by Sister Rosetta Tharpe to solemnize her third marriage in 1951. Over 20,000 "guests," most of them women, bought tickets and oohed and ahed over the $5,000 fireworks display. In addition to serial matrimony, Dinah Washington also indulged in peroxided wigs, crystal chandeliers and mink toilet-seat covers. Bessie Smith snacked on hot young men and cute chorus girls like so many chocolate truffles; so did Ma Rainey.

Bisexuality was no big deal—witness the unequivocal lyrics of Bessie Smith's restless "Jailhouse Blues":

Thirty days, with my back turned to the wall . . .
Look here, Mr. Jailkeeper, put another gal in my stall . . .

By the mid-fifties, wild, wild young men were garnering most of the head-lines with a new music called first rhythm and blues, and then, once the white boys took hold of it, rock and roll. Black women like Etta James (a.k.a. Soul-ful Miss Peaches) and LaVerne Baker, schooled in gospel and blues, were turning out ripping R&B sides. Ruth Brown's fusillade of hits, from "5-10-15 Hours" to "Wild, Wild Young Men" made the nascent Atlantic Records "the house that Ruth built." By 1955, Brown had sold an astounding 5 million records, a milestone celebrated in a lavish ceremony at the Apollo Theater. But in the fifties, vocal expression by women was about as segregated and schizophrenic as the rest of the Eisenhower years. Ruth Brown played one of rock's first-ever outdoor festivals to over 9,000 celebrants in Atlanta's Herndon Stadium with the likes of Ray Charles and B. B. King. But she never made it past the twenties in the white pop charts; Etta James's classic "Tell Mama" reached her personal best of #23, after a decade of hard rocking. White female cover records fared better; Peggy Lee's cover of Little Willie John's "Fever" shot to the Top 10. Connie Francis hiccupped cutely through "Stu-pid Cupid," and sweet Rosemary Clooney bounced through "Mangoes."

Post-war America was deeply conservative but giddily optimistic. It was a decade that embraced tight girdles and loosey-goosey hula hoops, Billy Graham's stern homilies and Detroit's finned and portholed excesses. But the greatest divide would prove generational. Though etymologists date the first usage of the word "teenager" back as far as 1935, that creature, as it is now described and understood in our culture, clambered to the hood of a souped-up, "chopped and channeled" deuce coupe, swiveled denimed hips and proclaimed its feisty arrival just after World War II.

Teenagers had begun to customize their not-quite-parallel universe with its own language, clothes and sound. The rise of real young people's music—rock and roll—had begun to strain the straight seams of domestic affairs, art and fashion. And though vast suburban sprawl had, for the first time in history, challenged the primacy of the cities, the subdivision tribes of Teen stayed connected by a wondrous new mode of communication that could preserve and disseminate the code from coast to coast.

By 1950, television sets were brought into American homes at the rate of about five million a year; by 1962, 90 percent of homes would have at least one set. Elvis Presley's appearance on *The Ed Sullivan Show* on September 9, 1956—the first of three—ushered in a new era of rock-based teen shows. Beneath all the screaming, advertisers heard the quiet euphony of folding money. And Marshall McLuhan, in his landmark *Understanding Media*, recognized some bold new signifiers in a younger generation determined to, like, *chill*:

> Part of the cool dimension of TV is the cool, deadpan mug that came in with the teenager. Adolescence, in the age of hot media, of radio and movie, and of the ancient book, had been a time of fresh, eager and expressive countenances. No elder statesman or senior executive of the 1940s would have ventured to wear so dead and sculptural a pan as the child of the TV age. The dances that came in with TV were to match—all the way to the Twist, which is merely a form of very unanimated dialogue, the gestures and grimaces of which indicate involvement in depth, but "nothing to say."

I can recall my father, a foxtrot diehard, hooting over the semi-detached dancing on *American Bandstand*. "They don't even look at each other. Look at that one—chewing gum, staring off into space! Which guy is she dancing with, anyhow?"

My reply was knee-jerk but heartfelt: *You just don't understand.*

Teen cool was further encoded in dress. And television also spread that style foment that shook up the fifties. A decade that began with Dior's corseted, wasp-waisted New Look would end with an industry frantically turning out blue jeans and mohair sheaths. For the first time in history, girls wouldn't have to dress in "junior" versions of Mom's prim shirtwaists. Department-store buyers, parents and teachers were all shook up. Blue jeans, particularly associated with real juvenile delinquents and the cinematic rebel ilk of Marlon Brando in *The Wild Ones* and James Dean in *Rebel Without a Cause*, had become so culturally charged that a 1959 movie about an unwed teenage girl was luridly titled *Blue Denim*.

The rebellious years were beginning to extend past high school; good girls were wondering if they had to go from Daddy's house to the marriage

bed with the customary dispatch. Briton Mary Quant, who would instigate
the Beatles-era "youthquake" with her kicky fashion designs within a few
years, told me of a restlessness that she and other fifties girls were feeling on
both sides of the Atlantic: "Certainly it had a lot to do with the war. There
was a generation that were expecting things just to settle back to the way it
was before. And, of course, that can't happen after such a major war as that.
The new generation approached things completely differently—and fresh."

To wit: In the mighty wake of wartime labor heroines like Rosie the
Riveter, the working girl was slowly being perceived as less of a transitory
creature—that trembling chrysalis who existed briefly between high school
and marriage, if all went well. "Until that stage," said Quant, "either women
would be their father's little daughter, their clothes paid for by their father,
or they were the wife of the doctor. This was probably the first time women
had their own careers—and therefore dressed for themselves."

Despite these post-war revolutions, the frivolities of poodle skirts and
bold conical advances of Maidenform sweater girls, feminism was still two
decades and a million tuna casseroles away. And the brief flaring of two
talents in the mid-fifties is testament to the sheer impossibility, back then,
of having it all. Patsy Cline, best known these days through the gorgeous
tributes of k. d. lang and a baby-boomer rediscovery of her boxed sets, was
a country singer so vibrant, so nuanced, that even the pop charts couldn't
resist her. Cline—born Virginia Patterson Hensley, a sweet-faced Virginia
girl—could get down and yodel up a barn-raiser, but her specialty was slow,
excruciating heartache.

Her ballads ("Crazy," "I Fall to Pieces") killed. And getting them out
there took everything Patsy had. Married twice, with two children, she
found herself so torn and breathless between domestic and career issues
that she recorded with broken ribs after a serious car crash; she cooked
madly when she came off the road. Somehow, she also found the time and
inclination to mother-hen another new singer with a hard life and sweet
disposition named Loretta Lynn. Anxious to get home on a foggy winter's
night in 1963, thirty-year-old Patsy Cline died in a plane crash.

*Elvis is in his mama's living room in Memphis, earnestly facing a pretty woman
with raven curls and blood-red lipstick. It's 1956, and the hopeful, hitless soon-to-
be-King is playing a stack of blues records for Wanda Jackson, a firecracker vocalist*

out of Oklahoma City who is holding her own at eighteen, recording in front of the
big country guitars of Roy Clark, Buck Owens and Merle Travis. Wanda and Elvis
have been touring down south.

"You should be doin' this kind of music," he tells her, and though she likes
the hard stuff, she demurs.

"I'm just a country singer."

El persists: "I am, too, basically. But you can do this."

Wanda did. But do you know her? Until I stumbled on her Capitol *Vintage*
Collection, I was unaware they were doing nuclear testing in fifties recording studios. Wanda's reading of that Lieber and Stoller chestnut "Riot in
Cellblock #9" shoots blue flames off the word "Raaaaaaht." She growls and
hollers through a brace of hard rockers. When Wanda whoops, it's the vocal
equivalent of Jerry Lee Lewis mulekicking his piano stool. Buck Owens's
guitar races to keep up with her devilment on the gleefully sassy "Hot Dog!
That Made Him Mad."

She was hot, she was great, but in the fifties, Wanda Jackson just didn't
fit anywhere. It seemed she had ideas as bold as her vocal delivery. She
insisted on touring with black piano player Big Al Downing in the segregated south. The night she played the Grand Old Opry in a little sheath
she'd designed with rhinestone spaghetti straps, an outraged Ernest Tubb
made her throw a jacket over them *nekkid* shoulders. She submitted, but
stormed off afterward and never played there again.

Wanda never found her Colonel Parker, never had a hit bigger than
1960's "Let's Have A Party," a two-minute frenzy so real so you can feel
the spilled beer seep into your shoes. She tried Vegas, more country, found
Jesus, then gospel. At last report, Wanda, a grandmother, is still shaking
several layers of naughty cowgirl fringe with the occasional gig near her
home in L.A. Like Patsy Cline, she rocked too hard and early, and had to
give it up too soon.

THE SIXTIES
from shoop shoop to lady soul

[At a Motown audition] Diana was with three girls. She was younger, she was skinny with sort of a whiney voice, but she had these great big eyes, and she knew that she had that appeal, and she used it. She used her eyes, she used everything. In her I saw this personality that could go far.
—Motown Records founder Berry Gordy on Diana Ross, 1998

Diana, Mary and Flo are rising out of the waves at the center of a craggy, foam-flecked oil seascape. It was painted by a fan as the Supremes rode the crest of sixties pop. Now it hangs on the wall of Mary Wilson's Manhattan apartment, across from the gold 45s for the likes of "Baby Love" and "Stop! In the Name of Love." Mary was the cute, sexy Supreme, the one, according to Berry Gordy, "that all the boys loved"—and the one a still-territorial Diana Ross brazenly shoved onstage during the taping of the Motown 25th-anniversary special in 1983.

A decade and a half later, Wilson and Ross are cordial during rare encounters, though they are no longer friends. When I ask Mary if she thinks she and Ross will be joined for life in fan's minds, she laughs and says oh yes, probably. But Diane, as Mary's always known her, is ... *Diane*. And thank God Miss Ross has had her big successes. Divahood suits a girl who wanted to look and sing pretty so badly she was a teen tornado of ambition: weekend modeling school, cosmetology studies, talent shows. Diana is still a drama queen—divorcing with dueling press releases, playing a pop queen in a glitzy TV movie with diva-in-training Brandy, emoting globally on *Larry King Live* after she was taken into custody for slapping a Heathrow airport employee.

In April 2000, music journalists on hand for the excruciating taping of the VH1 Diva tribute to "Miss Ross" offered a morning-after chorus of regrets. *The New York Times* headline: "Miss Ross is Ready, So Fawn, Baby

Love." Reported the *Daily News:* "She (Ross) oozed a surreal, air-kissing sincerity while delivering a host of New Age bromides like, 'It's all about enjoying your process.'" Refusing to use VH1's sound system instead of her own incompatible equipment, Miss Ross suffered static and pitched onstage ego spasms ("This doesn't please me"). Miss Ross psychobabbled further: "Where I'm at in my life is about giving you my love." Miss Ross gave the audience five hours of rump-numbing stops and starts due to incessant costume changes. Miss Ross publicly excoriated her own musicians. ("Where's my band? My band never leaves the stage before I leave the stage.")

In short, Diana Ross secured her long-standing reputation as Diva from Hell. Florence Ballard has been dead some twenty years now. And Mary Wilson is still on the road. "I am still trying," she says, "to establish myself as Mary Wilson." She is just back from a weekend gig at a Six Flags amusement park in New Jersey, where she presented her current mixed bag of Supremes hits, pop standards and the occasional Sting cover. Wilson, who once boarded transcontinental flights with a dozen wig-stuffed hatboxes, chaperones and chauffeurs, is traveling much lighter these days. She has been doing oldies shows, clubs and "corporate work" since the Supremes broke up in 1969. "I love singing," she says. "That's what I *do*. I'm out four days a week—every week."

And she has never stopped working, save for a hiatus in 1994 when her fourteen-year-old son was killed in a car accident. She didn't stay off the road long, though, says she *had* to go back. But she found herself singing Eric Clapton's tribute to his lost little boy, "Tears in Heaven," night after night. "I sang it for at least a year," she says, "because it was really hard to express that without talking . . . morbidly."

Losing a child is an unspeakable blow, and though Mary has carried on, performing, traveling and writing, the tragedy has muted the effervesence I recall from giggly, sushi-and-plum-wine ladies' lunches that we shared in the past. Since those days, Mary has also published two memoirs (now available in a new, updated edition by Cooper Square Press) that talked about the formerly unmentionable aspects of the Motown star system, about the Supremes' inner disharmonies due largely to Ross's extraordinary ambition, about the traumatic high school rape of Florence Ballard, who was never allowed to deal with the devastation. "That was a time when people didn't talk about rape," Mary says. "Flo didn't get outside help."

She tried gamely to work through the problems on her own, though, insists her friend. "I don't for one minute think Florence gave up. She was trying every minute. Desperately."

From all angles, Flo's seemed an uphill fight. Her tenor was so strong, so distinctive, that Lamont Dozier, who supervised the Supremes' backup vocals in the studio, used to move the mike farther away, so that she would not outmuscle and outsoul Diana's lead. When neither her temperament nor her body could fit the subservience and slinky fashions dictated by Miss Ross, when she behaved erratically and missed some engagements, Florence was asked to leave the group in 1967. (She was replaced by Cindy Birdsong.) After a fizzled solo attempt, Florence spiraled into alcoholism, a failed marriage, heart complications and death in 1970, at thirty-two.

Mary had her own struggles within the extremely patriarchal Motown star system. Like most girl groups, the Supremes were prone to the Big Daddy syndrome that pervaded the record industry in the sixties. Few if any girl-group singers wrote their own material; fewer still even owned their own names. At Motown, Berry Gordy's control was so absolute that Mary Wilson would eventually sue for the right to spend her own money; at one point, though the group was making millions, she needed Gordy's written permission to buy a car. Her 1977 lawsuit did win her a fifty percent right to use of the group's name—one she exercised once both Ross and Cindy Birdsong left.

Mary will still tell you that she feels she was one of the lucky ones. Before things fell apart, the Supremes had an astonishing run. Following their first hit in 1964, "Where Did Our Love Go?," they had four successive number-one hits: "Baby Love," "Come See About Me," "Stop! In the Name of Love," and "Back in My Arms Again." Only the Beatles could match them hit for hit, and by 1966, the Detroit girls had oooh-oohed their way into the British Hit Parade as well with five number ones. The beat was infectious, subtle as the two-by-fours banged together in the makeshift Motown studio to show all the white kids where to clap. The package was impeccable; introducing the Supremes, even the granite-faced Ed Sullivan seemed pleased to introduce this well-groomed, non-wiggling trio of proper young ladies. Plenty has been said about the extras lavished on Diana Ross, who walked off to a solo career on the boss's arm. Nonetheless, Mary Wilson has had enough of the revisionist history that puts down the very practical rewards of the fabled Motown charm school known as

Artists' Development. Flying first-class to London, the Supremes learned to scoop caviar daintily; traveling in the south, they were shot at in the Motown bus. Mary says she'll never forget the mortification on Flo's face when she ordered with a flourish in a swank Parisian hotel and wound up with a mound of raw chopped meat. People don't seem to understand just how far they traveled, and how much of the territory was scary and uncharted. "People would say the white community really backed the Supremes," Mary says, "because they would come to all our shows. Black people wouldn't. But black people *knew* us. They knew *everything*."

White women still come to her shows—often with their daughters—and they all have a ball together. But Wilson says it is black women who recognize her at airports and malls. They hug her and thank her for making America—the world—take notice when three black girls from the Brewster projects raised white-gloved hands and sang "Stop!" *Stop and look at us, will you?* Not long ago, Whoopi Goldberg told her, "You know, Mary, you girls are the reason that I'm here today."

And so, Mary likes to stay "out there." Today, Monday, is always a catch-up day after weekend engagements. She is booked for months; two assistants tend to details in other rooms. Retro rock and roll—and the public's longing to conjure their first, best times—can bring a woman alone a fine annuity. Respect is something else. Mary is still stung by her encounter with a young security gorgon who barred her way backstage at a Rock and Roll Hall of Fame event because she wasn't *somebody*. *Time* magazine had put Mary Wilson and her two girlfriends on its cover; Joe Eula painted her on a poster that now commands thousands; the Beatles demanded a summit when they came to the States. "Now it's all about laminated passes," she says darkly.

But quickly, the squall passes. She says that she is enjoying this period of her life because it is the first time she has felt truly independent. Divorced, she is "not eager" to remarry: "There's a certain freedom that I feel now that I've never had because I've been a child with parents, a female in a group, then a female in marriage. And then the children. I've always catered to other people's idea of who I was. Now I'm enjoying being by myself. I'm learning who I am." To that end, she is taking college psychology courses; she does her homework on a laptop, in limousines and airplanes. Perched in her home high above the Hudson River, amid the memorabilia of an astonishing life, Wilson smiles. "I feel that the things that the Supremes accomplished in history," she says, "were phenomenal at the time."

How right she is. And how it hurt, Mary told anyone who asked, when her old friend Diana announced a multimillion-dollar Supremes Reunion tour in the spring of 2000 with Scherrie Payne and Lynda Laurence, two virtual unknowns whom Mary had trained and taken on the road some years back. The genuine Supremes, Mary and Cindy Birdsong, were offered such disparate wages—a reported $3 million for Mary against a projected $15 to $20 million for Miss Ross (plus merchandising)—that they refused to climb on board. Diana dragged a clearly unprepared Payne and Laurence on to her VH1 tribute by way of promotion. And from the teleprompter she read, "Mary and Cindy I love you." Alas, plagued by poor reviews and a woeful box office showing, Miss Ross's love tour was quickly and quietly aborted.

The Supremes peaked in the middle of an extraordinary decade for young women who dared to rock. Not since blueswomen's triumphs in the twenties were there so many female artists at the fore. And this time, black and white, they managed to breach both the pop charts and the nation's consciousness. Audiences and playlists were open-minded enough to accomodate sandaled folkies, feathery English birds and sock-it-to-me soul sisters. The Rock Diva—that supernova realized so fully by the eighties—was just a glimmer in savvy promoters' eyes as Tina Turner, Cher, Diana Ross and Aretha Franklin took their first bold steps in strappy high heels and Janis Joplin fled a lacerating adolescence in Port Arthur, Texas, to wrap herself in blues and feather boas. By the sixties' end, things would get funky indeed. But first, as Mary Wilson says, there were the *girls*.

They came *shoop-shooping* onstage with a very fifties innocence—and firm foundation garments. The rise of the girl-group sound came at a time when those busloads of greased, conked and nasty boys—hormonal highwaymen whose appetites were as obvious as their tailoring—were in retreat. Chuck Berry was behind bars on morals charges, Elvis was in the army, Jerry Lee Lewis was riding low for marrying his thirteen-year-old cousin Myra. Buddy Holly died in a plane crash in 1959. And that same year, it developed that many of rock's hero deejays were being paid under the console.

Congressional payola investigations and parental backlash against the music's supposedly delinquent contagion delivered a devastating one-two punch to untrammeled rock and roll. Record men knew they'd have to clean up their acts. Thus fierce sharkskin suits gave way to fuzzy alpaca V-necks favored by the likes of Fabian, Paul Anka, Frankie Avalon and Bobby Rydell. These boys sang about puppy love and Venus in blue jeans. And, as fitting consorts, the hit parade embraced angoraed Daddy's girls and primly permed teen angels: Brenda Lee, Connie Francis, Shelley Fabares, Lesley Gore and that Mouseketeer-grown-into-a-C-cup, Annette Funicello. There were some nods to darker teen angst; Lesley Gore had her boyfriend stolen at her own bash ("It's My Party"). She could be feisty declaring independence from one possessive boor ("You Don't Own Me") and unabashedly vindictive toward her rival ("Judy's Turn to Cry"). Pre-marital sex and near rape was the unexpectedly adult subplot of the first (1960) spring-break movie *Where the Boys Are* (starring, and title song sung by, Connie Francis). Declared Paula Prentiss's beach-bunny character Truggle: "Girls like me weren't built to be educated. We were made to have children. That's my ambition: to be a walking, talking baby factory." Truggle did stipulate that it would be "legal, of course. And with union labor." Marriage was still the grail. And the majority of film and Top 40 teen fare was relentlessly wholesome. Even James "Butane" Brown popcorned restrainedly onto the set of the dorky film *Ski Party*—in a Fair Isle sweater!

All this good clean fun fit a massive new business plan; at the same time rock was slipping that "sanitized for your protection" band around its product, national programming and playlists took hold. With the rise of a Top 40 network, there would be no more quirky regional hits; everyone went national or stiffed. Production teams tinkered with a formula for mass-market success: Fewer moving parts onstage, lots of well-crafted hooks and cute, carbonated lyrics. The result: the girl-group sound.

Not that it was bad; it was delicious. Girl groups offered the record bin equivalent of those heavily frosted Kellogg's variety packs devoured by sixties pre-teens. There was sweet (the Honeys, the Cookies, the Jelly Beans, the Chiffons, the Dixie Cups, the Angels, the Toys), semi-sweet (the Orlons, the Supremes, the Shirelles, the Crystals) and semi-bad (the Ronettes, the Shangri-Las, Martha Reeves and the Vandellas, the Marvelettes). Their ranks were drawn almost exclusively from high school girls in urban areas whose other options held little promise.

"Until Motown in Detroit, there were three big careers for a black girl," Mary "My Guy" Wells told me. "Babies, the factories, or day work. Period." Her labelmate Diana Ross had a job as a restaurant busgirl in Detroit's Hudson's Department Store, which catered to the wives of auto executives from Bloomfield Hills and Grosse Pointe. Ross recalls walking through the four posh selling floors to the kitchen, pulling her coat closed to conceal the baggy uniform. On breaks, she studied the fashions and learned to sew them. And when she looked ahead, it was often into a mirror. "I didn't feel I was college material," she told me. "I couldn't select a career or anything. Really, all I wanted to do was sing and wear pretty clothes."

Many of these girls, as grown women, collapse into fits of laughter —tinged with a soupçon of horror—when they recount their first efforts at stage glamour. Slipping into buttery designer leathers after a concert one night, Diana Ross catalogued the Supremes' debut outfits: "I sewed them myself. They were black and gold, and we had a string of gold fake pearls from the dime store. You remember those balloon dresses? The skirt looked like a balloon? We made some of those in a very bright flowered print. And we had these bright orange shoes with big flowers stuck on the front of them . . ."

Look at us! The smiles aren't nearly as bold as some of the clothes in the early photos on the walls of the Motown Museum on West Grand Avenue. Outside its own enclaves, black Detroit had long been conditioned to adopt dull, protective coloration—on faceless assembly lines, in domestic day work that cast gazes downward at floors and laundry tubs. Looking the public straight in the eye—Gordy would dub his product the "Sound of Young America"—required preparation and vigilance. When the Motortown Revue left town for its first tour in 1964, said Ross, "they wouldn't let us off the bus until everybody had their makeup on. It was the day of the beehive, and your hair had to stay teased up like that for days."

When the Supremes headed abroad for their first Continental tour, Miss Ross deplaned in a pink suit with a caped top. There is a photo that still gets to her: "I thought I was *so* classy. Lord, you look at that picture now, with a Sassoon hairstyle. That picture didn't look like me at all. I mean, I have changed so much. I look at that and I realize what it was. I was just trying so hard to *please*."

There were so many like her, doe-eyed, stiff-haired and very, very young. A few years back, researching a history of rock photography, I sifted through thousands of old publicity stills in archival and private collections. If you line them up and study the poses and faces, frame them in a time of Johnson's fictional Great Society and Martin Luther King's mountaintop, of blond Beach Boys in white duck pants and Mississippi burnings, of Lester Maddox's segregationist pickaxes and a buoyant, julep-sweet *Hello Dolly* on Broadway, those girl group shots comprise one poignant funny valentine.

We were, all of us, headed for a time of shimmering visions dissolved by some of the bloodiest, most bitter days this republic has ever known. And these girls were dressed for dreams: adolescent tummies tucked into sophisticated sheaths, white debutante gloves on awkwardly posed black girls, coltish legs so unused to spike heels they pigeon-toed awkwardly. Many seemed to be teetering, physically, and otherwise. They were at the very edge of . . . something. Post-war American girlhood was beginning to change. These almost-women didn't mind being Daddy's girls—but could they *please* have the car keys?

The Professor Higgins for much of this pert pop maidenhood was a New York City photographer named James Kriegsmann, an Austrian immigrant who got his start in the thirties photographing the black showgirls and Cotton Club smoothies (Cab Calloway, Louis Armstrong) that other white photographers wouldn't go near. Kriegsmann gave the Cotton Club's "Chocolate Lovelies" the same glamorous treatment that George Hurrell bestowed on Hollywood's Harlows and Lombards. He turned a pock-marked kid with crummy teeth—Sinatra—into a jug-eared dreamboat, painstakingly retouching the ravages of adolescence, even making and attaching fake shirt cuffs of stiff white paper to make the cheesy jacket a bit sharper. No matter who the client, Kriegsmann doled out equal-opportunity allure. His 46th Street studio, a former Hungarian night-club, saw teen angels and Motown misses trip through an anteroom graced by more exotic Broadway blossoms: strippers Gina Bon Bon, Gypsy Flame (Goddess of Fire) and Jamie "Queen of Muscle Control" West.

When I visited Kriegsmann in his Forest Hills, New York, home in 1992, a stroke had confined him to a wheelchair, but his recall was photo-graphic. He shrugged off his determination to extend his star treatment to black artists when others warned him, "Jimmy, don't photograph niggers, it'll ruin your reputation." Kriesgsmann looked amused by the memory: "Such craziness. Photographing black musicians didn't ruin me—it made my reputation. They were a dream to shoot. Everything was *feeling*."

He was equally matter-of-fact about his skills in helping rock boys and girls look *clean*. "Rock and roll, in the beginning, was traditional," Kriegsmann said of those early portraits. Meaning that idols in training wore immaculate suits and fussy cocktail dresses. They'd bend an elbow—no more—for a pensive lean against the plaster Greek pillar in his studio. What nature didn't bestow, Kriegsmann conferred, with soft, indirect lighting and the retoucher's magic wand. He did all the lab work himself, said he even fixed "a botched nose job" for Connie Francis. When any record company needed a makeover for a gum-snapping ingenue in tight chicken slacks, a session with Kreigsmann was one-stop shopping.

Amid all the hopeful group portraits, standing firm and supportive as Kriegsmann's prop statuary, was the Unknown Stalwart of rock and roll. More powerful than a Stratocaster . . . able to leap songwriters' bridges on a single note . . . it's the backup singer. She shoop-shoops, doo-langs and ooh-wahs. She's dearer to a lead singer's heart than the most lubricious groupie, yet she is often uncredited, except in agate type. She is generally paid scale but is worth ten times her weight in industry platinum. And without her, there would be no rock and roll. Try to imagine Elvis Presley's "Suspicious Minds" without its menacing "ooh-ooh" fills, the Stones' "Gimme Shelter" without Merry Clayton screaming "Rape! Murder!" in the background, Aretha Franklin's "Respect" minus those pile-driving "Sock it to me's."

With a curtsy toward Gladys Knight's Pips and Presley's Jordanaires, it must be stated flatly that the overwhelming majority of backup artistry is female. And lest you think it's a snap to dip-da-dip an eighth of a note behind the beat—in six-part harmony—Luther "Never Too Much" Vandross will explain the finer points of the art: "Let's take a stunt pilot, metaphorically speaking," Vandross says. "They could go up and spin and dip, and do the loop the loop. But could they fly parallel with five other fliers and stay in exact formation? That is a whole other talent." And don't come to his audition saying you can sing any part—alto, soprano or in between. "Listen," Vandross says, "I don't want my dentist to remove my cataracts, and I don't want my podiatrist to give me a root canal. I like *specialists*."

And, above all, he loves Cissy Houston. These days, she may be best known as Whitney's mother, but since the early sixties, Miss Cissy has ruled as the empress of vocal enrichment. Her matchless stability has been the true rock for many; making his post-Hollywood Vegas comeback in 1968, Elvis Presley insisted on having Cissy and her Sweet Inspirations (Myrna Smith, Sylvia Shemwell and Estelle Brown). Houston remembers getting there weeks ahead of the engagement to rehearse: "Elvis came in, and he was just . . . beautiful. We all about fell out of our shoes. He was just so nice, too. Nobody had to tell us what he wanted from us. But I always added things on. I'd be standing onstage sometimes, and I'd sneak an obbligato in. I looked over at him, and he loved it—that wonderful smile he had."

The Sweets' only serious rivals for stage and studio time were the Blossoms, on the West Coast. My admittedly unscientific poll of artists and critics adds these unsung names to the roster of all-time studio backup stalwarts: Aretha Franklin's sisters Carolyn and Erma, Dee Dee Warwick, Fanita James, Judy Clay, Brenda White, Lisa Fisher. Some did go on to solo careers: Darlene Love, Minnie Riperton, Patti Austin, Chaka Khan, Merry Clayton.

But what is it about Cissy Houston that keeps her booking agents so busy? "She just gives it to you," says Vandross. "You say, 'Cissy, on that third bar, just hold the note straight, do not bend it; but on the fourth through the twelfth, go ahead and do your thing,' and she will say, 'All right, baby,' and you will have it, perfectly in the pocket."

Herewith, the tip of the mighty Houston oeuvre:

"Tell Him" (the Exciters, 1963), "Just One Look" (Doris Troy, 1963), "Walk On By" (Dionne Warwick, 1964), "Chain of Fools" (Aretha Franklin, 1967), "Brown-Eyed Girl" (Van Morrison, 1967), "Son of a Preacher Man" (Dusty Springfield, 1968), "Mother and Child Reunion" (Paul Simon, 1972), "I Wanna Dance with Somebody" (Whitney Houston, 1987).

When I asked Cissy to explain her enduring adaptability, she said, "When you are talking about a living thing—and I do believe music to be a living, breathing thing—you have to understand that it will push and change itself, just to survive. And if it's something you do every day, it's going to change right along with what's going down in your life."

* * *

Despite all the orchestrated primness, the girl-group genre's first smash was rather adult. The Chantels' "Maybe" was a scant two minutes of unremitting sexual anguish; sixteen-year-old Arlene Smith ripped her vocals atop keening, gospel-fired choruses. Just how she got it so right was a mystery. Years later, Smith admitted, "I was singing about a kind of love I didn't know; I loved my *parents*."

What the little girls didn't know, the record men took care of. With the speed and precision of Indy pit crews, songwriting and production teams custom-built hits, most notably in the stuffy warrens of Manhattan's Brill Building. In the main, they put their stuff out on independent labels like Philles, Red Bird, Scepter and Laurie. Towering over the genre was Phil Spector—aptly dubbed the "Tycoon of Teen" by Tom Wolfe—a small, intense man who blasted opera, particularly Wagner's bombastic "Ride of the Valkyries," when he was not making rock and roll. Spector built an empire with his dense, multi-layered "wall of sound" productions on the Crystals and the Ronettes.

The lyrics were pretty standard stuff. There is plenty of pledging, heartbreak and rhyming burnin'/yearnin' in the girl groups' short, 4/4 passion plays, from the Jaynettes' storm warning in "Sally Go Round the Roses" ("Sally don't you go, don't you go downtown") to the Dixie Cups' blissful "Chapel of Love." Romance—loving truly, tragically, unconditionally—was the subject at hand. And three married songwriting couples (Ellie Greenwich and Jeff Barry, Carole King and Jerry Goffin, and Cynthia Weil and Barry Mann) came up with endless Top 10 permutations.

Few gambits worked better than Loving the Wrong Guy. It was as if Teen Angel were still reaching for the fifties Wild One: the rebel who dressed like James Dean, flicked cigarette butts at pigeons—but kissed like a dream. Good girls loved the bad boys of "He's a Rebel," "Uptown" and "The Boy from New York City." And how many pop songs, since that death and dating soap opera, "Leader of the Pack" have echoed its Montague/Capulet plaint of loving the boy from the wrong side of town?

"Pack" was sung by the Shangri-Las, a trio of white chicks from Queens, New York, girls so tough they startled the Long Island–raised Greenwich. They showed up for work in tight pants and trailed a nicotine cloud; for them, Greenwich conjured a "good-bad but not EVIL" dream lover—with divinely dirty fingernails. The day the Shangri-Las performed in the cafeteria of my whitebread Connecticut high school, they looked out on a bland sea of Shetland-sweatered boys named Dusty and Miles—preppies whose eyes popped at the sight of these chicks in poured-on capris. Just outside the windows, the girl group's greaser Galahads—the auto shop guys, the skinny loners in black chinos and Cuban heels—smoked, indifferent and cool. The group played to them, beckoned them in with shiny, hot-pink manicures. The cheerleaders in plaid skirts took a long look outside and wondered . . .

Bad boys could be kinda . . . good. The same could be said for girls with harder looks but oh-so-tender hearts. When Phil Spector found a trio of mixed-race girls from East Harlem, they had some of the forbidden allure of Chita Rivera's Anita in *West Side Story*, and a bit of the awakening sexuality of Natalie Wood's dark-eyed Maria. It didn't hurt that they sang like angels—with smudged mascara faces.

Birth of the Perfect Pop Record, New York City, 1963. Writers Ellie Greenwich, Jeff Barry and producer Phil Spector are brainstorming at Phil's York Avenue penthouse. Veronica (Ronnie) Bennett, the Ronettes' lead singer is here too, hidden in a bedroom. Phil may already know he wants to make her his second wife, but right now she is his perfect, vibrant muse with a rat-tail comb.

It is a dependency he prefers to keep secret. But he's told her that he needs her nearby—right on the other side of the wall!—to get the feel for the song. It's got to be a cry from the heart of a good girl grappling with serious Passion. Ronnie doesn't know about sex yet, doesn't even venture downtown—and what's with calling a top-floor apartment a penthouse? With her ear to the plaster, she hears them talking. Talking about that girl.

"She's so innocent, she's from Spanish Harlem . . ."

"She has a grandmother who won't let her go out on the roof!"

They're writing about her!—an uptown Juliet who watched real life from her window and sweet-talked fictional dreamboats in the studio. They're building a bridge of promises—she'll make him so proud—higher, fiercer toward the chorus: "Be My Baby."

Ronnie is thinking to herself: I'm gonna sing it great.

Such was a vulnerability, a naïveté I never imagined of my personal girl-group queen in the days she first beguiled me. Ronnie Spector was the pioneering Tough Girl of Rock, with clouds of Aqua Net inflating her hair and a touch of sandpaper vibrato in her voice. Her look and her body English were revolutionary amid the cooing white-gloved doves of that day. She may have been Spector's cossetted Muse—and by her later account, a real prisoner of love during their four-year marriage. But live, on record and skittering across those corny TV teen stage sets, Ronnie telegraphed *power.*

Hers was the preternatural Girl Omniscience that led Madonna to wish aloud two decades after "Be My Baby" that she could look the way Ronnie Spector sounds: "sexy, hungry, totally trashy." With her piles of dark hair and her Cleopatra eyeliner, Ronnie looked impossibly exotic to white-bread teen America—an effect she credits to her mixed heritage: Her dad was Irish, her mom part black and Cherokee, her great-grandfather Chinese.

Up on my suburban altar, propped on the dresser against a jelly jar full of pale lipsticks and dark mascaras, Ronnie was the kohl-eyed goddess of Female Cool. The cover of *Presenting the Fabulous Ronettes Featuring Veronica* album was downright spooky; no matter where you were in the room, Ronnie's eyes seemed to be following, looking *right at you.* Talking to you. *Hey, girl* . . . Struggling with snappish garters—pantyhose was still a future comfort—I'd look up at Ronnie and pray for a swift end to girlish fumblings. Listening to the throbbing, operatic crescendo of "Walkin' in the Rain," we restless virgins were convinced. Ronnie *knew.*

Despite the intervening years spent developing a professional rock and roll cool, when I finally meet Ronnie, I find I have all the poise of a fourteen-year-old git. We arrange a rendezvous at a hotel between our homes in western Connecticut. Ronnie is remarried to her manager, Jonathan Greenfield, now, and they are raising two teenage boys. Waiting in the marble lobby, I see the Big Hair first—contemporized, but very Ronnie. Tiny feet in big heels; tiny woman. The dark eyes still catch and hold you—just like that album cover. We settle in the empty bar over coffee; the bartender peers, open-mouthed. Later, he'd ask me, "Oh, my God. Was that . . . *Ronnie?*"

Bill Clinton exercised less self-control when Ronnie, along with Eartha Kitt, Chuck Berry and Lyle Lovett, performed at the Colorado summit in June 1997. Ronnie says she felt his eyes on her throughout the show. She looked down and said in her best breathy Ron-ese: "And here's a little cha-cha-cha for Mr. Pres-uh-dent." Her Marilyn Moment. Ronnie giggles, telling the story: "And I did a little cha-cha-*cha* to 'Be My Baby' and he just went,

'*Oh God.*'" At a photo session backstage, the then-Boomer-in-Chief opened his arms to her and breathed, "BE MY LITTLE BABY!" Once he let go of her, Ronnie says, "Hillary grabbed me and starts crying in my arms."

What was *that* about? she wonders. It can get pretty weird, having to officiate at all the pyscho/sexual flashbacks Ronnie tends to trigger as she still works clubs and concert halls. Stranger still to know you once enraptured the leader of the free world. Ronnie is reeling off the riots she and the girls triggered—fistfights at the Apollo Theatre, when both black and Spanish uptown boys claimed the Ronettes as their own; real, testosterone-fueled terror when GIs in Germany were screaming at them, groping, "having orgasms on the floor," Ronnie says, until MPs removed the girls in an armored vehicle.

Ronnie's sister Estelle Bennett and cousin Nedra Talley were the other Ronettes. The Bennetts grew up in East Harlem, she explains, because "With my mother married to a white man it was hard for them to get an apartment downtown." The girls always practiced singing together in the mirror. But before they became the Ronettes, they sang with two other cousins. They watched the Hit Parade on the boxy black-and-white TV: "Theresa Brewer, Patti Page, Rosemary Clooney . . ." Forbidden to play—or even walk—in the mean streets, Ronnie says she spent much of her time lying beneath her grandmother's big Philco radio. She couldn't tell if Frankie Lymon was a boy or a girl, but his voice pierced her. Early on, she says, she knew: This could be a way out. Out of the crowded apartment. Maybe even the neighborhood . . .

She's gotta have it. Even Ronnie Bennett's mother understands the growing obsession of the scrawny kid who is developing such a fantasy life in front of the mirror. . . Mrs. Bennett is a waitress at King Donuts near the legendary Apollo Theatre, and almost every day she waits on Bobby Schiffman, the theater owner's son. He looks closely at her, won't let anyone else make his sandwiches, so when she finally asks if her daughters and their cousins can get a shot at amateur night, moony Bobby says he'll fix it up.

Mrs. Bennett knows the perils of amateur night at the Apollo, of audiences so tough, so mean, they call the balcony the Buzzard's Roost. She sends the kids to see her cousin, who works backstage, and he warns the wide-eyed quintet: Just remember, get off the stage because they will throw things at you if you're bad. They'll throw their own shoes . . .

Showtime, in the holding area, the kids look around, terrified. Grown men and women, other hopefuls, are sweating through thick pancake makeup. Ronnie's cousin Ira can sing like Frankie Lymon, so well that he always takes the lead. But Ira's not looking so good. And once they hit the stage, the worst happens. Ira opens his mouth and nothing comes out. The buzzards are starting to flap and cackle above these tender children when little Ronnie grabs the mike from Ira's clammy hand and sings into it:

Why do fools fall in love?

She charges ahead, loud and strong as she can, and from the darkness beyond the scarred stage apron, she hears a growing sound, an undefinable comfort she has been craving for so long.

"They applauded me," Ronnie says. "And that's when I first said, yes, this is what I want to do for the rest of my life. 'Cause if the black people could like me at the Apollo, I knew I had something."

In high school, the girls sang as Ronnie and the Relatives; they also danced onstage for rock and roll shows put on by New York deejay Murray "the K" Kaufman. Murray knew the one-track minds of the listeners in his "Submarine Race Watchers" club—K-code for the clammy-palmed tides of date-night teens who parked at beaches from Coney Island to South Jersey and groped their way toward heaven. One summer, Murray started talking up the Ronettes on the air as beach goddesses. Eventually, he would get them to dance in bathing suits for one of his promotional romps. "But at the beginning," says Ronnie, "it was just the radio, and Murray would tell the audience how we looked. He used to say, 'You should SEE these three things, I don't know what they are, what race, what color—but they're *beautiful!*'" And so they were introduced to Kaufman's huge, loyal armies—subliminal late-night visions, their giggles tinkling high and sweet just off-mike.

In 1963, Estelle got a meeting with an intense young man who was having great success with groups like the Crystals and Bob B. Soxx and the Blue Jeans. Things went pretty quickly after that. Sometimes Ronnie got a lead vocal down in one take. As for a look—well, they had been working on that for years.

Here I stop and caution Ronnie. Abashed but undeterred, I am probably going to ask her the same questions that curious girls wrote in to *Tiger Beat* and *16* magazines. But I have to know—how did they get their Look together? I need specifics. She laughs and says honestly, it's her pleasure. It was such fun. She describes an antic teenage seraglio in her grandmother's apartment, where she, Estelle and Nedra went every day after school until their mothers arrived to escort them home. Their grandmother, still besotted with the wartime Andrews Sisters, wanted her girls to call themselves the Darling Sisters. And just never mind what she thought they should wear. *Have mercy.* But though they were all but cloistered in upper Manhattan under an old woman's strict, pious eye, the girls employed a wide-angle camera obscura. "I got my ideas from looking out my grandmother's window on Amsterdam Avenue and 104th Street," Ronnie said, "seeing all the Spanish girls with cigarettes and big hair. I loved that tough look."

These external street images were flashed almost immediately into their grandmother's mirror as they worked variations on the glistening lip colors that stained all those cigarette butts they trod on the way to school, experimented with the hot flashes of fuchsia stretch pants, the towering hair constructions that even an icy blast off the East River could not intimidate down there on 104th Street.

If hair has been a symbol for potency since Delilah, it's also been rock's key signifier—a point the hit hippie Broadway show *Hair* underscored so raucously in 1966. Even when the prudish Ed Sullivan showed us only the above-the-belt Elvis, El's sly, hormonal 'do shook and shone in floppy, greased defiance. Conventional and flyaway, or fashionable and sculpted, hairstyle speaks. It's capable of wit, lust, aggression, irony. Racial, political and sexual orientations are deconstructed from do's. Organic, yet malleable into the most unnatural states, hair would become the specialty of populist shock troops: DA'd greasers, Afroed Panthers, skinhead Oi! boys, Mohawked punks and dread-ed rappers. In the girl-group days, the Ronettes' Big Hair was pretty strong sexual semaphore. It hollered: Untamed!

But before Ronnie got creative with all those cans of—yes, it *was* Aqua Net—she had to go straight. Her family's genetic shake and bake had made the Bennett girls' hair extraordinarily thick and curly, unmanageable for a working mom who needed to get them off to school in a hurry. Rendering it workable required some funky chemistry. "When we were really young, we used to have to go to this hairdresser that lived in the basement—my sister and my cousin and me—just the three of us, 'cause a lot of the other cousins weren't half breeds. We had to get it straightened out. This lady would curl it and put it in paper bags to roll it up. And get it in a real *flow*. That started the three of us looking in the mirror together, seeing who would get their hair to the waist the fastest."

And who could wrap and tease it the highest. They had a ball, but it didn't play well at school. "I didn't want to go out because kids would beat me up," Ronnie explained. "Especially the black girls. If you had long hair and light skin you were trouble."

Ronnie's signature insurrection hinged on a loose hairpin; letting her hair down may have been a red flag, but she was stubbornly committed: "I loved my look even though I got beat up a lot and my braids were cut off in school. I loved being different. And when I got with the Ronettes, we didn't do like the Supremes. Our hair would be up in these big beehives with intentions for it to fall down during the show. I always made sure the pin wasn't tight. I loved getting *messy*. Now, my eyes are a little Chinese. I wanted them ALL the way out. The three of us would sit in the mirror and see whose eyes would get out the longest with the eyeliner."

The Ronettes used black Revlon liquid eyeliner; they sat forever, waiting for it to dry. And once they started to sweat onstage, it would melt and run into their eyes. They always left the stage looking like they had been in a fight. And in a way, they had. Spector's multi-layered Wall of Sound was a painstakingly crafted studio construct. And while all girl groups labored to reproduce their records credibly in live shows, the Ronettes faced an almost insurmountable gulf. It helped that most often the house band at the Brooklyn Fox Theater was that of the mighty saxman King Curtis, who could funkify a nursery rhyme if you gave him three bars. "It was a big, big band," Ronnie says. "But it wasn't as big as the records. That bothered me. So I'd tell the drummer to go bump-de-BUMP, and the bass. And I realized then that my looks were important—my movements—because that took over for what was missing."

Of all the girl-group pinups, Ronnie *incited* onstage; having shaken it for the most progressive of Manhattan sock hops including the famous Peppermint Lounge, the Ronettes never locked themselves into the sorts of demure steps and hand gestures taught by veteran hoofer Cholly Atkins at Motown. Sometimes the Ronettes quarreled about it; Ronnie wanted them to be "more rock and roll." Ask her how she choreographed her knowing hand-flick-followed-by-hair-toss and she says, "Smoking." Over and over, she mimed those street-corner mamas, with their haughty, *so-then-I-told-him* head snaps, until she got it right.

If girls idolized her, boys had other ideas. Ronnie has written her own book, *Be My Baby: How I Survived Mascara, Miniskirts and Madness*. And it details the priapic indiscretions—and abject apology—of John Lennon, her wild one-nighter with David Bowie, her nightmare marriage to the manically possessive Spector. Enough has been said about her days and nights in his Los Angeles fortress to let it rest on a single image from her autobiography: Lest she travel anywhere alone and seem unescorted, Ronnie was compelled to drive her car around Los Angeles with a blowup male dummy in the passenger seat as silent, humiliating enforcer of her husband's mad love.

Men were crazy about Ronnie, but they also proved to be stalwart friends, especially those wild boys who shared her fealty to the beat. She snuck the Beatles out of their beseiged Manhattan hotel room to the greasy abandon of a Harlem chicken joint. ("People in my neighborhood just thought they were some square Spanish guys.") Thirty-five years after the Ronettes toured England with the Rolling Stones, she says they are still friends; Keith Richards happily joined her in the studio to work on a solo record slated for 2001; Joey Ramone was just as pleased to produce Ronnie. Murray the K helped her get back on her feet when she returned from Los Angeles after the divorce. During Bruce Springsteen's mid-seventies performing hiatus owing to a titanic management dispute, Ronnie says he would put on Southside Johnny's red jacket by way of disguise and leap onstage with her in Jersey clubs, gleefully escaping his legal muzzle, if only for a song or two. In 1981, Billy Joel would write a song about Ronnie's split with Spector, "Say Goodbye to Hollywood"; it was a hit for him, and she says he got it so right she had to record it herself. It was a fitting bookend to "Be My Baby."

Ronnie says that years of therapy have been invaluable, but it is her marriage to Jon Greenfield, and their boys, that have finally made her feel safe—at last. When she and Jon come in off the road, she likes to tell the boys everything; the noise from their boom boxes has, in turn, introduced Ronnie to Coolio, R. Kelly, Counting Crows. Her touring band—two backup singers, two guitarists and a piano player—is mostly female, and she likes it like that. "It's like being balanced for the first time in my life. My entire life in the sixties, I couldn't talk about anything. I couldn't talk about my shows, about the guys going crazy over me. I couldn't talk about women. So it was a very limited life. Now I have everything. I'm not rich, but I have enough to support my children and have dinner on the table and buy them their jackets for the winter. Yeah. I have everything now."

She confesses to one lasting addiction: compulsively reading biographies of other women artists— Eartha Kitt, Billie Holiday, Patti Labelle, Mary Wilson—"to see how they handled things." She says she wrote her own, mercilessly detailing her own descent into pill and alcohol abuse and back to "close the chapter" on the Spector years. There is just one thing from those days she can't live without.

"I love the road. It's so great when you meet people who can't even speak your name but they realize what you're singing about. It's something I can't do without. I get crazy if I'm not onstage for like, say, two months. I'm like, 'God, when am I going to be *free?*' That's why I can't do a routine in a studio and then go do it onstage. Because the audience *makes* you. When they go, 'Ooooh,' your hands go a certain way. It's *now. That's* rock and roll to me."

Solo acts also scored with the girl-group sound. Betty Everett and Shirley Ellis hit with cute novelty songs—"The Shoop Shoop Song (It's in His Kiss)" and "The Name Game," respectively. Miss Mary Wells was just seventeen when she stepped up to a mike at the Motown studios and the producers told her, "Mary, sing it like you are really *hurt.*" Mary's front teeth are chipped beneath the tentative smile of her first publicity still. But her subsequent *My Guy* album cover was soul's Mona Lisa, circa 1964. She's smiling broadly beneath a carefully teased bouffant, almond eyes drawn into a near Egyptian slant by twin strokes of eyeliner. Mary was mohair and sequins, vulnerable and tough. The Beatles adored her and persuaded her to tour with them.

Mistakenly thinking she could chart her own course, Wells walked away from Motown's hit-making machinery at twenty-one; she had no songs of her own and less business savvy, and she never got her groove back. But years after her greatest successes, she, too, was still touring, supporting three children from two failed marriages. And though it was tough, like Ronnie Spector, she said she wouldn't have it any other way. One night, as she reached for her mascara wand in another small Manhattan club, Mary looked at me in the mirror and explained, "Some women just can't be at home. I can do both. I like to come home, clean the house myself, enjoy the kids, help them with their homework. And then go back out there and work. I just cannot be idle. It makes me feel like I want to climb the fuckin' *wall*. I think a lot of people feel that way, don't you? That's why you be runnin' *all* the time . . ."

Gotta go . . . Mary stayed out there until her voice literally gave out and she died of throat cancer in 1992.

Girl groups ruled for just half a decade. Some were broken up by record-company politics and the whims of powerful producers. Others fell to gentler foes. "When people say what happened to the Vandellas, I say *men* broke up my group," Martha Reeves told me. "I get one cute and all properly trimmed and some man comes along and say, 'Wow, that's a hot number.' And before I know it, she's gone."

It went so fast, they'll all tell you. The transitory nature of these girl groups, packaged and arranged by male Svengalis, is a common subtext in conversations I've had over the years with assorted Vandellas, Ronettes and Supremes. But Martha, one of Motown's more soulful, hard-charging acts expressed it best in a 1965 smash. "Nowhere to Run" was one of Motown's rare adult songs that went past teen longings to serious sexual frenzy, the kind that left a woman in a blind alley with the relentless breath of passion on her neck.

The singer says it's not love she's running from, but the heartache she knows will come. Can't tame it; can't quit it. Martha could be singing about a man, but later, she found she was singing about the music itself. Motown singers, girls and boys, came of age in a raging sea of adulation. How baffling, how unbearable, then, was that sudden stop when the kids, the radio stations, even the Motown "family" itself could easily, blithely do without you—especially when Martha found her own passion undiminished. We were talking about it one night after an oldies show in Manhattan, in a frigid, unheated theater, when Junior "Shotgun" Walker strolled by and told Martha the evening's version of "Nowhere" was HOT. She smiled and allowed that "Some part of every day I'm like that song. I feel like that every single day."

It's the rocker's pact with the marketplace devil: Choose a restless, fickle medium and learn to live with the sudden stops—or get a straight job. In the sixties, it was easier for eclipsed male artists to drift into production and management careers—men's work. Transitions were not so simple for women who didn't even own their stage names. Darlene Love—a former Blossom and Crystal—has made the point that since producer Phil Spector owned both those names, he could put anyone he wanted out on the road or on record—and frequently did so. Martha told me that the Marvelettes' name was lost one night in a poker game between Gordy and other Motown guys: "That's how easily your life can get tossed from one place to another," she said.

Mick, Keith and the boys are hungry. The Rolling Stones have come to New York craving a serious hit. But more than that, they wanna meet James Brown! And maybe Ronnie Bennett can fix that. As it is, they've just passed another uncomfortable night sleeping in the offices of her label, Philles Records, in Manhattan. Phil Spector's secretary has kicked them out, as usual, at the start of business hours.

The Stones take the train to Flushing Estates and show up at the house Ronnie is renting with her mother. Touring together in the foggy U.K., the two groups used to knock on doors when the thick mists halted their funky caravan. Blinking mums in flannel robes would heat up a scone and some tea for these pasty boys with big lips and the trio of polite café au lait girls with shocking great hair.

Those bony Brits still look hungry as Ronnie's mom lets them into her kitchen.
"You boys want some scrambled eggs?"
"Yes, Mrs. Bennett, if it's not too much trouble."

How sweetly they welcomed their conquerors. Plenty of sixties singers—and rock histories—have attributed the demise of girl groups to the British Invasion, but that's a bit shortsighted. A wider look at the sweeping plains of pop suggests it was a more natural attrition—that restlessness again—rather than the dominance of shaggy foreign boys. After all, how long did surf music rule? Or bubblegum? Or punk?

There was a smaller, more demure female British Invasion. The interlopers were all pale and blond and rimmed with enough black eyeliner pencil to rewrite the Magna Carta. Petula Clark was a fab little dollybird, all eyes and incisors. Her brightness and bounce brought her fifteen big hits in the U.K. and the U.S. Clark's "Downtown" was the swingin' London flipside to the Crystals defiant, ghetto-proud "Uptown," and it hit #1.

No one came roaring across the big pond with a better understanding of root American pop than Dusty Springfield, born Mary O'Brien in London in 1939. According to writer Lucy O'Brien, young Mary told her convent school teacher, at age eleven, that she wanted to be a blues singer. Outraged nuns walked out of her talent show rendition of Bessie Smith's "St. Louis Blues." For a time, childish dreams yielded to the realities of the marketplace and Springfield began her career in the fifties as part of a cutie-pie outfit, the Lana Sisters. But the solo hits that eventually made it across the Atlantic had a deeper, more soulful feel, especially "Son of a Preacher Man," which featured Cissy Houston on background and phrasings that seemed far more delta than Celt. Springfield's finest example of what would become known as "blue-eyed soul" was her 1968 album, *Dusty in Memphis*. Her talents were much larger than the British bird flirtation, but though she kept working intermittently, it would be as a critic's favorite—not in the Top 40. She died in 1999, after a long struggle with breast cancer.

Marianne Faithfull, best known then as Mick Jagger's sometime girlfriend, had a solemn, quavery hit in 1964 with "As Tears Go By." High times, heroin and what girl groups would call a bad *repu-tay-shun* would pillory Faithfull in the London tabs as "Naked Girl at Stones Party." Being a performer and a famous rock girlfriend could be a double-edged sword back in those unsisterly days when teens slavishly copied Jane Asher's thick-lashed, dollybird makeup—and longed to tear her heart out for dating Paul McCartney. And the music business could be brutally dismissive to a chick singer who hung with the band. The Stones' manager Andrew Loog Oldham was blunt in explaining why Faithfull got her chance: "I saw an angel with big tits and signed her," he said.

Faithfull's post-Jagger tailspin—a fairly standard substance abuse fable by now—could easily have ended in the London shooting galleries where her heroin addiction had landed her. But she'd later describe hitting bottom as affording a certain kind of relief. As she explained in *Faithfull*, her 1994 autobiography, after all the rock and roll shamming and posing, being packaged in what she called the "angel doll" persona, being a street junkie was the first time she felt she was leading an honorable life, without PR or pretense.

Though her life was a prolonged train wreck for another decade and a half, Faithfull put out a shockingly brilliant album in 1979. The woman who wrote and sang *Broken English* was no angel doll. She looked and sounded more like a torchy Miss Havisham—with a syringe or two impaling the ruined wedding cake. The sixties tremor had deepened into a knowing vibrato; the speaker was more coarse than coy. Having walked through more fire and rage than Alanis Morissette or Fiona Apple would ever invent, Faithfull had erupted as rock's own volcano goddess Pele. Molten anger hissed out of "Why'd Ya Do It?"; regret and ash lay thick in cuts like "Guilt." In my own disbelief—could this be the same person?—I went through two copies. In later years, Faithfull's affinity for Kurt Weill's music led to some recordings and live cabaret-type performances. I finally got to see her perform live during one of those Weill evenings at the Brooklyn Academy of Music. She was wry, wonderful, thrillingly hoarse. Faithfull's casual irony—the honestly acquired kind—moved one young man to scream out, "Why couldn't YOU be my mother?" Watching this older, decidedly unpretty woman effortlessly captivate, I marveled at a glimpse of the early Angel Doll that I had just seen on video.

The Rolling Stones' Rock & Roll Circus was filmed in 1968 but kept in the can until 1995. Mick Jagger is the ringmaster; John Lennon is the featured clown. Two famous rock girlfriends—and late bloomers—perform.

In't she loverly? Her blond hair pulled into a French twist, feathery fake lashes casting shadow on her alabaster cheeks. Marianne Faithfull is prettily arrayed in a purple gown. Golden and unmoving as a trophy, singing somberly, she gets a scant two minutes before the fire eater comes on. Then, as the band "Dirty Mac" is jamming (John Lennon, Eric Clapton, Keith Richards, Mitch Mitchell), a hand reaches down and pulls a tiny black-clad figure onto the stage. Her face is barely visible beneath the thick scrim of black hair. But suddenly she is screaming into the mike.

Ahhhhhhh . . . aieeeeeee, eeeee——yah.

WHAT THE HELL? The screams are disconnected now, not bothering to hang with the tempo. Eiiiiieeeeee. And as the number ends, she forms words within shrieks:

GIVE ME . . . GIVE ME . . .

What the hell *did* Yoko Ono want? Who did she think she was? This caterwauling proclaimed the beginning of one of rock's great love stories, a total collaboration that would include bed-ins and bread baking, the Plastic Ono Band, albums, films, marriage, concerts and a son. Unlike Faithfull, Yoko Ono would arrive on the rock scene with her own fully formed aesthetic. But she, too, would have to overcome the rock-girlfriend classification that belied another, three-dimensional persona. Before she met Lennon, Ono, the Tokyo-born daughter of a well-to-do banker, was a classically trained musician. And she was an entrenched part of the Manhattan avant-garde art scene before the Beatles had their first hit in 1964. She made films—notably a montage of 365 derrieres called *No. 4, Bottoms.* As a performance artist, she invited audience members to scissor off her clothes.

Yoko was no shrinking violet, but she knew little of rock and roll before she met John Lennon. She has said she started screaming so hard, high and loud to compete with those strange electric guitars. It would take a while, but the B-52s and, later, a slew of woman-dominated bands like Hole would cite Ono's primal screeches as a root influence for their own howls-from-the-whirlwind sound. But not before disgruntled fans would lay at Ono's doorstep the ultimate (and false) Rock Sin: *She helped break up the Beatles!*

As the sixties wore on, other female voices would grow more insistent and adult. To explain the glamorous arrival of Miss Dionne Warwick, I leave it to today's foremost connoisseur of divadom, Luther Vandross. He says he was thirteen, living in the Alfred E. Smith projects in downtown Manhattan, when he went to the Brooklyn Fox Theater to check out one of deejay Murray the K's amazing Christmas shows—the kind where the Angels would roar out on a motorcycle. Here's Luther singing their big hit now:

"My boyfriend's back and you're gonna be in trouble" . . . It was really cool. So the next act was about to come on and . . . [Luther is humming here, some familiar introductory chords] And this woman with a very exotic look and a red spaghetti-strap dress—chiffon!—started singing . . . [He sings it: "Anyone who ever loved . . ."] And I am telling you, she is single-handedly why I wanted a career. She pierced me. The sheer beauty of her voice is what carried me and her away.

Queenly, sloe-eyed Dionne glided to stardom on the butter-smooth pop compositions of Hal David and Burt Bacharach: "Walk On By," "Anyone Who Had a Heart," and "I Say a Little Prayer." Dionne had come up singing with her sister Dee Dee in the New Hope Baptist church choir, directed by her aunt Cissy Houston in Newark, New Jersey. Theirs is a powerful female dynasty in modern pop; Dionne was a standout session singer before she went solo. And before long, toddling around the studios, singing around the Houston home before Sunday supper, there would be baby Whitney.

As soulful artists amassed more and more sixties hits, black American life was venturing into wide, uncharted territories. And bigger, bolder voices were keeping up with the rising barometers of political and social change. In Los Angeles, in 1967, Phil Spector produced a gloriously bombastic record by Ike and Tina Turner. "River Deep, Mountain High" set Tina's flamethrower vocals atop a combustible booster rocket of sound—strings, voices, screams. It was a spiraling, vertically built record that went straight to the top of the charts in the U.K. but fizzled at #88 in the U.S. Furious and embittered, Spector would go into seclusion for two years; Ike and Tina kept touring relentlessly, slowly building a following for Tina's heartstopping live act that would take another decade and a half to pay off.

In New Orleans, the marvelous Irma Thomas put a gale of tears and two centuries of Crescent City musical infusions into "I Wish Someone Would Care," and Fontella Bass demanded "Rescue Me" with a high estrogen urgency. There was Maxine Brown, Brenda Holloway, Carla Thomas, Gladys Knight and Marvin Gaye's soulful partner, Tammi Terrell. But no one was quite prepared for the force that was Aretha Franklin.

She had recorded gospel at fourteen, had endured six frustrating years at Columbia trying on everything from jazz to standards to limp R&B before Atlantic Records, long a soul powerhouse, sent her to Muscle Shoals, Alabama, with a greasy mixed-race studio band and producer Jerry Wexler in early 1967. They released the first cut a month later, in February. Newly licensed, I ran my first red light the moment I first heard that voice singing "I Never Loved a Man" from the tinny dashboard of my mother's

Chevy II. Aretha's voice was so arresting, her delivery so immediate, that "Never Loved" sold a quarter-million copies within the first two weeks and went gold shortly after. It was the beginning of an astonishing run that pushed music that was deeply, unreservedly and powerfully black to the center of the dial.

Aretha's soul united pop and R&B audiences from black neighborhoods and white universities. In the clubs and in the charts, her hits came like cannonballs, blowing holes in the stylized Motown sound. Here was a voice with a sexual payload that made the doowop era, the girl groups and the Motown years seem like a pimply adolescence. It was a new kind of sexual lament that had the pain and knowing of the blues, without the resignation. Lady Soul was a fighter, but she was no quitter, perhaps owing to that gospel habit of holding out hope. In the war of the sexes, Lady Soul was a healer. The balm was homeopathic and applied directly. RESPECT.

They were just records—albeit big hits—but in some quarters they took on anthem quality. "Respect" boomed through inner-city black culture and activist centers; "Chain of Fools" chugged across the airwaves as General William Westmoreland sent more troops to the mouth of the Mekong Delta. Grunts packed field kits with C-rations, morphine and Aretha cassettes. For years, Aretha told me, Vietnam vets would come up and thank her, and recount the horrors she helped them through.

Aretha saw it this way: "I sing to the realists, the people who accept it like it is. I express problems. There are tears when it's sad and smiles when it's happy. It seems simple to me, but for some people, I guess feelin' takes courage. When I sing, I'm saying, 'Dig it, go on and try. Ain't nobody goin' make ya.'"

Soul was not the only barricade music. And as in any decade, some of the most interesting action took place far from the pop charts. Coffeehouses and folk festivals were becoming more and more crowded as young America strayed farther from *Leave It to Beaver*land. For them, intriguing sirens crooned in clear, unretouched voices. Odetta's severe cropped hair and high, round Bessie Smith cheekbones were as striking as her bluesy folk. Alabama-born, but educated in Los Angeles and San Francisco, Odetta Felious landed in New York, at the Blue Angel, in the fifties, with a repertoire that took in folk standards and gospel classics such as "I've Been 'Buked and I've Been Scorned," sung in a way that resonated with the increasingly restive times. Her performances echoed both Woody Guthrie and Thomas Dorsey; she was classically trained and politically inclined—a loud, strong presence at the 1963 march on Washington when Martin Luther King, Jr., delivered his "I Have a Dream" speech, and in the wave of anti-war rallies that increased with the U.S. war effort in Vietnam. Odetta has sung with symphony orchestras and at Carnegie Hall, but she became best known for raising her powerful voice in the streets. Even tempered but immovable, Odetta was a counterweight to the wiggy irascibility of Nina Simone, a singer with a scary, thrilling alto and a temperament to match. Both women had hit New York in the mid-fifties; Simone had also trained in the classics at Juilliard. Both were committed activists—Simone's composition "Young, Gifted and Black" was a barricade classic. But it took a younger woman more willing to try on designer gowns and Top 40 stylings to earn the title Queen of Soul.

Midnight on a mid-sixties evening and Aretha Franklin, nearing the end of her ill-suited years at Columbia Records, is restless. The label executives have hauled her here to Puerto Rico—another convention full of more fast-talking suits just like the ones who keep trying frilly pop tunes on the nascent Queen of Soul. They are all downstairs in the hotel, heady with Big Plans and top-shelf bourbon, courting the radio-station smoothies that make her want to scream. Aretha is staring down at the beach; she notices a lone figure walking up and down, up and down. So alone. She sees it's that scarecrow with an acoustic guitar also signed to Columbia, Bob Dylan. And she thinks to herself, "My, he must be havin' a ball, and here I am miserable . . ."

Later during the convention, in the few words Aretha said she had with Dylan, she sensed that the raggedy Jewish folkie from Hibbing, Minnesota, was as disoriented as she was. "Believe me," she recalled, "neither of us was what you call—ah—mainstream."

The folk revival that had embraced Dylan was decidedly leftie, but it had its icons like any other genre. If Odetta was its bedrock mother figure and Dylan its scrappy, mutinous Huck, we also revered Saint Joan. A committed pacifist, tireless activist, beautiful and headstrong, with a voice as clear and brittle as glass, Joan Baez also became the musical and romantic collaborator of the freewheelin' Dylan, whom she introduced to the 1963 Newport Folk Festival. They plied the cafés and festivals together in the august company of Odetta and Pete and Peggy Seeger. Watch them together in D. A. Pennebaker's landmark 1965 Dylan documentary, *Don't Look Back,* and you see a tight, self-contained juggernaut of creativity and caustic social observation. They were in such a hurry, and the music came so hard and fast:

In a London hotel room, a silly Brit photographer is trying to get a bead on the dark, Scottish-Mexican beauty better suited to the lens of Dorothea Lange. Ordeal passed, Joan is strumming, singing idly, her eyes flitting now and then to the hunched, chain-smoking Bob. Mindless of the cameras, the hangers-on, the crystalline beatitude of Joan's voice, he is pounding out new lyrics on a battered manual typewriter. His elbows scissor over spent cigarettes and coffee cups. Louder now, her voice cuts through the din:
   "And love is just a four-letter word . . ."
   He's still noodling, shoulders moving slightly to her song. "Oh GOD!" she says. "You've finished it eight different ways. If you finish it, I'll sing it."

So many times, onstage and on record, she did, giving a newer, more independent life to songs set loose from Dylan's idiosyncratic delivery. *Any Day Now,* Baez's 1968 collection, revealed the melodic strengths of Dylan compositions and showcased Baez's powers of interpretation. More striking is the strong sense of self in the journals Baez kept of those years and the letters she sent home to her mother. They show a quiet but emphatic shift in Woman's Place—the Muse who knows all your secrets and may let you break her heart but won't stray from her larger convictions.

Baez did jail time for her pacifist resistance. She appeared on the platform with Martin Luther King, Jr., at the march on Washington. Romantically, Bob would play Joanie dirty—treat her, in fact, like just another rock girlfriend. Later, she'd laughingly compare two-timing notes with Dylan's wife, Sarah. But musically and politically, Baez never blinked. Ten years past their time together, standing toe-to-toe with Dylan on his 1975 Rolling Thunder tour, she prodded him, challenged him—and made the grouchy old leadfoot *dance.* Though not an accomplished songwriter, that same year Baez wrote and recorded "Diamonds and Rust," her rueful elegy for the youthful passion Pennebaker caught on film. Younger women, from Mary Chapin Carpenter to the Indigo Girls, still measure their sharper-toned harmonies against Baez's quavery soprano onstage. *Ring*

Them Bells, a live album made from a series of performances at Manhattan's Bottom Line, is a loose-jointed, nicely imperfect valedictory for the long journey of the female singer/songwriter. Baez sings with the likes of Janis Ian, the McGarrigle Sisters, and the Indigo Girls. The harmonies are tight, the circle updated—but unbroken.

There were other clear sopranos venturing forth with just an acoustic guitar. "Folk pop," industry categorists were calling it, a lyric-heavy form well suited to the airiness and clarity of a female voice. In 1968, Judy Collins had a hit with "Both Sides Now," a circumspect tune written by a fiercely intelligent Canadian named Joni Mitchell. Another singer/songwriter, Laura Nyro, was nonpareil at writing songs other artists could get a hit with, from "Wedding Bell Blues" and "Stoned Soul Picnic" (5th Dimension) to "Eli's Comin'" (Three Dog Night) to "And When I Die" (Blood, Sweat and Tears). Nyro, who died in 1997 at age forty-nine, was best at singing her own darker, introspective compositions. She took liberties with language, pushed her voice and her piano further than she should have some nights. Still, it must have been lacerating when, at the legendarily groovy love-in that was the 1967 Monterey Pop Festival, the crowd booed this earnest Bronx-born troubador.

There weren't many other women on the bill there. During the apotheosis of sixties rock held over three December days on a foggy California peninsula, delirious celebrants saw Jimi Hendrix, Otis Redding, the Who, Ravi Shankar, the Grateful Dead, the Steve Miller Band. They cheered wildly for Jefferson Airplane, beloved of Bay Area bands, fronted by the indomitable Grace Slick.

The daughter of a well-to-do Palo Alto banker, Slick learn to serve tea properly at tony Finch College, alongside first daughter Tricia Nixon. Who knew that, shortly after, Grace would be dosing the Darjeeling with the finest Ousley windowpane acid and composing the Airplane's hallucinatory "White Rabbit" while tripping to Miles Davis. The ivy on countless college dorms shivered beneath the stereo onslaught of Slick's loud, commanding chorus, "Feed your head!"

Very few women had the guts and the vocal power to front a big loud band then, but Slick proved a daunting Valkyrie, all flying dark hair, silk and leather. Her vocals flared like Day-Glo runes above the band's guitar-heavy psychedelic rumble and whine. The opening of the Airplane hit "Somebody to Love"—the de facto anthem of the fabled '67 Summer of

Love—caught the stinging disillusionments inherent to sixties activism and "free" love:

When the truth is found to be lies
You know the joy within you dies
Don't you want somebody to love?

It was a straight, simple delivery and it played well. But complications would set in. Love, drink, disenchantment and Slick's unrepentant bad behavior would break up the Airplane and spin off a series of other bands and fitful resuscitations. In those willfully uncertain times, it was hard to keep any band of Haight renegades together, coherent and content to sing behind a tempestuous siren. Yet another young woman, newly arrived in the Bay Area, was determined to make it work.

If ever there was a girl who had to sing, and had to leave home to do it, it was Janis Joplin, who came yowling into the world in the stinky refinery town of Port Arthur, Texas, and lit out for the West Coast just as soon as she could. "They laughed me out of class, out of town and out of the state," Janis told Dick Cavett in 1970, months before her death.

She was riding high at the time, with a string of hit albums, a global following and the ability to splurge on $300 silk tie-dyed sheets. Sitting down to assess it all with her TV host in his blue blazer and desert boots, Janis cracked: "You're a real swinger, I can tell by your shoes, man." Then, on national TV, she dropped the bomb: After years of exile in the wilds of San Francisco, she was headed home to her 10th high school reunion. Since her parents had sold Joplin's bed as soon as she left, she had to sleep on a cot. But facing the gathered media, she was upbeat, as news footage revealed.

Janis sits, a purple and rose hothouse orchid, a bit florid on the old videotape. She is surrounded by ferrety men in blocky Dry Look haircuts and boxy dark suits, women with sprayed blond helmet hair peering suspiciously over the rims of their plastic cups at this vision lit by TV lights. Janis blinks back at them through tinted lenses, feather boas floating from the very top of her head, her sister Laura by her side. She is dry, she is wry, but if you watch her eyes, it'll make you weep, especially when Laura confides that Mama really did say nice things about her now and . . . yes, the family owned three of her records—though two got misplaced.

"Aw, man," Janis gamely commiserates, "my stuff gets ripped off all the time . . ."

Flamboyance may have been Janis Joplin's marquee legacy, but when you go back and listen to her speak, it's clear that humility helped her rock. Hers was a careful and willing apprenticeship to populist American music. She presumed nothing but her own limitations: "With the blues, I felt there was an honesty there that Peggy Lee was lacking," she explained to a British TV interviewer. "Billie Holiday, Aretha Franklin, they are so subtle. They can go just from A to B and make you feel like they've told you the whole universe. But I don't know that yet. All I've got is strength. Maybe if I keep singing, maybe I'll get it. That's what I think."

Janis was one of rock's first poster girls, a wisecracking, good-natured muse to hip photographers who came to adore her appealing candor. Like Ma Rainey, Janis didn't mind looking a mess onstage—sweaty, straining, face screwed up like a root-canal patient—in order to sing it right. Lost in the boogie, she'd shake her rump at camera angles Whitney Houston would sue over. She lived just as hard, let cowboys with big rough boots tear up those satin sheets. Her tango between vulnerability and bravado is characterized by two well-known portraits that papered dorm rooms, head shops and hemp-filled theater lobbies. Peering out, mischievous in one shot, bereft in another, she mirrored the frustrations of being whipsawed by strange days.

Bob Seidemann's lovely semi-nude shot of Janis, made into a poster during the Summer of Love, sold over 150,000 copies—unheard of at the time. Operating in San Francisco out of an $80-a-week storefront, Seidemann and his partners also sold posters of the Grateful Dead and that band's loveable psychopath pal, Pigpen. That one amazing summer, they made $250,000. And Janis was the best-seller by far.

She wore nothing but a fringed cape and love beads, coyly arranged. Mid-session, Joplin yelled, "Hey, Seidemann, I wanna take it all off!" He shrugged, she did. "It was so on the fly," he said later, "that you can still see the elastic mark from her underwear." He said that Joplin was surprised when she saw the contact sheets. "Do I look that good?" she wanted to know. It made her a psychedelic pinup overnight.

"She felt she was ugly," Seidemann recalled. "She wasn't pretty; she was a fucking mess. And the lighting doesn't make the pockmarks look as bad as they usually did. She had terrible skin and a kind of big flat nose, fucked-up hair. The inside was fantastically far-out, but in terms of what she looked like—ask a hunchback why he's insecure."

One night, backstage, Jim Marshall took the other photograph, a shot of a sad-eyed Joplin clutching a Southern Comfort bottle. It is often cited as a postcard from the times: too much, too fast, in a too-screwed-up world. Marshall told me that he has shots of a sunny Janis grinning just fifteen minutes after it was taken. But when he handed her a print of the sad one, she told Marshall: "A lot of people won't understand this, but I do. That's how it is sometimes. Thanks, man. 'Cause that's how it is."

The medical examiner's report said she died of a heroin overdose in October 1970, but those who knew her well have sworn it was a terminal case of the blues. And it's a strain peculiar to the road-weary blues mama. She described it herself to *Rolling Stone*'s David Dalton:

"I was the same chick, because I've been her forever, and I know her, and she ain't no star: she's lonely, or she's good at something. I have to get undressed after the show, my clothes are ruined, my heels are run through, my underwear is ripped, my body's stained from my clothes, my hair's stringy, I got a headache and I got to go home, and I'm lonely . . . and I'm pleading with my road manager to please give me a ride home, please, please, just so I can take these fuckin' clothes off, and that ain't no star, man, that's just a person."

Aretha said it more simply: A woman's only human. *You should understand . . .*

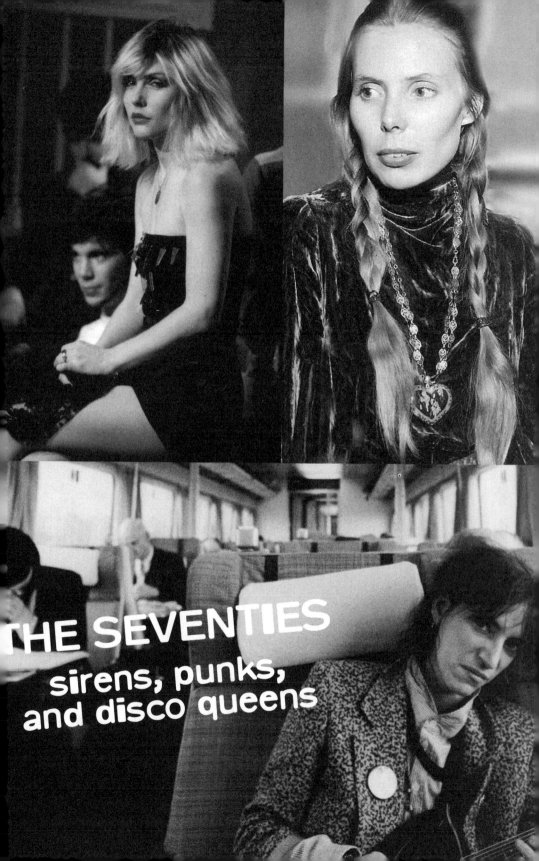

THE SEVENTIES
sirens, punks,
and disco queens

For a while it was assumed that I was writing women's songs. Then men began to notice that they saw themselves in the songs, too. A good piece of art should be androgynous. I'm not a feminist. That's too divisional for me. . . . This guy came up to me . . . and he said to me, "Joni, you're the best woman songwriter in the world." And I went, "Ha . . ." And he insisted, "No, you are the greatest female singer/songwriter ever." And I walked off. And he thought it was because I was being modest. But this whole female singer/ songwriter tag is strange. You know, my peers are not Carly Simon and these other women.

—Joni Mitchell, 1991

I f you do remember the seventies, you must remember the *noise* at their outset. As the Vietnam war continued to escalate, Young America bellowed its outrage in the streets outside the White House. Inside, Richard Nixon hunched over a televised Redskins game, insulated by its roar. By the spring of 1970, bombs had begun to fall on Cambodia and a sense of futility had begun to outpace activists' energies.

Who didn't long to quit the barricades and head for the hills? What a balm to be—or be with—those ethereal California girls. Not those cute, sun-bleached wahines with helium between their ears and beach tar on their toes that the Beach Boys had lusted for circa '65. But Ladies of the Canyon.

Lady—as in "my old lady"—was a sexy and respectful honorific then. I can recall lying on a cold linoleum dorm floor with *Ladies of the Canyon,* Joni Mitchell's 1970 album, on the tinny portable stereo; for an escapist moment I was one of her willowy tribe, a thoughtful being in gauzy clothes, well read, well loved, experienced. The canyon lady was a modern woman who tended her own garden: liberated but committed, informed but serene, re-reading *The Second Sex* while bread rose in the whitewashed adobe kitchen and the old man—a guy who can whip up the right mix of sex and sensitivity and flip it for you like the perfect omelette—snoozed, handsome, beneath the heirloom quilt.

Okay, she was an ideal, but she did glide convincingly through the passion plays and romantic disenchantments of my California heroine's songs. If Jane Austen had been around to limn the fractured morays of womanly existence in the 1970s, she might have sounded like the acutely observant Joni Mitchell. Call it *Sense and Sensimillia*. Once many of us picked up Mitchell's work and found ourselves, we just couldn't put it down.

It was a sensibility and a sound that appealed to both sexes. The same wry, enlightened resignation that would buoy Mitchell's "Big Yellow Taxi" would also power Carole King's "You've Got a Friend," leaven the Eagles' "Best of My Love," aerate Linda Ronstadt's "It's So Easy." Mellowing out seemed the only sane thing to do. And it was predictable that this Call to Chill would come from artists settled amid the wavy tectonics of laid-back California. California beamin' was a hit. The Eagles captured the lighten-up ethos succinctly in the aptly titled "Take It Easy."

The song signaled a retreat on all fronts, political, intellectual, and musical. It was a groovy kinda nihilism—with the comforts of a frozen margarita and maybe an ocean view. That Eagles' anthem suggested the young no longer even *try* to understand. It was recorded as the Vietnam war lurched toward a ceasefire in February of 1973; there may have been plenty left to protest, but there were few volunteers. Even rock festivals had become fat, uncomfy sprawls. Traffic headed to see the Grateful Dead at Watkins Glen raceway was snarled for one hundred miles. Why not just pop a cold one and drop *American Beauty* on the turntable?

Joni Mitchell was at the forefront of this California wave, but it would be wrong to classify her as mainly mellow; her music was jazzier, artier, edgier than most of the easy-chair pop that would flow from the L.A. scene. There was nothing MOR about this singer accompanying herself with guitar tunings that were just a smidge—but perfectly—off center. In her, the clear stream of singer/songwriter talent that has so recently widened found its natural source.

For all her devotion to California, Joni Mitchell was not a native of the canyons. Roberta Joan Anderson was born in Alberta, Canada, in 1943 to an ex–Royal Canadian officer and a schoolteacher. She was stricken with polio at age nine; the enforced stillness turned her toward the arts and left her with the urge to *move.* "In my teens, I loved to dance. I instigated a Wednesday-night dance 'cause I could hardly make it to the weekends. For dancing, I loved Chuck Berry, Ray Charles's 'What'd I Say?' I like Elvis Presley . . . the Everly Brothers. But then this thing happened: Rock and roll went through a really *dumb* vanilla period. And during that period, folk music came in to fill the hole."

She and her friends said "later" to Frankie Avalon's beach-blanket blandishments and sat around singing Kingston Trio songs. "That's why I bought an instrument," she explained. "To sing at those parties. It was no more ambitious than that."

Joni was headed for art school, but after she finished her commercial coursework, the music beckoned again. She sang in Toronto cafés, married a singer named Chuck Mitchell, and wound up in New York when the marriage broke up after two years. She was first successful as a songwriter, turning out material diverse and idiosyncratic enough to fit Tom Rush, Judy Collins—and Buffy Sainte Marie.

She began recording in the late sixties and had her first hit album with *Ladies of the Canyon.* She continued to produce prodigiously—almost an album a year, so much a presence that *Variety* dubbed her the day's greatest "chirper/cleffer." *Blue* and *Court and Spark* won her critical raves and a fanatical connoisseurs' following that today includes the likes of Chrissie Hynde, Janet Jackson, Madonna and Prince. Like Bob Dylan, Mitchell could write and record sheaves of great songs with astonishing ease and speed.

Her art has been a graceful pas de deux between emotion and intellect. Poet, painter, performer—a woman of such magnetism that *Rolling Stone* dubbed her Old Lady of the Year and printed a most unfortunate chart of her romantic rock liaisons, from Jackson Browne to Graham Nash. Years later, after her self-imposed exile from the offending magazine's pages—and after she had titled one of her albums *Don Juan's Reckless Daughter*—she would laugh about it in *Rolling Stone.* "The people that were involved called me up to console me. My victims called first. That took some of the sting out. There was a lot of affection in those relationships. The fact that I couldn't stay in them for one reason or another was *painful* to me. The men involved are good people."

Her difficulties as a lover, she decided, involved the same character trait that prodded her art past the blander boundaries of pop: "I'm a con-

fronter by nature," she concluded. "I have a tendency to confront my relationships much more often than people would care. I'm always being told
that I talk too much."

But once those pesky challenges were honed, harmonized and directed into a microphone, no one would dream of suggesting she pipe down.
Or stay put. To those of us tethered—to school, to parents, to more conventional female paths—Joni was a light-footed and enviable vagabond,
at least in her songs. At a time when much of this country's youth was mortified by its ugly, uncool American-ness and at least dreaming about the
ex-pat life, when legions of liberal-arts malcontents were taking up bee-
keeping and talking about "buying some land" far removed from their
parents' smug zip codes, Mitchell sang about being "unfettered and alive"
in Paris, falling headlong, in "California," for the sly advances of a Greek
satyr who stole her heart—and her camera.

In so many ways, our wine- and gesso-stained minstrel *got around.* On
the heels of a decade that revered, overused and abused the word "free," she
seemed to have found a workable definition. But she did not feel it was rooted
in any feminist inclination. Years past her furthest romantic and lyrical
rambles, she would tell interviewer David Wild, "Miles Davis and Picasso
have always been my major heroes because we have this one thing in common: They were restless. I don't know any women role models for that."

Such artsy inspiration might have been confined to the coffeehouses
if it didn't swing as well. Mitchell turned out records that teemed with metaphor and melody. Way back in 1971, in a song on *Blue* ("A Case of You"),
she was singing about a lover. But she could have been describing the dicey
position of intellectual rock in a relentlessly commercial market:

Just before our love got lost, you said,
"I am constant as the Northern Star."
And I said, "Constantly in the darkness
Where's that at?
If you want me I'll be in the bar."

Shining in the dark would prove an apt and durable metaphor for
singer/songwriters in a constellation that stretches from Laura Nyro
through Joan Armatrading, Tracy Chapman, et al. Mitchell never felt com-

pelled to pull an Ani DiFranco, putting out a steady stream of indie albums from one buzzing room in Buffalo, New York. Her early hits afforded her fame, money and the relative luxuries of experimentation. But Mitchell's further explorations—including collaborations with techno-Brit Thomas Dolby and late jazz great Charles Mingus—left the critics and some fans decidedly cool. In 1994, she sent forth her seventeenth album, *Turbulent Indigo*, which was set on the more familiar ground of its color-coordinated progenitor, *Blue*. Recurring polio effects have slowed this restless daughter; concert appearances are rare enough to qualify as Events. Mitchell has spent much of the last few years in quiet reassessment, catching up with the grown daughter she gave up for adoption in the late sixties, putting out a book of her poems and lyrics and completing a memoir.

There were more and more ladies putting out records in the cavernous sound studios that were expanding all over Los Angeles. They plied the clubs in West Hollywood where pockets of A&R men pondered the music over long-necked Mexican beers. These women wrote and sang in a more accessible pop mode than Mitchell and found a huge audience. It was no accident that one of them enjoyed her first success as a Brill Building songwriter, tailoring hits for the likes of the Cookies and Aretha Franklin. She was comfortable singing her compositions for artists about to record them, but never considered performing herself—until she, too, moved to California.

James Taylor, that lanky boy from Carolina given to suspenders and acoustic idylls, is gently winding through his set in a Los Angeles club. It is an adoring crowd; the vibe is mellow when he turns to the curly-maned woman accompanying him on piano in the shadows. He says to her, "Why don't we play one of your songs?" Shyly, she agrees, and the crowd gasps with recogition as they begin to sing.
   The song was "Up on the Roof."

This song had become an urban classic when the Drifters recorded it in 1962. The piano player was Carole King, who had spent the sixties writing girl-group hits like "The Loco-motion" and the Shirelles' "Will You Still Love Me Tomorrow." She was eighteen when she married her writing partner Jerry Goffin; they had two children by the time King was twenty. Transplanted to Los Angeles with her young children, King was not all that keen on the rigors of performance, travel and the graceless dance of promotion. She was working on song demos, singing them herself with no intention to venture outside the studio, until Taylor—a friend to a musician she'd been working with—coaxed her into the light. "I was pre-loved," King said later of that night, "because they already loved James. And they knew the songs, so it was really a no-lose situation."

Still, it was a fateful embrace. It felt so very good. King went back to the studio, kept noodling with her demos, sat at the piano and performed the songs herself. Released in 1971, *Tapestry* sold over 10 million copies and yielded a brace of pop evergreens ("You've Got a Friend," "It's Too Late," "I Feel the Earth Move"). Unlike King's early teen confections, *Tapestry* was a record that dared look youth's disillusionment in the face, sigh and get on with it. After the love-ins came . . . the mortgage? Orthodonture? Hard rock might never admit to stretch marks and alimony blues, but that wasn't Carole King's constituency.

King was divorced from Jerry Goffin and raising her children when she wove personal uncertainties into a confident, hook-laden pop statement. After all, she'd also written the decidedly adult "Natural Woman," frank and fiery enough to become a signature song for Lady Soul. And there were legions of Woodstock post-grads who heard her, loud and clear. In May 1973, when King gave a free concert in Central Park, over 100,000 fans crowded in. Soundman Chip Monck was obliged to up the wattage; he used six times the equipment that the Rolling Stones carried on their '72 U.S. tour. Though none of King's next dozen records fared particularly well, her debut success and the bounty of song royalties made it possible for her to retreat to the comforts of a sprawling ranch out west with her family.

As the seventies tripped forward, the media drumbeat grew louder: Single women were supposed to be free—and swinging, if they had the urge. *Cosmo* said so, as did the newly founded *Ms.* magazine. But if you went to the movies, the message wasn't so upbeat. Diane Keaton paid for her abandon by dating a psychokiller in *Looking for Mr. Goodbar*, Jill Clayburgh got dumped like a bruised cantaloupe in *An Unmarried Woman*, and Ellen Burstyn sponged down miles of sticky diner Formica before Kris Kristofferson showed up in *Alice Doesn't Live Here Anymore*.

Amid all these dour portraits, there was a poster girl for well-adjusted, moderate feminism. She was another West Coast canyon dweller. Arizona-born Linda Ronstadt stepped into the spotlight as a healthy, attractive single woman with a roaring career and an active love life that included Jerry Brown, Steve Martin and George Lucas. She started out fronting the L.A. band the Stone Poneys in 1964. Not long after their 1967 hit, "Different Drum," she skated off to a solo career built on her confident readings of country classics ("Silver Threads and Golden Needles") and torchers ("You're No Good," "Love Has No Pride").

"It's so easy," she sang in her hit song of that title, but according to Ronstadt, it never was. In the beginning, she said, she had great difficulty bossing men around for the sound she wanted: "When I got to L.A., I was so intimidated by the quality of everyone's musicianship that instead of trying to get better, I chickened out and wouldn't work."

Ronstadt's self-esteem didn't keep pace with her popularity and her sales: "When *Heart Like a Wheel* went to #1, I just walked around apologizing. I could see that my supposed friends resented me. I went around going, 'I'm not that good of a singer.' . . . And I got so self-conscious that when I went onstage I couldn't sing at all. It almost made me go crazy . . . I mean, I needed a lot of help."

She began seeing a therapist and grew bold enough to pose for the cover of *Rolling Stone* in filmy scarlet lingerie. But here is her description of her triumphant 1976 tour: "I threw up on the way to the airport and for the first two weeks of the tour. I had taken six months off because I'd become a physical and emotional wreck . . . I just didn't think I was good enough."

Somehow Ronstadt got through the tour, but even though the ordeal was done, her assessment sounded a lot like Janis Joplin's chick-singer blues: "They haven't invented a word for that loneliness that everybody goes through on the road. The world is tearing by you, real fast, and all these people are looking at you like you're people in stars' suits. People see me in my 'girl singer' suit and think I'm famous and act like fools. It's very dehumanizing."

Fame and its particular rock and roll absurdities may have been as disorienting to men. But most of the big rock acts of the day were male bands that offered some ready-made camaraderie; there were also growing tribes of female groupies to help them make it through the night. Listening to Ronstadt, to Joplin, mindful of the increasing economic and musical pressures of their fronting bigger and bigger shows in evermore yawning venues, it's easy to understand the eighties advent of huge backstage entourages that would become standard issue for every arena-class rock diva.

But when Ronstadt assumed the responsibilities of hugely anticipated tours and roaring adulation, tour outfits were still experimenting with the crude prototypes of today's laminated, holographic, encoded and color-dated backstage pass. Personal trainers did not materialize with clanging weights and purred encouragements to help blunt the anxiety. And nobody had developed a set of specs for fitting 20,000 sets of screamed expectations onto a pair of size-six shoulders.

It was a curious dilemma for an avowed introvert like Ronstadt who suddenly found herself incredibly and widely loved. But the ferocity of the embrace made sense. If Aretha Franklin had to cross over from soul and Janis Joplin from the hippie fringes (a white trash chick singing black like Elvis), Linda Ronstadt looked and sounded like the girl next door who'd slipped the traces—just a little. Women and men seemed equally smitten by a performer who could be alternately tough and kittenish. Her harmonies were informed and delicate, but she could also sing about the deepest hurts ("When Will I Be Loved?") with the brio of Ethel Merman belting "Everything's Coming Up Roses." Ronstadt was so beloved, the Los Angeles Dodgers insisted she sing the national anthem for the '77 World Series there. By the following year, she was the highest-paid woman in rock; her bankability rested on the multi-platinum successes of albums like *Heart Like a Wheel, Hasten Down the Wind* and *Living in the U.S.A.*

Then, not long after becoming one of the first rock artists ever to "ship" double platinum (2 million copies), Ronstadt decided to step out of that stress-inducing spotlight. She turned on her tooled boot heel and walked off to experiment in less pressured, less lucrative streams. She recorded a rather ill-fitting punkish album in Los Angeles (*Mad Love*) and lovingly interpreted the ranchera music of her part-Mexican father. Such pricey experiments were the privilege of an established hit maker, one who still performs rarely, and most often in concert with her close sisters in harmony, Dolly Parton and Emmylou Harris.

Manhattan-bred, high-strung and working three thousand miles from the mellow epicenter of the California sound, Carly Simon suffered severe stage fright, stemming in part, she said, from a childhood stutter. Her mother taught her to sing her way through the affliction, and on record she laid it down without reserve. A songwriter with canny pop instincts, Simon scored a huge hit in 1972 with "You're So Vain"—long rumored to be a scold of über-playboy Warren Beatty—and slid neatly into the easy-listening slipstream. That same year, her marriage to (and recordings with) James Taylor and motherhood made her one of rock's first hot mamas: a capable woman who could bring home the bacon, fry it up in the pan— and pose for an album cover with another kind of sizzle.

Ever the genial host, L.A. photographer Norman Seeff—the man known for creating the raunchy seraglios on the Rolling Stones' Exile on Main Street *album cover, for sessions that unfold like happenings, drawing film students, musicians, hangers-on—has poured a glass of wine for Carly Simon. And another. He is talking to her with the hypnotic, penetrating gaze that even the tough-minded Lily Tomlin worried would "penetrate to my core!" And the more he talks, the more clothes a giggly Carly is discarding. Now she is in just a sheer black teddy and high boots, leaning back, fists and thigh muscles clenched with the kind of telegraphed tension that can set off the neighborhood dogs.*

Shortly after the album, Playing Possum, *appears with this come-hither black-and-white photo on its cover, Simon is accosted in Bloomingdale's by an outraged matron. How could she? A mother herself . . .*

In fact, Simon's sexy mama played well in a time when the majority of female artists seemed in no particular hurry to rock the cradle before they cracked the Top 10. "Having it all" was just beginning its life as the career woman's impossible mantra. And even in the pampered nests of wealthy rock stars, domesticity wasn't having the greatest decade.

It began with Elvis and Priscilla's divorce in '73. Two years later, Sara Lowndes Dylan, mother of five and the inspiration for songs like "Lay, Lady Lay" and "Sad-Eyed Lady of the Lowlands," began bitter and sometimes bizarre divorce proceedings against Bob. After scalding singer Al Green with a pot of hot grits as he sat in the bathtub, Green's girlfriend, Mary Woodson, shot herself to death at his home in Memphis. Sex Pistol Sid Vicious killed his girlfriend, Nancy Spungen, in Manhattan's Chelsea Hotel with two thrusts of a knife. In London, singer Marsha Hunt slapped Mick Jagger—loudly—with a paternity suit. Even George Jones and Tammy

Wynette announced their breakup (only to reconcile and issue a single, "We're Gonna Hold On"). And on that bicentennial Independence Day of 1976, after years of beatings and abuse, Tina Turner, with just 36 cents and a Mobil credit card, walked out on Ike.

Compared to all these nasty smashups, the shifting erotic permutations of Fleetwood Mac were a mild soap opera, belied by the group's easy, laid-back sound. It was unabashed California pop, smooth as guacamole and great for a snack. Mick Fleetwood and John and Christine McVie, British ex-pats who had resettled in L.A., teamed up with Californians Lindsay Buckingham and Stevie Nicks.

In Nicks, they found an appealing frontwoman. Blond, wide-eyed and possessed of a light, skittery voice that cracked now and then like tinder-dry mesquite, Stevie Nicks was the Canyon Lady gone a wee bit over the cliff. Her vocals, her trailing, spidery dresses and her possessed body language were a determinedly witchy foil to Christine McVie's grounded, more soulful sound. The sales of their successive albums *Fleetwood Mac* (1975) and *Rumours* (1977), spiced by rumors of their ever-changing romantic linkups, gave new meaning to the term supergroup.

In the main, fans fell for the warbling, whirling, tambourine-shaking Nicks. Her lead vocals on "Rhiannon," about a Welsh witch, larded with theatrical incantations, made that single a huge hit. Onstage and off, Nicks played the part even more, her blond hair flying higher, chiffon capes swirling, midnight-blue boots stomping in possessed druid jigs; she claimed to have been harassed by ghosts. Once, citing her fascination with the Beauty and the Beast myth, she dressed in a black cape and mounted a borrowed white steed, intending to play-haunt the Gothic grounds of the L.A. recording studio/retreat Le Chateau. 'Twas a bonnie vision —until the horse bolted and nearly pitched her into the very 20th-century parking lot.

Overall, the group's mix of slick, buoyant production and mystic dabbling bewitched its Top 40 audience; *Rumours* sold over 15 million copies. There was no fern bar anywhere in America, no fitness center, no dry cleaners' counter that didn't vibrate to Mac's bromide, "Don't! Stop! Thinking About Tomorrow!"

* * *

Despite all those easy-listening sounds drifting in from the west, the national climate remained far from balmy. Few decades have been more tempest-tossed in terms of fashion, politics and sexual identity. We hounded Nixon out of office and got . . . Gerald Ford. Cocaine had become such a popular recreational drug that suburban matrons bought sterling coke spoons—yet the Justice Department was still trying to deport John Lennon on a sixties marijuana charge. The nation suffered crippling oil shortages, yet petroleum-based fashion ruled: little Quiana nothings that could mold a thigh like Saran Wrap during a steamy Latin hustle. Over it all crashed the first blue wave of denim distressed by commercial process rather than plain hard work.

On the East Coast—that bastion of enlightened pessimism—no one caught this ball of confusion and ran with it better than Bette Midler, a nice Jewish girl from . . . Honolulu. Named after that drag queens' icon Bette Davis, the Divine One got her start singing in her lingerie at Manhattan gay bath houses. She emerged as the patron saint of the Confused and Abused, an outsiders' moll who could score with the forties camp of the Andrew Sisters' "Boogie Woogie Bugle Boy" and torch her way through a standard rocker like "Do You Want to Dance?"

When he saw her at a club one night, Atlantic Records' Ahmet Ertegun says he knew instinctively that she was more than a novelty act. The woman could sing. He went backstage and offered to sign her. It took eight months to make her debut, *The Divine Miss M,* but it was an instant hit. Soon her tiny caricature body—short but stacked—and her busy, over-size and overpainted mouth would rule the most prestigious rooms; gay men followed her from the baths to Broadway and brought along their mums. And we all laughed together.

Midler's licentiousness was witty, nuanced and well art-directed. But a Millie Jackson show in the seventies could be a rough ride, even by R&B standards. Jackson was raunchier than a cathouse loo after a busy Saturday night. She was given to racial and sexual diatribes as the mood struck her. Nor was her body language subtle, favoring squats and spine-cracking grinds. And given her penchant for aerobically challenging spandex, it was quite a sight.

But everyone was getting their ya-yas out, weren't they? Mick Jagger was riding a bucking, forty-foot inflatable penis on one of the Stones' megatours. LaBelle had adopted Space Age glitter vamp, and nailed a hit about a French Quarter whore called "Lady Marmalade." Flat-topped, gilt-lipped Grace Jones prowled in sprayed-on catsuits, purring ominously, "I Need A Man," then commanding, in a huge disco hit, "Pull Up to the Bumper."

It followed that seventies rock visuals were all about sex—very little of it conventional. Rock style embraced androgyny, cross-dressing, gay disco, straight disco. Sequins were in for both Elton and Cher. Look-alike rock couples like David and Angie Bowie, Mick and Bianca Jagger, seemed more about self-love than marriage. Androgyny was, in its way, autoerotic. Sexuality could also be burlesqued; showbiz rock, born beneath the gaudy corona of Elvis's Vegas excesses, delivered a clutch of glam goddesses extreme enough to keep drag performers well salaried for decades.

"Stunning! Cele, this is stunning. I can tell you I am fully amazed."
Cele, a sixty-five-ish matron in a wheelchair, is being pushed by a silverhaired ladyfriend in a beige Ultrasuede pantsuit. The pair's voluble delight is so contagious that an amused style coven of black-clad students is following them through the "Unmistakably Mackie!" costume exhibit at Manhattan's Fashion Institute of Technology. Though the lighting is subdued, the rooms are ablaze with sequins and bugle beads, millions of them, flashing stop-sign red from cleavage, rippling, blue-green and watersmooth down a hip . . .
"Who sewed these, Cele? Women must have gone blind . . ."
Most of designer Mackie's famous rock mannequins are represented: Tina Turner, Diana Ross, Madonna, Bette Midler, Elton John. The largest section by far is devoted to Cher, the perfect gaudy flowering of Mackie's art. And though it is the fall of 1999, many of the mannequins wear vintage seventies Cher—fantasmic Cochise headdresses, Cleopatra getups, a chorus line of peekaboo gowns improbably held together by what is called "nude illusion" fabric. There is a good deal of belly exposed.
"Cher had babies, yes?"
"Two," says Cele. "Remember little Chastity on their show?"
"God bless, you can't wear that dress with stretch marks."
They have reached the infamous Oscar-night ensemble—the black spiderweb bodice, the ebony feathers spurting from the headdress like a wild, lustrous gusher of Kuwaiti crude. It made the cover of Time *and kept America tsking for weeks.*
"I remember that night, Cele. Murray had his bypass two days later."

God bless. One woman's outrageous vanities are seared into the American brainpan. The person who inhabited all these dresses—short, tiny-waisted, but able to support her weight in rhinestones—will tell you she's been pleased to serve as a winking pop-culture milestone for millions of the rank and file. She's been out there for almost four decades. Cher's people cover a wide demographic, from admiring hausfraus to deeply ironic drag queens. One museum visitor, aggressively pierced and violet-haired, spoke for all of them:

"Hallelujah, the bitch doesn't quit."

Dare to deconstruct Cher and the Crystal Palace comes to mind. The same dazzle that lured London hordes out in 1851 to goggle at the glass and iron achievements of its Industrial Revolution would draw post-sixties Americans to a figure clad in translucent glass bugle beads. The miraculous pavilion and the smiling, shiny woman were both reassuring exhibits for scary new eras. Both aesthetics are technology-dependent, but nonthreatening. Neither demands the wholesale embrace of some discomfiting new ideology.

Though her solo rise coincided with the growing Women's Movement, Cher was no rampart feminist, just a woman who Knew What She Wanted. Hers was a sexuality that could pass network censors; to mask the naughty parts, there were yards of that flesh illusion fabric. Cher's celebrity was so made-for-the-seventies that when she mounted her triumphal 1999 summer tour, she commissioned trunksful of Mackies, ordered up giant lava lamps and tacky lounge chairs, instructed her tour designer to make it "very seventies, very Cher."

For her fans—and they are still legion—Cher's husky contralto was never the main attraction, though its lowest registers did manage a certain smolder. Her material often bordered on the overwrought or corny; hits like the 1967 divorce ditty "You Better Sit Down Kids" and '73's interracial plaint "Half Breed" (you can imagine the outfit) seemed to take a page from Elvis's "In the Ghetto" mode. And as Cher's private life unfolded publicly, only El could rival her for tabloid space and speculation.

Californian Cherilyn Sarkasian LaPier had started off singing backup on girl-group records when her boyfriend, Sonny Bono, worked for Phil Spector in the early sixties. She was seventeen when she began hanging out at L.A.'s Gold Star Studios, where an excited Ronnie Bennett dragged her into the ladies' room to spill the details of the Ronettes' 1964 British tour. "Ronnie came back with Beatle boots and leather skirts and poor-boy T-shirts and I nearly died," wrote Cher in the introduction to Ronnie's autobiography. "It was like she'd gone to Nirvana and brought home souvenirs."

Ever the clotheshorse, Cher had come up with those matted-dog fur vests she and Sonny wore to warble "I Got You, Babe," their 1965 breakthrough. But over thirty years later, Cher told me the look that got them so clamorously noticed was, at first, accidental. "The truth is," says Cher, "we didn't realize what style could do in the beginning. Our stage clothes were really conservative. Our regular clothes were really *insane.* The first time we ever wore our real clothes was up in Oakland. The plane lost our luggage. So we went on in our bell-bottoms and our suede. Sonny didn't have his bobcat vest then, but he was wearing corduroy pants and Cuban-heeled boots and a poor-boy hat and a striped shirt. The kids went wild."

Soon, so did their parents, in a less demonstrative way. By 1971, Sonny and Cher—those longhaired weirdos—had morphed into America's improbably Cute Couple on prime-time TV. They were about as counterculture as Ozzie and Harriet by the time they got their network variety show. But rock had already been safely sitcommed for family consumption, from Ricky Nelson's deadpan performances on his parents' show through the made-for-TV Monkees and that cloying Partridge Family in their Mondrian-painted bus. In a twist that could make Chuck "Sweet Little Sixteen" Berry weep, the Partridges shook their polyester booties with their *mother* (Shirley Jones). The Jackson Five became a deadly Saturday cartoon.

It may have been dorkily scripted, but the co-opting was widespread, network-funded and complete. And Cher, who had seemed so exotic and outré at first that Salvador Dali insisted on dining with her, became part of a seventies Burns & Allen act with a spin: Sonny was Gracie—without the charm. In cartoon form, they guested on *Scooby-Doo.*

It can safely be said that Sonny and Cher stayed together for the sake of their careers; their relationship was always far from ideal. Back when Bono had invited broke, teenage Cher to move into his place, he told her, "I don't find you particularly attractive . . . just keep the apartment clean and do the cooking." Cher would confess to writer Lynn Hirschberg, "It's impossible to explain Sonny's hold on me. . . . We became Sonny and Cher so quickly, and then we had a kind of decline, and then I got pregnant. For five years before I left him, I wanted to leave, but the *Sonny and Cher* show was so popular that I was afraid. And when I finally did leave, he said, 'America will hate you. You'll never work again.' . . . All we did was work . . . That was our relationship—*work*."

Picking up, perhaps, on the stinky chemistry, their TV writers hit a winning formula: the wisecracking, raven-haired beauty and her hapless, hairy little beast. It worked on several levels. By the time Cher walked off the show and out of the marriage in 1975—notably on the arm of record mogul David Geffen, who talked of marrying her—she was a huge star. Geffen would decide he was gay, Cher would go on to win an Oscar; Sonny had to settle for a bit part in a 1986 horror flick, *Troll.* As he'd put it later in his autobiography, "I used to be the jockey, but she quite nicely shoved the saddle up my ass."

Sonny would find new careers, first as a restauranteur, then as mayor of Palm Springs and finally, astonishingly, as a member of the House of Representatives. When I spent time with him on his Capitol rounds in 1994, the *Washington Post* was hailing him as "the idiot savant from way beyond the Beltway." He was having a grand time, giving Janet Reno heck about the Waco raid, ordering twenty pizzas to break up a tense committee meeting, dragging me to Newt Gingrich's office to see the nasty raptor fossils on display in its anteroom. Sonny was Vegas/Zen about his career ("I just watch and listen. And *it reveals itself* "), still mad for rock and roll and wryly, sweetly nostalgic about his crazy trip with Cher. In 1998, when Sonny skied into a tree—even death refused to take him seriously—Cher was accused of made-for-CNN crocodile tears after she delivered her shattered eulogy. The truth was—if you had talked to them both—that they just couldn't be done with each other. And even if they had been, we were not. The indecorous powers of pop myth put Cher and not Bono's widow, Mary, with him on the cover of *People's* hot-selling death issue. Then came the mini-series . . .

They had both said, separately, that the most bitter time was just after the split. While a solo Sonny worked crackerbox clubs to gin-soaked indifference, Cher touched down in Vegas's biggest rooms, reinventing herself in a blaze of feathered headdresses, cosmetic surgeries, tattoos and a new wave of rockin' boyfriends (Greg Allman, Kiss's Gene Simmons). With her bombastic rock productions and Mackie's sorcery, she became the self-appointed Doyenne of Dazzle. Beneath it all, Mackie told me, Cher is a canny, practical girl. She regularly held garage sales to resell the beaded and hand-tooled remnants of her gently used former selves.

No longer a bubbly, ingenue Supreme—and henceforth, always and imperiously *Miss Ross*—the seventies' other glam diva was more Tattinger's than tattoos. When Diana Ross blazed into her solo career, she indulged her long-standing penchant for showbiz schmaltz. She arrayed herself in fluffy show tunes, masses of maribou and the kind of stage presentations that sent high rollers back to the craps tables muttering, "HELLUVA show!" In Ross's hands, Marvin Gaye and Tammi Terrell's soulful "Ain't No Mountain High Enough" became a huge, saccharine production number. Licking a finger, laying it on a sequined haunch, she'd declare herself HOT with a well-miked *"Tsssssssst!"*

It played, and to very large venues. When the times required it, Miss Ross climbed into more spangles and the carefully prescribed rhythm track and went disco—notably with "Love Hangover" (1976) and "The Boss" (1979). And like Cher, she kept up the big stage shows. During one early-eighties concert tour in Europe, I asked Miss Ross about Cher. Was theirs a sequined sisterhood? They had plenty in common: Both were given to lavish stage shows averaging six to eight costume changes, mainly by Mackie. At the time, they were both raising their children alone. They had both dated Kiss gargoyle Gene Simmons, albeit at different times. And in the grande-dame tradition of Mae West, Judy Garland and Joan Crawford, both enjoyed a substantial gay following. Theirs is the most democratic of divahoods. Exaggerated female signifiers, rather than real sex, seemed to be their currency.

"I get a lot of gays at my shows and it's my pleasure," Ross told me. "They can dress up like me; they can put on makeup and probably look like Diana Ross. Cher has a female impersonator in her show. His name is J.C. This guy has all my moves. He's quicker than I am. I watch *him*, and I see how I look."

In their way, the seventies glam queens fulfilled the same over-the-top mandate as the latter-day Elvis—the once-wild boy confined beneath the jeweled, caped and belted carapace of legend. His would become the defining megastar dynamic: the hot, youthful Rock of Rages cooling into

Rock of Vegas. This is the same American transit that has seen James Brown's finger-popping 1965 exhortation "I feel good!" selling laxatives to aging and bound-up boomers in the nineties. Cher would issue a mortified mea culpa on national TV for her hideous infomercials without suffering a drop in her Q-factor. Such is the redemptive power of camp: *All is forgiven, Dorothy. Come on home . . .*

Gracing the pages of *Rolling Stone* —and starring in pneumatic similitude in countless drag clubs—was the seventies' unlikeliest glam crossover. Country queen Dolly Parton arrived as a 40DDD conundrum—a honey-voiced, Bible-quotin' sweetheart with a wicked gleam beneath those heavily Maybellined lashes. She sang divinely: sad songs, corny songs, true yarns about coming up hard-but-loved as one of twelve kids. Dolly's bell-bottom jumpsuits were unabashedly Elvis-inspired; her monumental cleavage was the great refuge of *Tonight Show* joke writers and her own stage humor. ("Honey," she told me on tour in the late seventies, "I'd like to go joggin', but I'd black both my eyes.")

Early in my wanderer's profession, it was Dolly who literally took me by the hand and led me to my first backstage catering table, a bubbling, steaming langiappe set up during sound check. She pointed to a volcanic tray of lasagna, some equally suspect turkey in gravy. "Don't you have no truck with *that*." She went for the mashed potatoes and advised me to follow suit. "Stick with white, pasty, squashy and safe," Miss Dolly instructed. "Think of it as pure fuel. Whether you're back on the bus or in front of a mike, it's not gonna come back at you at an *inconvenient* time."

For a long time—until New Age catering outfits began laying out whole-grain breads and poached salmon—I lived by her words gratefully, and without antacids. Dolly, whose huge, hardscrabble family did not keep the Sears, Roebuck catalog in the outhouse for reading material, has a way with plain truths and practical solutions. And even if she was got up in a fuchsia ruffled jumpsuit with more vents than a fast-food fry station, when Dolly sang "Jolene" in some yawning cow palace, the notes fell like a spring rain in the Blue Mountains. Women would cry. Tough men in tractor caps would mutter a wondering "Damn." You had to love her. Leaping off her tour bus in deepest Wisconsin, I dashed into a Wal-Mart to fetch her a fresh supply of mascara. And after three days with Dolly, I felt like I was carrying the Olympic torch back to her impossibly frou-froued domain.

Dolly's traverse from Nashville, where she had been partnered and promoted by Porter Wagoner, was expertly guided by the savvy management of Sandy Gallin. But it was Dolly herself who sat on Johnny's nubby divan and charmed America. A decade before that advertising major Garth Brooks eclipsed rockers and rappers in millions sold, Parton and Gallin saw the possibilities in crossing over to pop. And unlike Emmylou Harris, Dolly was more than happy puttin' on the glitz. Country had always had deep drama, lots of wailin' guitars and a serious fringe and glitter habit. In 1975, Glen Campbell's "Rhinestone Cowboy" had made it to number one on the pop charts. And increasingly, cowgirls were rocking some of the biggest, most lucrative showrooms.

Las Vegas in the late seventies. Loretta Lynn has gotten through the evening's early performance, but now, in the late or "cocktail" show she knows she has it: the dreaded "Vegas throat." Desert aridity, air-conditioning and cigarette smoke has her all but gasping just as it's time to go into the tribute medley to her departed girlfriend which forms the core of her 1977 album, I Remember Patsy. *Despairing, Loretta looks up into the rigging, and there is Patsy Cline smiling down at her, as Loretta would tell friends later, "with her little boots on." Loretta starts singing and the notes come easy and whole:.*

"I fall to pieces . . ."

Later, having tried to explain the vision of her mentor and great pal, Loretta said, "People think I'm crazy, but I saw it and I felt it. I got offstage and there was nothing wrong with my throat."

Patsy had offered Loretta $50 to join her on her last engagement—and its fatal trip—but Loretta had an offer in Memphis for $75. Patsy told her to go on and take it. What girl didn't need $25 more? Loretta Lynn wrote her tearjerker "This Haunted House" sitting on the steps of Patsy Cline's house the night after her friend died in the plane crash. It was a new house, one Patsy was very proud of, and the day she left she had taken Loretta out front to look at it. "Isn't it beautiful?" Patsy said. "I won't be happy until I put Mommy in one like this." Loretta said she wrote the song in twenty minutes, then went inside to play it for her friend's widower. She took his tears as approval and recorded it two nights later.

Despite their wardrobe excesses, beyond their trumped-up rivalries, the women of country music have retained a certain kitchen-table solidity, one that boasts big hearts and bigger hair. Oh, Loretta Lynn and Tammy Wynette had their differences: Nixon booster Wynette—she of "Stand By Your Man"—released "Woman to Woman" in 1974, which counseled a close-your-eyes-and-do-it-to-keep-him-home sexuality. Then came Lynn's "The Pill," which was banned as licentious by many Bible Belt radio programmers. Country had come a long way since Maybelle and Minnie Pearl. And some younger women were coming home—to country—with a sigh.

Nashville, 1976. Emmylou Harris has come to Porter Wagoner's Fireside Studios at the invitation of Dolly Parton, who is just finishing an album. Parton thinks her friend would like to hear the final tapes because one of the cuts is a cover of "Boulder to Birmingham," a song Emmylou wrote in tribute to her late duet partner and mentor Gram Parsons. Emmylou has steeled herself for its impact, stands in the darkness of the studio waiting for it, but suddenly, the cut before "Boulder" has her lip trembling.

It's wellspring clear, it's country, another woeful tale of an overworked, neglected mountain wife and mama with an O. Henry twist that takes Emmylou's breath away. In the final verse, insteading of dying tragically like any proper country heroine, this one up and leaves home—with a curt note to Daddy. "I have needed you so long, but I just can't keep holding on . . ." Dolly's vocal sweetness makes the last line a honey-dipped pile-driver: "Goodbye to Daddy!"

Harris later told writer Ben Fong-Torres that the song devastated her that day; she hardly paid attention to the next track, her own composition, remembered thanking Dolly after the listening session, hugging her, stammering something about the song to which her friend replied, "That's about my mama." "To Daddy" so compelled Harris that she recorded it right away.

She had long declared her fealty to "out of left field" songs, the kind that carry near-impossible odds in the hit derby. At the time, with California cool and disco ruling the charts, Harris stuck Dolly's domestic fable on her 1978 *Quarter Moon in a Ten Cent Town*, one of the quirky, not-quite-rock, not-quite-country albums she was making during that period. And when I first heard her version of "To Daddy," I felt sucker-punched as well.

We were all used to runaway girls in rock songs, but never—ever—a mature woman with grown children. There she was, calmly writing a farewell note in the house she has kept so long, so faithfully and silently, for a cold and distant man—then disappearing forever just before dawn. Where? How? Throughout the song, her stoic, epic loneliness is more heartbreaking, more shocking than any Family-of-Five-Killed-on-the-Way-to-Church wreck on the highway. As a testimonial to feminine pain and triumph, it would have dwarfed Helen Reddy's execrable anthem "I Am Woman"—if anybody had been listening.

Released as a single, "To Daddy" was a modest country hit for Harris, and it resonated with a certain melancholy tradition. The recognition of the tragic sitting right down to table with the commonplace, presented in an almost deadpan way, betokens a starkness of vision that goes back past the Carter Family. And it surfaces, every now and again, to snap the casual listener's head back. A whole nation was captivated in 1967 when another twangy bit of Southern Gothic hit the pop airways. Bobby Gentry's "Ode to Billy Joe," set on "a sleepy dusty Delta day" was memorable not so much for its announced tragedy—today Billy Joe McAllister jumped off the Tallahatchie Bridge—as for the offhand way the news is delivered to his lover over a humdrum farm lunch. Folks sigh and pass the biscuits.

Perhaps Emmylou Harris was drawn to such thrumming aural tableaux because, in the early seventies, she *was* a country song: Born in Alabama in 1947, she blew the sax in the high school band and became a committed folkie who learned nearly every Woody Guthrie song on her tinny little Kay acoustic guitar. She tried plying the folk scene in Greenwich Village, tried true love. And by 1971 she found herself a divorced mom on food stamps—moved back in with her parents!—and singing six nights a week to an audience too small to field a bowling team. Then— bang—a crazy boy, a rich Florida-born hippie with a George Jones obsession named Gram Parsons walks into the bar—Clyde's, in Washington, D.C.—just as she's singing "It Wasn't God That Made Honky Tonk Angels."

It was a harmonic convergence. Parsons, who had been knocking around the L.A. music scene pursuing an elusive rock/country fusion sound with the Flying Burrito Brothers, was looking for a duet partner who could come up with the kind of close harmonies that made Ira and Charlie Louvin's classic duets sound like they'd climbed into each other's souls. He felt he had found her. At Parsons' urging, Harris headed to L.A., where he steeped her in more country: the Carters, Tammy Wynette, lots of Louvins records. The resulting Parsons/Harris duets were stunning, pristine draughts of pure country, all reeling hawks and smoke-ringed mountains.

When Parsons's assembly, calling themselves the Fallen Angels , hit the road in 1973, the men were protective, even courtly toward their doe-eyed Emmylou as their bus crossed America. After all, she was a mother. Nightly, her voice grew more confident and captivating. If, as Johnny Cash asserts, the otherworldly Anita Carter was the best female voice in country music, Emmylou Harris is her direct heir—with a decided leftie turn. Linda Ronstadt, with whom she has dueted often (most recently on a 1999 album, *Western Wall: The Tuscon Sessions*) likens the sound to cracked crystal. Listening to Harris's splintered, keening "All My Tears," my nine-year-old son burst unaccountably into tears of his own, then asked me, "How did that happen?" Harris is that good a singer; her high notes can pierce the listener the way the Santa Ana winds drive straw through wood and ping the tight-strung neurons of L.A. traffic cops, waitresses, alley cats.

Harris was soaring, helping Parsons lay tracks for his planned LP *Grievous Angel,* when their roadshow hit a sudden stop. In September 1973, Parsons—a man given to flying long hair and garish rhinestone suits by Nudie—died alone, one of those "mysterious rock deaths," in a motel near the Joshua Tree Monument in California. It was first attributed to heart failure, then a drug overdose. He was only twenty-six, and had lived his last few years in the wild-man mode of Hank Williams—by way of Margaritaville. Apparently, someone felt he should leave the world like a Viking; his friends stole his coffin and set it afire in the Mojave Desert.

For Harris, Parsons's death was, she said, "like falling off a mountain." She went to Nashville and started all over. In 1975, she did what few women in the hit-hungry record business dared: She made a totally honest record. *Pieces of the Sky* gave her an unlikely first hit in the single "If I Could Only Win Your Love." The triumph was not lost on Harris, who said, "It was like, God, here's this old Louvin Brothers song and it's got a mandolin solo. Remember mandolin? At that time, it was like, 'Don't put a mandolin on it. People might think it's actually country music.' Musically, I think I've always managed to be kind of an outsider anywhere I would be. I've always managed to do whatever I wanted."

For all her talent, Emmylou Harris has never become a huge star. But she is surely a musician's musician, and a sort of patron saint to lonesome travelers with Stratocasters. I've heard her album *Wrecking Ball* played in post-performance dressing rooms and on motor-coach night rides as exhausted rock shamans trust Emmylou to take them, gently, back to the world. And she is always sought after in the studio for her peerless harmonies. One of Harris's fan clubs estimates that she has done 283 backup recordings for other singers. Imagine the joyful sounds, on New Year's of 1977, when Dolly Parton invited Harris and Linda Ronstadt to her Nashville home to woodshed for a studio project (the three have done two albums together). Bob Dylan loved Harris's harmonies for his *Desire* album so much he had them mastered at full strength rather than muted background.

It takes a singular, secure musician to devote so much to the *blending* of voices; currently, the Indigo Girls and Lucy Kaplansky practice this kind of selfless artistry. I found Emmylou's own explanation for her longtime devotion to harmony as I flipped through the liner notes on a Louvin Brothers collection I've played over and over (*Radio Favorites '51–'57*). She writes: "What is it about two really good voices coming together to make something so wonderful, something greater than the sum of their individual parts? Perhaps, in this world of discord, it makes us feel that, yes, we can get something right."

In 2001, in reasoned hindsight, this makes sense. But during the Me Decade, it was a notion way behind those narcissistic times. Or perhaps too far ahead.

Sweet harmony really wasn't the point of the seventies' obsession with sex. Sex—be it tantric or parking-lot quickie—was being recast as a brave new way to Self. As in first-person singular. *The Joy of Sex*, that *Kama Sutra* for the tract ranch set, ruled *The New York Times* best-seller list for an astonishing 362 weeks beginning in 1973. It sold over 10 million copies. Enterprising women abandoned all that burping Tupperware to host naughty product parties: chewable fruit-flavored panties, massage oils, livid pink French ticklers. After all, the Pill had been around for ten years; Helen Gurley Brown's *Cosmo* manifesto, *Sex and the Single Girl,* had been in the Dewey Decimal System just as long, and disease, in the forms of herpes and AIDS, had yet to cast its pall over the new sexual freedom. Sex, artfully simulated, was selling everything from extra-long smokes to steel-belted radials. On album covers and Sunset Boulevard billboards, lingerie ruled; boys and girls drooled. It seemed anyone could do it—with whomever or whatever they pleased.

The frenzy all came together beneath the copulatory, boogie-oogie-oogie thud of disco, a most inclusive genre. Donna Summer snapped her choruses over booming rhythm tracks that moved the artfully tied construction boots of gay men and the teetery hetero platforms of the *Saturday Night Fever* disco hordes. The BeeGees made that movie's soundtrack a monstrous hit singing about macho triumphs in nosebleed, girlie falsetto.

For the most part, the disco era was one long Ladies' Nite, from Donna Summer's "Bad Girls" to Gloria Gaynor's Moog operatics and the joyful party-down adventurism of Sister Sledge (Joni, Kathy, Kim and Debbie Sledge). And, given disco's synthesized, overwrought productions, it was a time of musical co-dependencies. Like many girl group singers, disco queens were deeply reliant on the multi-layer engineering of male producers such as Giorgio Moroder and Nile Rodgers.

Those factory-stamped rhythm tracks, synthesizer beeps and gusting psuedo-strings provided the background urge for Gaynor's anthem "I Will Survive" and Chic's "Le Freak." Designed to induce a boogie trance sustainable through a 12-inch extended cut, disco was hardly a lyric-driven form. *Time* magazine reported that Donna Summer's vocalizing on "Love to Love You Baby" consisted of twenty-one distinctly moaned orgasms.

Disco was primarily a black thing, in terms of performance, but the seventies did see some straight soul survivors. Aretha Franklin scored some moderate hits; Minnie Riperton's astonishing high notes on "Lovin' You" floated above the din, and the ever-classy Gladys Knight, freed from years of benign neglect at Motown, turned out her signature "Midnight Train to Georgia," beginning a string of lush, achy ballads on her new label, Buddah.

Chaka Khan, a wild-haired, ebullient sister, was born Yvette Stevens in 1953, more than a decade after Gladys and Aretha. She came up in Chicago with a perspective that had plenty of rhythm, but far fewer adult blues. After a brief stint in a girl group, she took on the Zulu name of Chaka, meaning "fire," in high school. Then she became the lambent life force fronting the funk band Rufus. Khan took any stage by storm, a bumping, whirling vision in jangling bracelets, vests and bell-bottoms, approximating the width and locomotion of a modest tornado. In 1978, her "I'm Every Woman" combined the infectious repetitions of disco with a spark of timely, womanly brag. Two decades later, Whitney Houston's more antiseptic version couldn't compete. Like the formidable Tina Turner, Khan could get soulful and she could rock; hers is a flexibility that helped her bounce into the eighties with a remake of Prince's "I Feel for You" and a rousing duet on Steve Winwood's "Higher Love."

Plenty of soul singers have blamed the corporate tyrannies of disco for the demise of their own free-form vocalizing. It's partly true, of course. Over the years, I've collected a few dozen versions of what I've come to call the Disco Diatribe. Even the strongest voices can get lost in the whirlwind of a dance craze—particularly if it has strong corporate backing. And disco did huge business. But there were some notable breaches in this wall of sound. To punch through, it helped to be very loud and extremely rude. And until rap, only white kids could get away with it.

BOLLOCKS! Punk came hurtling through all disco's stylized hormonal displays, through all that mellow formatted rock, like a fat, juicy spitball. What an astringent moment when Poly Styrene whispered a girlish intro about little girls should be seen and not heard, then roared into a mike, "Oh Bondage, Up Yours!" Not to be cowed by their musical limitations, the Slits, a brace of female Brits opening for the Clash at London's Roxy, invited critical audience members to take over their instruments while the band hit the floor and danced. Sometimes a riff could sound like a tray of silverware hitting the floor. This lot knew they often sucked; that was very much to their point. *So what?* Despite plenty of critics intellectualizing on this new, oh-so-simple aesthetic, the fact remained: Technical virtuosity might carry the same weight as attitude or choice of trousers. Besides, they were all relative beginners. And many could at least manage the kinderchords that characterized the Beatles' naif "I Wanna Hold Your Hand" period.

By the late seventies, there were few standards, anyhow. And playing for posterity was a dodgy concept: The King had toppled, dead, off his bathroom throne. Rock deaths (from Janis Joplin to Jim Morrison, Keith Moon, Florence Ballard, Tim Buckley, Bobby Darin, Jim Croce) occurred with the speed and randomness of a kozmic demolition derby. Punk's nihilism had its appeal in an age when the Village People could fill Madison Square Garden and Debby Boone's "You Light Up My Life" hit #1. For most young people, the seventies were either numb or reactive—depending on your sixties experience. And for punk kids, the stance was decidedly anti. Anti-melody, anti-fashion—and the aggressive buzzing feedback of onstage antipathy.

When it came to chord changes and costume, minimalism was the other punk ethos. (Unless, of course, you counted up all the fussy bondage trousers, piercings, studs and dog collars. This was a genre that knew how to accessorize anger.) Anti-fashion did find a gorgeous pinup in a Jersey girl who split for Manhattan's East Village and fell in with the right wrong crowd.

"Eeeeuuuww. You goin' out like that?"

Downtown designer Stephen Sprouse is addressing his neighbor, a singer named Debbie Harry. He has seen her feeding the feral cat that lives in the ceiling of their Bowery apartment house. They meet "somewhere near the toaster oven" in the communal kitchen and become further acquainted as she tosses Tender Vittles into the insulation above Sprouse's bed.

"You got a better idea?" Harry, who has about a million black T-shirts, admits she does need something special to wear for performances with her band, Blondie. They huddle. Sprouse takes a pair of black stretch pants with stirrups and somehow converts them into a black one-shouldered minidress. He hangs pins and razors off the hem and delivers an ultimatum: "You have to wear this with thigh-high black boots and black tights."

Within months, the dress is famous. Harry wears it on a record jacket. The name of the song: "Rip Her to Shreds."

One gloomy winter's day a decade past that glorious rock and fashion Moment, Harry and Sprouse recounted their past collaborations for me in the bar of New York's Gramercy Park Hotel. She was in a torn T-shirt, sweatpants and running shoes. Her hair was bleached blond with its trademark dark roots and Sprouse's dyed ink-black. Sprouse wore a black hankie safety-pinned to his black painter's hat and black polish on the fingers of

his left hand, à la *Berlin*-era Lou Reed. They seemed to be in a wry, nostalgic mood, happy to cackle over their early conspiracies.

The long afternoon turned into a coffee-fueled style symposium;
Sprouse, who once dressed Park Avenue ladies as a Halston assistant, allowed that he was a committed minimalist. His own go-anywhere, day-
for-night rock uniform was simply "torn T-shirts and black eyeliner."
Harry was a bit more voluble: "I've always thought rock and roll is fifty
percent music and fifty percent visual. That's not to say the music doesn't
come first. But I've always expected a *look*, if it was Elvis or Sigue Sigue
Sputnik."

She has never argued the fact that her own extraordinary image was
crucial to Blondie's success. The look? A deft hybrid of cultural icon and
throwaway chic. Red lipstick and peroxide made historical sense of her
remarkable face; it was Marilyn, of course. But Debbie's clothes were secondhand, mix and match or just wittily weird. Five years before Madonna
tried it, Harry wore a wedding dress onstage, then tore it off to sing "Rip
Her to Shreds." She did jokes: Woolworth's accessories, dresses made from
pants. Big face, small dress—Robert Palmer would clone her proportions
for his guitar-toting video molls. In the era preceeding $10,000-a-day styl-
ists, Harry's costuming was very do-it-yourself: "We shopped some," she
said, "but we pulled a lot of things out of Dumpsters."

A couple of years past that style council with Sprouse, I had another date to
meet Debbie; she was releasing a solo album, *Def, Dumb & Blonde*, more than
ten years after Blondie's high-tide hit "Heart of Glass." The band had broken up a few years before, and Harry had become Manhattan's most whis-
pered-about rock MIA since John Lennon dropped out to bake wheat bread
high above Central Park West. As it turned out, she was nursing her former
lover and Blondie collaborator Chris Stein, who had fallen dangerously ill
with pemphigis, a rare skin disease. And where was she now that he was recovering? Harry dissolved into her deep, huh-huh chuckle: "Just write, 'She's
living alone. Somewhere below Forty-Second Street.'"

To avoid the hackneyed chat-in-the-manager's office, I coaxed a
leather-jacketed Debbie to a Museum of Modern Art retrospective on her
late pal Andy Warhol. We walked over, and no one recognized her wrapped

against the cold. But inside the museum, plenty of inky-clad art lovers stopped staring at the soup cans and turned their gaze to Harry. Those runway cheekbones were still unmistakable beneath her shades and wool scarf. It was one of those mirror-crack'd moments, strolling with one pop icon through the brash, vibrating oeuvre of the Master.

Everything—the silk-screened car crash photos, Warhol's infamous "piss paintings"—seemed to trigger vivid memory for a girl so downtown she used to get the bends above 14th Street. Harry turned the corner to find herself smack in front of "Marilyn Six-Pack." Monroe in lavender. A mint Marilyn. Lemon . . .

"Ah . . . ," she breathed. "Our Lady."

As an adopted child in New Jersey, brunette Debbie Harry fantasized that her real mother was Marilyn Monroe. As a bad girl in a band she had resurrected the dream and bellowed it in "Platinum Blonde," a "blondes have more fun" homage to silver-screen goddesses like Marilyn, Jean, Mae, and Marlene.

"Andy. Jeez. Sometimes I think I'm just a child of his imagination."

She really misses Warhol and his determined celeb choreography. He did one of his iconographic silk screens of her face in 1980, with raging turquoise around the eyes, orange hair, a painted cupid-bow mouth. But when she first encountered Warhol's artsy mob, it was a boho nightmare. This was in the mid-sixties, when she crossed the Hudson to lower Manhattan after a stint in junior college.

"It was the beginning of the hippie invasion," she said. She was living in an Italian/Ukranian neighborhood on St. Mark's Place, singing with a folkie group called Wind in the Willows and paying the rent by picking up change at that scene-maker's boîte, Max's Kansas City. Nightly, gaggles of Warholites like Nico, Ultra Violet and the protean Velvet Undergrounders flung themselves into the scarred black booths and made her cry into cocktail napkins. "I was just a hysterical waitress," Debbie said. "I was so timid in those days."

We were just turning the corner from the Marilyns, Debbie just ahead of me, when she whispered, "Oh my God, oh, c'mere!"

She grabbed my coat sleeve and hauled me to a silk-screen of S&H green stamps, a long-defunct consumer incentive that had millions of sticky-fingered suburban moms dreaming of 4-speed blenders and cute chip-'n'-dip bowls. It was a simple sixties equation: Spend, get green stamps from the supermarket, paste them in the books; trade them for stuff.

Debbie was transfixed. Seemed she'd worked in an S&H "redemption center" near Paramus, New Jersey. "It was near Route 4. I wore little rubber things on my thumbs to separate the pages. I handed out toasters. Lawn chairs. Cookie jars. TV trays for your frozen dinners."

Presiding over these redemptive if tacky rites of retail was, she confessed, far more satisfying than her other incarnations as waitress, shampoo girl, Playboy Bunny, aerobics instructor. She pointed out that every chick rock singer she knew had paid dues and the rent with numbing straight gigs, and of course, she was right. Janis Joplin punched out IBM cards, set down foamy glasses of Schlitz, Emmylou Harris served up flaming pu pu platters—who *didn't* wait tables? New Orleans soul queen Irma Thomas sold auto parts at Sears, Grace Slick modeled and Bette Midler sold women's gloves at a Manhattan department store.

Debbie the Timid Waitress gained some confidence by joining a girl group, Pure Garbage—later reinvented as the Stilettoes. She says she walked back into Max's with a bolder step, "serious makeup" and outfits that melded convent school and Frederick's of Hollywood. The Stilettoes sang their own compositions, including "Dracula, What Did You Do to My Mother?"

"I got to be a rock singer," Debbie said. "But, whooeee, first I was, um . . . AN AMERICAN GIRL!"

We both laughed. Amid all that logoed Warholia, I'd had my own flashback to the gas station owner who promised me a summer job—if I'd pump high test in hot pants. In the seventies, Miss American Pie was one puzzled creature. All those recent revolutions had left us with nothing but choices, and relatively little equipment to help one do the right thing. Birth control was dispensed like Chiclets, but true love had a higher price tag than ever. *Our Bodies, Ourselves* was a feminist best-seller, but guys were poring over it as a user's manual.

Out-cheesing the assholes—platinum hair with black roots, lyrics like chainsawed ad slogans—may have seemed the best defense. Debbie and her cohorts thought up their band's name after some trucker hollered at her on the street, "Hey, blondie, how about a blow job?" Record stores and college dorm rooms everywhere were plastered with posters of Debbie in distressed vinyl minidresses. Camp feminity, as Dolly Parton knew, as Debbie Harry, then Madonna, would demonstrate with such aplomb, could function as a useful, inscrutable mask. The semiotics suited the lusty ogler or the nascent feminist. And if the mask kept the singer safe, the fan could grope at its intrinsic mystique.

Debbie says she did not fully appreciate the power of rock style—how her brand of severity redeemed those silly seventies—until one night, circa '77, when Blondie played L.A.'s Whisky a Go Go and she transformed its fash-addict audience instantly, like some punk fairy godmama:

"Everybody was there in bell-bottoms. And we did a couple of shows. Then the girls were there in tight pants and minis. They had SCOURED the secondhand stores. It was bing, bang, BOOM, shooooooom." Harry lunged, imitating the greedy grasp of Melrose Avenue thrift shoppers plucking vintage chicken slacks off a rack.

"It was funny. It was cute. It was really overnight."

Ask Debbie for an overall impression on the workings of rock style and she doesn't stop to cogitate.

"IT'S COMPOSTED!" she hollered, then laughed.

Things reconfigure and bubble back to the surface?

"COMPOST!"

As Debbie would later write: "A torn T-shirt made it all dangerous again."

Their lead singer's runaway iconography did lead the group to its cranky PR campaign reminding the public that "Blondie is a band." (To wit, guitarist Stein, bassist Gary Valentine, keyboardist Jimmy Destri and drummer Clem Burke.) And working as such, Blondie was spinning out tough, chewy little hits. Sometimes the band's imagery seemed culled the way Harry built her wardrobe; their lyrics were scavenged from decades of cultural landfill. Songs like "Contact in Red Square" and "Eat to the Beat" were soldered together willy-nilly from literature, sitcoms and soap ads.

Debbie aptly characterized their music as "aggressive pop." "Call Me" was suave enough to play behind Richard Gere's Armanied stud-muffin in *American Gigolo*. "Heart of Glass" was pure disco, smoothed by synthesizers and Debbie's soaring, charged moans. "One Way or Another," a sort of punk Sadie Hawkins take on getting a guy, always made me giggle when Debbie stomped and mugged her way through it onstage in 1978. Nearly twenty years later, when the song welled up in *The Rugrats Movie* (as the hideously aggressive toddler Angelica hunted her missing doll), I howled along with the rest of the parents in the theater. The joke was on us: Blondie's not-quite-punk was always a PG-13 product—humorous, accessible and absolutely unashamed.

Nor was the band afraid to put out Jiffy-Popped versions of other, fiercer styles. Walking down a graffiti-scarred city street for an early video, Debbie rapped—albeit awkwardly—in "Rapture." A reggae beat moved "The Tide Is High" to number one. Such thrift-shop songwriting would reach its digital apotheosis in nineties hip-hop, which made sampling an art form. But in its punk incarnation, the aesthetic was appropriately crude: Whatever works.

Blondie broke up in 1983; when they reconvened in 1999 for a new album (*No Exit*), a VH1 concert and U.S. and European tours, I burrowed front and center for the cable taping at Manhattan's Town Hall. And it was an electric, whistle and stomp moment when Debbie took the stage in a sharp suit and shades. She danced like the sprite she no longer is, sang like the cheery bohemian she's always been and behind her, the band was as fluid with its new material—notably the infectious hit "Maria"—as with the clamored-for chestnuts. It was great, undiminished, stand-up rock and roll. Blondie further showed its bratty resiliency—and its undiluted sense of humor—at a millennial New Year's show on Miami's South Beach. Ten thousand people roared at a post-midnight encore that featured Debbie and the boys (clothed) amid a naked dance troupe. Still sampling, they punched out some "Auld Lang Syne," jump-cut with Irma Thomas's R&B classic: "Time Is on My Side."

Blondie didn't own the franchise on instant, wash 'n' wear irony in the late-seventies. Some female punk performers even borrowed brand names, like the aforementioned Ms. Styrene and Slits' drummer Palmolive. There was a deep love/hate relationship between punk kids and the processed cheese they'd grown up on. Tarry at Lower East Side punk bars back then and you could invariably find some sodden, scarified rudeboy demanding to ogle that Velveeta bitch Marcia Brady on the tube before he crashed, facedown, into an overfilled ashtray. Anything was fair game amid this Rubik's cube lyricism. Punk bands plundered surf music, girl-group la-la, rap and reggae. The kids had great fun and left the semiotic analysis to fusty rock critics.

Like the sixties, the punk era enjoyed a foreign exchange program with the UK; this time, instead of moptops and dollybirds, it was rudeboys and sluts. That canny fashion and rock trickster Malcolm McLaren, who masterminded the Sex Pistols, had conspired earlier in Manhattan with the crossdressing New York Dolls. (McLaren's former wife and co-conspirator Vivienne Westwood told me—rather huffily—that she was sure he'd also nicked the torn T-shirt idea from New Yorker Richard Hell during that sojourn.) Along with these matted, stinky boys (Johnny Rotten was known to wear a moldy Lurex jacket for three weeks straight) came a louder, shriller, more intensely costumed bevy of rubber-wear babes: Poly Styrene (of X-Ray Spex), Siouxsie Sioux (and her Banshees), the Raincoats, the Slits, the AuPairs. They were singular; Siouxsie, who'd jumped the traces of secretarial school to follow the Sex Pistols around in a van, performed topless once she formed her own band, and accented her *sod off!* insouciance with thoughtfully placed swastikas.

Like a stubborn case of acne, punk would enjoy sporadic breakouts. On the L.A. scene, Exene Cervenka (of the band X) was a literate, Rubenesque punkette who tossed her zebra-streaked mane and occasionally smiled through the heady poetry of "Real Child of Hell" :

Men of flesh hitch a ride
Shorts & tans & greasy thighs
At night drive into slimy bars
And piss it out on our front yards

Punk poetics were determinedly pustular: *Be a carcass; be dead meat.* Early on, it was clear that pre-emptive gross-out could be a girl's game— an impulse that persists today in L7's *Hungry for Stink* and Bikini Kill's little incest lullaby, "Suck My Left One."

The very notion of a punk legacy should be an oxymoron. But the nineties would see a riotous effloresence of bent chords and carefully considered skank—especially among young women. And in the early eighties, there was the well-muscled and mohawked Wendy O. Williams of the Plasmatics, a former topless dancer who chainsawed wrecked cars onstage to sweeten the mix. Williams had her own McLaren, a Times Square sex entrepreneur named Rod Swenson. Ten years after the death of Jim Morrison, who had been arrested for exposing himself onstage, Wendy O. went him one better: The Milwaukee police hauled her off for "simulating masturbation with a sledgehammer." Her brief, unpretty life was a punk saga that ended ugly and far, far from the roar of any sort of crowd.

Requiem for a Chainsaw Princess:
(From Billboard, *April 18, 1998)*

Wendy O. Williams, former vocalist for New York shock rock band the Plasmatics, died of an apparently self-inflicted gunshot wound April 6 in Storrs, Conn. She was 48. Her body was found in the woods near her home by her manager and companion, Rod Swenson.

Williams, a former nude dancer who was brought into the music business by Swenson, often appeared onstage in various stages of undress, "clothed" in some cases with strategically placed strips of electrical tape. The band also engaged in attention-getting spurts of onstage destruction which ranged from chain-sawing TV sets to, on at least one memorable occasion, blowing up a car.

Williams's terse, weird obit was a capsule summary—albeit an extreme one—of the hard-rocking woman who could not stand the quiet. Male ghoul rocker Alice Cooper plays golf and opened a theme restaurant; semi-retired wild man Ted Nugent hunts and plays with guns. What outlet for a girl better aquainted with a chainsaw than a Cuisinart?

Born in Rochester, New York, the daughter of an Eastman Kodak chemist, little Wendy had begun her career at age six as a dancer on *The Howdy Doody Show.* Swenson, a Yale graduate who ran Captain Kink's Sex Fantasy Theater in Manhattan, met her in 1976 when she was working there as a dominatrix/dancer. Forming the Plasmatics, which debuted at CBGB at the height of the punk scene in 1978, they made ugly music together—forthright little ditties like "A Pig Is a Pig" and "Sex Junkie." Wendy wore a white Mohawk and sometimes a nurse's outfit. Or just daubs of shaving cream and/or well-placed Band-Aids. In one stunt, she leapt from a Cadillac just before it exploded and hissed into the Hudson

River. The music was bad, but the band's stagey aggression got them as far as blowing up that car on Tom Snyder's *Tomorrow* show. "Elvis Costello, I enjoyed," Snyder later grumped. "Wendy O. Williams, I didn't get."

Like many novelty acts, Williams did a slow fade. She and Swenson moved to Connecticut, where she worked at a health-food co-op and in an animal-rehabilitation program. In the late nineties, when pissed-off young women in neo-punk groups like Hole had begun to make so much noise for so much profit, friends and family said Wendy got quieter and sadder. Swenson explained her suicide this way: "She felt she was past her peak and found it difficult to lead a normal life."

Amid all the Cocoa Puff cosmologies and well-miked belches, some folks did get torqued up on intellect. Given the macho, head-butting physicality of the doings at that Manhattan punk palace CBGB, it was amazing, one night, to peer through the stinky blue haze and realize that the Talking Heads' rather businesslike bass player was female. Tina Weymouth, brainy art student from the Rhode Island School of Design, had played her way into the job over classmate David Byrne's reservations. But she was more than capable, holding a steady tiller beneath the tempests of Byrne's twitchy, Tourette's syndrome vocals. ("Psychokiller, *qu'est-ce que c'est?*") More than anything, Weymouth's inclusion sent a bulletin across those hot rooms packed with pouty, pierce-lipped anomie: Girls can be *in* a band playing as well as vamping out front.

They could also be poets. The plain white shirts and black pants, the skinny naked body of Jersey guttersnipe Patti Smith were photographed as monotint Art by her pal and soulmate Robert Mapplethorpe. Smith lifted hairy armpits to Lynn Goldsmith's camera for the cover of *Easter,* wore tight rubber pants with circus-tent T-shirts, prizefighters' belts and frankly undone hair. It was decidedly anti-diva and sometimes almost girl-dismissive, a kind of cross-gender cool that mimicked the macho nonchalance of her idol Keith Richards. Patti's distant sisters were the Shangri-Las and the Ronettes, the first girl groups to invest in matching pantsuits. Her more contemporary echoes are Joan Jett and Chrissie Hynde. They're all women whose clothes bespeak the hassles of singin' in the boys' room.

A former factory worker, Smith was self-educated in the works of great men—from Baudelaire to Coltrane, Camus and Bob Dylan, with whom she seemed obsessed. Arriving on the New York scene, she was almost the polar and physical opposite of Nico, the blond German ex-patriate who starred in Warhol movies, sang on her own records (notably, *Chelsea Girl*) and performed with Lou Reed's Velvet Underground. If Nico's chilly beauty and her art were deeply, smokily boho-femme, Smith's frantic stage evangelism seemed closer to the absinthe reveries of randy-boy poets like her hero Rimbaud.

Smith affected the poet/dandy's thin black tie and, sometimes, suspenders. On *Horses*, her 1975 debut album, her turbo-charged remake of Van Morrison's "Gloria" seemed to out-macho that Hibernian he-man. She was most comfortable collaborating with men, a gender preference that still has feminists and riot grrrls scrapping over her alleged betrayals and/or revolutions.

Smith did like to play with the boys. She wrote a song for the cheerfully misogynist Blue Oyster Cult. One mad weekend with Sam Shepard at the Chelsea Hotel, they co-wrote an entire play (*Cowboy Hat*) that they would perform together. Her band, the Patti Smith Group, was all-male, and her only Top 40 hit, the incendiary "Because the Night," she recorded with Bruce Springsteen. Offstage, Smith took her simmering bard mien seriously; once, she refused to talk to *Rolling Stone* writer Charles Young—equipped with only Luddite pen and notebook—until a tape recorder was procured. The reason: She sometimes spoke in what she called "spontaneous poetry" that must be recorded verbatim.

Rock narcissism knows no sex; stars of both genders have long been given to bouts of self-love that range from lingering video closeups to five-story billboards. But Patti Smith did flabbergast even the mighty road warrior Young with her comment that she liked to masturbate to her own photograph. "I've never heard anyone say anything quite like that," he told her. "I'm trying to figure out if you're actually that sexually attracted to yourself."

"No," she answered, "it was just one of those moments, ya know. It was the photo for the cover of *Easter*. I thought if I could do it as an experiment, then fifteen-year-old boys could do it, and that would make me very happy."

Besides its value as hands-on market research, Smith pointed out that she viewed sex as a religious experience. Young couldn't resist:

"You jerk off to the Bible too?"

"Definitely."

Smith was irritating, compelling and, when she was amped, a fabulous rock performer. Her delivery was alternately incantatory, pugnacious, sacrificial. And she was self-aware enough to enjoy her role as Trickster figure in a growing religion of celebrity. She carried around a postcard of the painter Amedeo Modigliani and told people he was her boyfriend, this European guy who painted long, skinny women just like her. She palled around with oil scion J. Paul Getty III, the rich boy who had part of his ear sliced off in an infamous kidnap caper. For a time, Getty traveled with her band. Explained Smith: "We're the media generation. I know him like I know everybody who's been twisted and redesigned by people. We immediately connected because we're both walleyed. Our eyes travel in our heads. It's an exciting handicap."

Further confounding her media analysts—and upsetting plenty of her fans—Smith left the national rock scene for domesticity and the unhip Midwest. She spent nine years quietly raising two children with her husband, MC5 guitarist Fred "Sonic" Smith. He died in 1994, and when his widow reemerged a year later with a studio album, *Gone Again*, it was as strong and revelatory as her first "resurrection" album, *Easter.* (That record was released in 1978 after a stage accident shattered her neck and sent her to the hospital for months.) *Gone* was so quiet and introspective that critics were calling it folkie. Smith toured briefly behind it, sharing the bill with one of her inspirations. And in each of those shows, Bob Dylan kissed her onstage, with tenderness and respect.

Opting out of the clamor that would characterize the eighties, staying out of range of the new, intense and sometimes misogynist lens of MTV, was a comfortable—and affordable—choice for confident artists like Linda Ronstadt, Joni Mitchell and Patti Smith. Chrissie Hynde, in contrast, seemed to grow louder, feistier and more confrontational.

No female has a more amazing rock-life dossier than Hynde, who grew up idolizing the Kinks' Ray Davies as a teenager in Akron, Ohio.

She spent three antsy years at Kent State University—infamous for the 1970 murder of student protesters by the National Guard during Hynde's tenure there—then got herself to the Swingin' London she'd longed to see. She began a series of rock adventures there that would include having Davies's child almost twenty years after she first fell in thrall with "You Really Got Me."

Hynde got a job as a rock journalist with Britain's *NME* (*New Musical Express*). But after a series of assignments that included meeting teen idol David Cassidy's plane, Hynde decided that she preferred a more hands-on approach. She had also been working at Sex, one incarnation of Malcolm McLaren and Vivienne Westwood's little shop of punk horrors; she fashioned earrings of tampons and condoms and hung out with the Sex Pistols. Hynde offered Sid Vicious £2 to marry her—so she could get her green card. (They called it off when the registry office was closed.) She also played with one of McLaren's instant, microwavable bands—Masters of the Backside—until she formed her own group, the Pretenders. Their first single, in 1978, was a slamming, harsh cover of the Kinks' "Stop Your Sobbing."

Visually, Hynde seems the love child of Ronnie Spector and Roy Orbison. She was lean and mean: a shock of short black hair over much serious black eyeliner, and the businesslike T's and trousers of most serious male guitarists. And black leather, of course. Her sound was just as muscular—loud and speedy with just enough melody to pull it out of deep punk and into the charts, with singles like "Brass in Pocket."

The dossier also takes in the overdose deaths of two Pretenders band members, the end of the affair with Davies, a brief marriage to Simple Minds vocalist Jim Kerr (and a second child), creepy public rants that were alternately anti-feminist, anti-PMS, anti-meat and -fur and anti-image (she once trashed Debbie Harry for her Blondie look). Still rocking hard in her mid-forties, getting arrested at animal-rights protests, raising her children alone, she described her quiet life to writer Amy Raphael: "The girls go to bed. I go to my room. I light a candle. I smoke a spliff. I do my yoga. I go to bed and read." Still, Hynde's occasional nights out don't go unnoticed:

In December 1995, Joni Mitchell has decided to celebrate her fifty-second birthday with an "informal open rehearsal" at Fez, a small Manhattan club. It's an event: Mitchell has not toured in twelve years. Within hours, the word has spread, and the room is packed with Famous Fans, such as Natalie Merchant, Carly Simon—and Chrissie Hynde, who begins the evening by screaming, "Let it out, Joni!" Hynde keeps screaming throught the performance, and, seated in the next booth, Carly Simon asks her to stop. Hynde is up, she's grabbed Simon by the neck, pointing at Mitchell, announcing to her astonished captive, "That's a real singer up there!" As a male audience member suggests, none too gently, that Hynde have another drink, the crowd sings "Happy Birthday" to Joni. Carly Simon goes home early.

At the tail-end of the seventies, in bopped a new singer/songwriter, a slurry-voiced runaway named Rickie Lee Jones who could not begin to dream of what lay ahead for a rock and roll girl about to meet the eighties. This was no canyon lady. Her California was urban and Chandler-esque, all fly-specked diners and lumpy motel beds. The characters in her songs had pockets full of tobacco flakes and pawn tickets: Chuck E., Sal the Weasel, Cunt Finger Louie. . . . Before she settled in the marginal Echo Park section of Los Angeles, she had been sleeping in parks and up in the hills behind the famous Hollywood sign. By the time she reached her tatty corner of the City of Angels in 1973 at age nineteen, she felt she'd been on the road a lifetime. She waitressed, too, in an Italian joint in Echo Park.

Rickie Lee was the daughter of two orphans—a waitress and a soda jerk—who raised four children of their own but found difficulty making their house a home. The Joneses moved from Chicago to L.A. and back, then Arizona, and finally Olympia, Washington, where they divorced. By fourteen, Rickie Lee was a habitual runaway; one stolen car escapade found her in Phoenix in a juvenile detention center. Bad attitude got her expelled from high school for insubordination. She listened to a lot of Janis Joplin, then Laura Nyro. Later she would write a song ("Skeletons"):

Some kids like watching Saturday cartoons
Some girls listen to records all day in their rooms . . .

Forty-three-year-old Rickie Lee has a new record of original songs out when we arrange to meet in 1997. We first get acquainted by e-mail,

a form she enjoys and hammers at prolifically and often. She is just starting a string of club dates in support of the album, traveling with a small
band, a portable collection of stage props culled from thrift shops and
New Orleans botanicas—plaster saints and voodoo lights. Often, her
eleven-year-old daughter Charlotte comes along. One night, Rickie Lee
writes from the road:

*I guess that it's not a question of needing to do this. It is what I do. Traveling
to play the music I have written is more than, well, I could have believed, and
yet did believe that I was meant to do. I travel as light or as heavy as I am. I
stay in the world of waiting to play, and afterwards, waiting to play again. In
the hotels are bibles and boxing matches. In the clubs there are always nice
people moving very heavy things around, and on the walls are written the great
literary notices of my peers. The dressing rooms smell bad, and the toilets are
often missing . . .*

   *Tomorrow I play. Sometimes I feel like the Statue of Liberty. The fog coming
in . . . soon autumn.*

And a few days later, Manhattan. Rickie Lee has found us a shady
spot in Central Park. The summer day is fair and watermelon-crisp, and
she's hugging her ankles above sensible brown oxfords, laughing at the
thought of replaying the tape that's running on the bench between us. It
will pick up the hiss of Rollerblades, a sharp bongo crescendo, a quartet of
gently cursing boys, and the tale of her strange little trip. "We can put this
out later," she says. "It's like a poetry piece."
   And it's not unlike the new sound collages she's releasing now, jazzed
and looped, alternately broad-stroked and painstakingly pointillist. Her
songs have long been painterly aural landscapes, peopled with greasy spoon
lowlifes and other L.A. exotica on early albums like *Rickie Lee Jones* and
Pirates. The lyrics of *Ghostyhead*, still glide along, then stop and start fit-
fully, still a jazzy olio of dreamlike verses and infectious choruses. There
is a mordant humor to "Roadkill," wherein "a mystical vision got dressed
up one night" and headed out, only to get splattered by a Corvette ("Moon-
light on the hill and the future is a roadkill . . ."). The title cut is all mists
and aural celtic runes. It has hints of the Irish singer Mary Black. And it
sounds very, very old.

Rickie Lee smiles when I tell her that. She is only realizing how much is in the blood, how spooky and comforting this minstrel gene can be. Her father, an itinerant musician, was the son of a chorus girl and a one-legged vaudeville dancer named Peg Leg Jones. An on-the-road e-mail talked about the connection: "What I take with me is this: I am meant to be here. My grandfather was here, my grandmother, too, and the spirits of my ancestors dream of me."

Peg Leg's granddaughter took things further than all of them. Nineteen-seventy-nine was a fevered springtime for Rickie Lee Jones. She was flush with a hit ("Chuck E.'s In Love"), in mad love with fellow hipster Tom Waits; she was a dishy, big-boned *naiad du jour*. Tripping along in short skirts and Matterhorn heels, she'd get blindsided by the high-speed rock commerce of the dawning MTV age within two years. In hindsight, Jones says she was woefully unprepared. Her embrace was so instantaneous and extreme. Folks took her personal style—fishnet! lingerie! berets!—and set it out for the masses to try on. "It was a big *phenomenon*," she says now. "There were berets in windows."

It was too much. The boho street chick singer/songwriter cant played well in the magazines; the little-girl voice and ancient hoodoo perspective was a winsome, intriguing combination. "It was so confusing because it penetrated society so deeply, so fast," she says. "And then nobody was quite sure what to do, because in fact I *wasn't* a pop personality. But they had already embraced me as such. They were very attracted to the appearance and *idea* of me. . . . But I didn't turn out to be as sweet as I first appeared to be."

She was the Christmas puppy who ruined the carpet: There were chemical misadventures, the end of the affair with Waits that sent her to bed under Mother's care for months; some boozy, train-wreck performances that set even adoring critics to shaking their heads. By the mid-eighties, Jones was headed for a dryout, retreat and motherhood, in that order. We've left Charlotte, a wise soul in a Rugrats T-shirt, back at Jones's hotel with friends. Having her baby in 1986, says Rickie Lee, made Mother mend her ways.

"I think I had already tired of my habits," she says. "I was pretty tired of myself then." She was sick of the songs, too—she felt she was imitating herself. And she kept hearing her sly, irregular cadences everywhere: "Suddenly there were so many women who were singing in that style that it wasn't necessary for me to maintain it anymore. It had gone out into the world and taken root. And it wasn't mine anymore. That bothered me at first because they were making a lot of money and I wasn't. But now I think, how fantastic. It gives me the chance to leave it and do something else. Thank goodness."

She knew she had to change her off-meter tunes but says she couldn't write for years—until Charlotte led her back. They lived in rural, groovy Ojai, California, outpost of organic gardeners and crystal healers.

"Canyon ladies?"

Rickie Lee shoots me a look, then laughs. Yes, there were play groups, other moms. Some of them were a bit overwhelming. Charlotte went to a vegetarian school that treated the errant tuna sandwich in a lunch box as a capital offense. "Sometimes left-wing vegetarians can become very conservative and right-wing," Rickie Lee sighs. At times the parenting correctness wafting through those righteous canyons made her nuts. But, for the first time in years and years, she found she had a close female friend. She felt like, well . . . talking to people again. "She connects me to the world," Rickie Lee says of Charlotte. "She makes me have faith and hope in the world. I must trust that the world will take care of her. So it's created incredible hope. Yeah."

Last night, Charlotte came to the taping of PBS's *Sessions at West 54th*, a popular showcase for rock's less mainstream acts in a no-frills studio setting. The little girl stood in the wings, haloed, intent as her admittedly edgy mom finished a brave, well-received set. As soon as the red camera light blinked shut, Rickie Lee made a beeline for her baby; her bony black-draped shoulders drooped with relief as Charlotte clamped her in a hug.

She is feeling so strong, this California artist, that she and Charlotte have left the canyons and moved back to town, to West Hollywood. "And it was a big step," she says, "because I don't smoke, I did not drink, I was very strict and I went back into the middle of it all again. And I felt confident I could retain my health amid all the debauchery . . ."

She loves it in those hills alive with invigorating kooks and espresso bars, loves working again and says she is ready for the next step: "I never wanted to be motivated by money. But now I think that's not so good. I think the need for money, to not be poor, is a great motivator to do brave work." She grins. "Yeah, you have to have an earthly gain."

If only she'd been hip to that in the eighties, she says as we head out of the park toward rushing Fifth Avenue traffic. Not that she'd have gone *vavoom*. "I don't know," she's saying. "I still watch some of those videos and I wonder. How did those girls *do* that?"

THE EIGHTIES
provocateurs, boy toys, and fierce mcs

Tina Turner © Henry Diltz/CORBIS

My older brothers were incredibly rebellious, they got into drugs and trouble with the police. One of my brothers ran off and became a Moonie and the other one joined the Army. I became an overachiever. I had it programmed in my mind: "I don't care if I have to live on the street . . . and eat garbage. I'll do it."
—*Madonna, in* Spin *magazine, 1996*

e's been calling. And calling. He's interested in her music—this guy could actually sign her! She's left her demo tapes with countless aggressively hip receptionists, endured the chilly, glazed indifference of so many record men in black collarless shirts and stupid-ass shoes. And maybe that's over now. She's at the door of his swank East Side apartment, she's inside, they're both smiling and . . .

Within minutes, the quid pro quo has announced itself. Blam! Madonna Louise Ciccone has shut herself in his gleaming bathroom, gulping for air and wisdom. He's made it quite clear: a blow job, then the record deal. What's a girl to do?

The eighties would present some hard choices for fresh faces. With the advent of MTV—unleashed at the stroke of midnight on August 1, 1981—Madonna and her contemporaries were swept into a media juggernaut that would loose a stampede of instant divas in that go-go decade. Some would hire a savvy stylist and a hot video director and jump to it: Those who embraced the form would in short order be rewarded with a stunning global visibility (in Mandarin! Hindi! 24 hours a day!). Immediately, even radio was in MTV's sway; a hot video could almost guarantee drive-time airplay in a way that even great lyrics and a hook never could.

Commerce and art had rarely enjoyed such a close, torrid tango. The eighties were no time to be coy about living in the material world. Selling out and selling short were suddenly sexy as hell. Elton John turned "Sad Songs" into a jeans ad ("Sassoons say so much") by changing two letters. Co-opting made a comeback as black break dancers were used to accessorize magazine fashion spreads and otherwise unhip videos. On TV, flashdancers sold sanitary pads and Grace Jones bit Adam Ant's ear for Honda.

As the fashion industry turned out LaCroix poufs the size and price range of Goodyear blimps, as Gaultier sweet-talked Rodeo Drive matrons into twin warhead bustiers, Cyndi Lauper and Boy George vied for best Kabuki makeup. Dour, carrot-topped Annie Lennox jackbooted around in cross-dresser's chic; Stevie Nicks now fluttered as a solo act in weedy, diaphanous dresses that evoked Ophelia by way Melrose Avenue. The guitar-wielding, female-dominated bands that had seventies incarnations in Joan Jett's Runaways, in Suzi Quatro and early Heart, found a more telegenic and marketable incarnation in tiny shag-cut Pat Benatar. Tina Turner rose from the ashes of the Ike years, a long-stemmed and independent Colossus of Hose.

In the same vein, some female singers cultivated a return to Big Hair and copious eyeliner as the eighties saw a modest revival of girl groups. And in their winking homage, they put a reverse twist on the vixen look. White girls dipped back into ditzy lyrics and beehive kitsch: The B-52s punked it up and Bananarama, the Go-Go's, the Bangles all had fun, fun, fun with the form. Much of the music was unabashed novelty pop: Vivid red lips chomped big ripe bananas in Bananarama's "Cruel Summer" video. The Bangles got middle America to "Walk Like an Egyptian." They all sang agreeable harmony with Cyndi Lauper's chick power anthem, "Girls Just Wanna Have Fun." And in a go-go time when money men floated junk bonds like so many Frisbees, when restaurant madness made idols of chefs and cruel dominatrixes of their black-clad urban hostesses, such giddiness played well.

Though they came snarling out of the L.A. punk scene in the late seventies, the Go-Gos were America's New Wave sweethearts by 1981. Their *Beauty and the Beat* was the first number-one album by an all-woman band, selling over two million units. It held the top spot on the *Billboard* list for six weeks, spinning off singles "Our Lips Are Sealed" and "We Got the Beat." It seemed that maybe they could best the average girl group's maddeningly short life span.

Early in May 1985, Go-Go's lead singer Belinda Carlisle and guitarist Charlotte Caffey are walking home down Sunset Boulevard from SIR recording studios, where the band has been rehearsing for its fourth album. Nothing is working. The band has two new and shaky members and a history of ego-fueled snits.

Carlisle has been fending off press assaults on everything from her visible weight gain to her drug and alcohol problems. Caffey, the band's other drug user, has finally kicked along with Belinda. Clean and sober but sad, the two women trudge along reliving the session until they reach this fatal crossroad:

"We can't make another record."

The Go-Go's broke up a week later, on May 10. Carlisle and Caffey told the other two group members in a sterile room at their management firm. It was Kleenex and recriminations all around—yet still such a blood-lessly corporate end for a bunch of unregenerate garage girls. So un-rock and roll. Surely, the group suffered from the too-much-too-fast syndrome that has KO'd bands—girls and boys—for years. But this crack-up had a new wrinkle: The real lives just didn't match the pictures. Women who came up in smudged mascara on the L.A. club scene couldn't maintain all that MTV *Pretty in Pink* glow.

Said Carlisle, "I got tired of being cute, bubbly and effervescent all day. I just didn't feel like being bouncy anymore." Bassist Kathy Valentine put it this way: "There was a real desire on the part of the media and society for us to be nonthreatening and wholesome. . . . We could have done more to try to control the way our image was thrust on us, but for some reason, that had to be part of the package in order for us to be accepted."

Madonna would writhe before she walked erect on MTV. In 1984, her video for "Lucky Star" was a study in bare-tummy floor exercises. "Borderline" was bland but bouncy—a description that fits much of the early oeuvre. The not-yet-blond ambition that her early bandmates and club cohorts have complained of paid off. Seymour Stein signed Madonna to Sire Records. And when, in 1982, I talked with Michael Jackson's über-agent Freddy DeMann, he groused good-naturedly that this girl Madonna had simply browbeaten him into taking her on. It was DeMann who took Michael, during those *Thriller* days, to corporate megastar status. He would get Madonna there as well, if she wanted it enough. And did she? I asked him. DeMann laughed. *Are you kidding?*

No, Madonna assured me, she would never say that her gender was a handicap. "I felt like Seymour [Stein] totally respected me," she says. "I never felt I was being treated in a lesser way because I was female. Maybe that's because a gay man signed me to a label."

But wait—what finally happened that night in the record guy's bathroom? What were her thoughts when he proposed his sloppy little transaction?

"I was like, '*yuck*,'" she says. "I was horrified. I contemplated whether I would be able to do such a thing to get a record deal. I couldn't, so I left."

It was one of many sober acts of self-control exercised by a woman the Catholic Church would soon condemn as the essence of wantonness. Understandably, Madonna would not gratify the baser urges of some record-company sleaze—but she would, with cameras rolling and for full theatrical release, demonstrate her fellatio technique on a bottle in her tour documentary *Truth or Dare*. "I am an enigma to most people," she told me.

By the time she turned 40 in 1998, Madonna's was the most scrutinized female life of the 20th century—with the possible exceptions of Diana Spencer and Jacqueline Kennedy Onassis. Since the myth of Madonna (the motherless Catholic girl from the Midwest, the headstrong modern dancer, the brilliant urban opportunist) is now more familiar to schoolchildren than that of Betsy Ross or Eleanor Roosevelt, I offer an economy rendering of that herstory—with a few asides from Madonna herself.

The restless and willing architect of her own notoriety, Madonna Louise Veronica Ciccone was born in 1958 to a homemaker and a Chrysler engineer in Bay City, Michigan. The family moved to Pontiac, where their home was fiercely Catholic: Mrs. Ciccone taught her girls that it was sinful to have pants that zipped up the front. She slept on wire hangers, knelt on uncooked rice to pray during Lent. Such piety proved no defense against earthly disease, and she died, after a long struggle with cancer, when Madonna was just six. The big family—six kids—got a new stepmother two years later when their father married his housekeeper.

Madonna learned the facts of life from her stepmother one night at age ten, as she was washing the dishes. She says she was horrified, turned the water on full force every time she heard the word "penis" to drown out the very sound of it. No tampons, the older woman warned—until *after* you're married. Even family fashion was repressed. The four Ciccone girls went to church in matching dresses made from McCall patterns and bargain bolts of Kmart fabric. White ankle socks. White shoes. Madonna's teen years were committed to a single goal: getting out of the house—and Pontiac.

"When I was *five* I knew I wanted to move," she corrects. "I knew that I was living in a really sheltered world. In high school I decided that as soon as I graduated I was getting the hell out of Dodge. I had a choice between going to the University of Michigan and moving to New York. I went to UM for a year and I liked it a lot, but I decided to cut to the chase. So I moved to New York. I was eighteen. I didn't know anybody in New York."

A taxi dropped her off amid the honk and hustle of Times Square. And before long, this dance student/singer was hawking her demos like any pushy hopeful. When I ask her what she found most trying about being ambitious and poor, she laughs. "Not having a place to take a shower or bath. Having to go out to dinner with idiots so I could come home and use their bathrooms. Living a hand-to-mouth existence didn't bother me so much. Not having a huge amount of comfort for me was like the bathroom problem, you know. I lived in the Music Building for a year—I was bascially squatting illegally. I was only supposed to be rehearsing. There was only a sink and toilet on each floor. Trying to make that work and feel clean was a bit of a nightmare . . ."

Thus Madonna's scene in the movie *Desperately Seeking Susan,* wherein her vagabond character is seen drying her armpits in the blast of a ladies' room hand dryer, was hardly an acting stretch. An eighties rock ingenue could run up against some of the same hygiene problems that dogged thirties vaudevilliennes. The difference: Madonna didn't have to wash out dainties in borrowed sinks for very long. Ever the practical girl, she used her first royalty check to buy a synthesizer and a bike.

Why was it so perfectly Madonna's moment? Since entire symposiums have been designed to assess her cultural impact, let us simply, succinctly regard her as the leather-bustiered Hale-Bopp that hurtled smack into the Information Age—at an astrologically and technologically propitious moment—and rendered us all slightly awestruck, whispering among ourselves in the dark, a little afraid but ultimately glad that she's up there glowing.

Mainstream pop, feminist issues, fashion, the rising cult of celebrity would all cluster in the forcefield of Madonna. Without seeming to be, she was incredibly accommodating. Like Madonna the star, her music—pretty pop, stylish dance cuts, reasonably wrung ballads—has always been extremely flexible and market-savvy in its refusal to stay in one groove. In this way—and especially with her danceable empowerment anthems like "Express Yourself" and, later, "Vogue"— Madonna was a crucial bridge between the vital club scene and less flexible corporate rock. She was a huge star with the obligatory (and allowance-laden) teenybop fans, but the downtown demi-monde could claim her as well.

Video sealed the mad affair with a big close-up kiss. Though her big-screen career has been lackluster, Madonna has a deep sense of cinematic instinct perfectly suited to the short digital form. Liz Phair neatly explained the girl-appeal in *Rolling Stone*: "To me, video art began with Madonna. I watched MTV in high school, when it was a new, happening thing, and the only videos I cared about were Madonna's. I learned the dance for 'Lucky Star.' It made me feel sexy, like a woman, to emulate her. She was cool and independent; she had muscles and boobs."

Lightweight songs were anchored by appealing video fables: Danny Aiello played the parental heavy in "Papa Don't Preach," about a teen pregnancy; no expense was spared for the "Diamonds Are a Girl's Best Friend" homage of "Material Girl," a tongue-in-cheek eighties anthem that branded Madonna with the nickname she now loathes intensely. Her records and her videos have, for the most part, been meticulously produced, with some of the best talent available to her deep checkbook. And the same hiring acuity that first paired her with the streetwise producer Jellybean Benitez led her a decade and a half later (1999) to chose William Orbit to shepherd her mature, introspective electronic tapestry, *Ray of Light*—a record that won her three Grammys and long-awaited critical praise. In wisely acceding to their star's smart, if expensive, instincts, Warner Brothers' serious investments paid off handsomely in record sales and visibility. By the end of the eighties, Madonna was bigger than Michael Jackson, who had begun his tabloid descent.

Madonna's economic side effects were not lost on youth marketers. Once MTV began its direct sell of rock styles—in sometimes indistinguishable videos and ads—a cheerily complicit mannequin could move warehouses full of bustiers and leather hair scrunchies. The two-way traffic was musical and visual. Trickle-up street fashion was all too visible in $1,000 Chanel biker boots clomping down the runways.

By the eighties, street chic had gone from a curious oxymoron to a furious form of cultural and currency exchange. If Madonna was its most skilled style manipulator, the kids kept up their end—with a little help from the rag trade. The same sort of retail sharpies who had turned out all those Swingin' London vinyl miniskirt knockoffs and Beatle boots seized Madonna's street-slut look and rode it to market. And that first look—born both of Madonna's limited means and later, the ministrations of her early stylist Maripol—was readily accessible. She piled on stretchy skirts and tube tops, junk jewelry, bustiers, rubber bracelets and lace gloves—a look little girls could put together on Saturday-afternoon scavenger hunts. Before Macy's made it easy with Madonnaland, the kids were ransacking Retail Slut, on Melrose Avenue in L.A., and Manhattan's Unique Clothing Warehouse and Screaming Mimi's. If they didn't want to be an exact copy of their idol, they at least were seeking desperately to be *interesting.*

Did they want to be sexy? Well, sort of. But not . . . *too.* "Like a Virgin," the single and the video, offered up the most clichéd images of the madonna/whore archetype to date: cute girl writhing in wedding dress, big cat prowling, boats in canals. Ooooh! For the under-sixteen set, it was scary/safe in its glib, small-screen packaging. And it would stand as a marketing blueprint for the likes of Britney Spears, who began her video life as a bruised-peach schoolgirl, then boasted on the first single of her second album, "I'm not that innocent"—while still claiming chastity in the teen mags. Deflowering by degrees—in this case, album sales cycles—can make dollars and sense.

In 1984, Madonna's breakout year, America—and MTV's growing global audience—felt the full flowering of makeover madness. It was a year of artful and antic juxtaposition: Anti-fashion became fashionable, genders were bent, trash beatified, Doonesbury yuppified, punk tamed for shopping mall sensibilities. Boy George and Annie Lennox raided each other's closets and shared a *Newsweek* cover, complete with a photo documentary of George's beauty makeovers. At twenty-six, he'd had more paint jobs than a Times Square billboard. In the ruffled tradition of Jimi Hendrix and Rick James, Prince got exquisitely dandified in eyeliner and lace—and thus, more deliciously *dirty.*

Cyndi Lauper was making being unusual all the rage; she summed up all this recombinant ID-swapping succinctly: "We all dress in *versions* now."

Pound for pound—and pop bead—Cyndi was every bit Madonna's equal. And in 1984, she made "Girls Just Want to Have Fun" as sizable a hit as "Like a Virgin." Cyndi dressed in glorious Goodwill Technicolor to Madonna's dance-student black. Cyndi sang about girls pleasuring them-selves ("She Bop") half a decade before Madonna dry-humped on a bed set at the centers of 70,000-seat stadiums on her 1990 Blond Ambition tour. Long in advance of World Wrestling Federation madness, that kooky Ital-ian Lauper girl from Queens accessorized her videos with her grapplin' pal Captain Lou Albano, who thoughtfully punched rubber bands through his face for festive close-ups. If MTV fans preferred to dress like Madonna, the girls would surely opt for Cyndi's pajama party; she was genuinely girl-friendly.

Musically, Cyndi was the stronger singer and writer. Besides the cartoony "Girls," there were tender, vocally sophisticated ballads like "Time After Time" and that future Kodak campaign, "True Colors." Just why Madonna left Cyndi eating her stardust rests with some indecipher-able ratio of ambition and opportunity; Lauper has always bemoaned the fact that she can't sell herself. But if she lost her chart position in the crunch of eighties corporate rock, she did not lose her way. She said she was grate-ful to go home every night to her husband and cats. And on a more human scale, she kept plying the Road.

What can she be thinking, running breakneck up the aisle at Radio City Music Hall? Cyndi's hair is Pez purple this night in 1997; she is barefoot and her magenta, glow-in-the-dark floral sheath is stretched over a clearly pregnant belly. She is opening for Tina Turner's Wildest Dreams tour. Tina, who has performed while in the family way herself, says she's been a bit concerned for Cyndi since the outset. All that morning sickness. And now, girl, those dresses . . . .

(Imagine, here, Tina's Acid Queen laugh.)

With some effort, Cyndi clambers back onto the stage, says in her Bugs Bunny New Yawkese, "This gives new meanin' to the phrase 'barefoot and pregnant . . .'" She settles on a stool. There are two women in her band, a long-haired violinist and a hot, slick guitar player in leather pants and a halter. Cyndi straps on an electric guitar and, reaching across her vast expanse, attacks it hard. She is singing the title cut from her latest album, Sisters of Avalon, *and it rocks.*

The crowd is on its feet for her, hollering, "Cyndi, yeah, go girl."

What is in Cyndi's carry-on bag for this tour? Guitar picks and prenatal iron supplements? A dog-eared copy of What to Expect When You're Expecting? *Whatever the mix, it is clear she will keep on moving until a small, unseen hand stills her in a way that chart vagaries and shifting pop vogues could not. Bobbing now inches beneath the vibrating steel strings, the kid will doubtless have timing. Cyndi is grinning over the rippling thickets of raised arms.*

"Well, OK," she pants, waving back. "Gotta go!"

Somewhere amid all the mad vamping of Cyndis, Madonnas and over-dressed haircut bands, there was also room for generic cool. Keds were reissued in more colors as designer-jean sales slipped. American flags could be seen waving at Springsteen shows and, after years of being hideously unfashionable, being born in the U.S.A. became at least acceptable. What emerged in those arenas ringing with factory songs and paeans to Jersey girls was not the stretch-limo, patriotic chic of the Reagan White House, but its opposite: a mongrel American stance, alternately proud and mortified—and fated to puzzle forever over a dubious birthright. If fantasy's signifier was Michael Jackson's sequined glove, reality's was the baseball cap hanging out of Springsteen's back pocket. For girls, Madonna was a brilliant mediation of the two: One *could* achieve fabulousness on baby-sitter's wages.

Such spirited and detailed reinvention of self could well have been a hiccup of the self-absorbed seventies. But it was likely a reactive impulse as well. A helmet-coiffed bastion of white privileged adulthood had just resoundingly reasserted itself. Rock and roll kids on both sides of the Atlantic recognized the eternal Square enemy in the American actor and his mannequin wife, and in the stiffly permed Toryism of Margaret Thatcher. As the second-term Reagans swept out the last vestiges of the Carters' mortifying polyesters and homespuns and reinstated couture, the kids—those eternal sans culottes—were inputting a staggering load of images to come up with revolutionary looks of their own. After all, fantasy—call it anti-fashion, androgyny, anarchy—always sells better when the rich get richer and the poor go window-shopping.

And my, the neighborhoods they visited. Just like Elvis in those boxy-blue-suited Eisenhower years, white eighties sharpies made a left turn toward the ghetto. Suddenly, suburban pre-teens were affecting the baggy-pantsed ghetto look; black hip-hop kids were looking to Polo, long the somber haberdashers to New Jersey tax accountants. Prefiguring the hugely profitable cross-dissing of the nineties, those skinny white boys of Aerosmith joined rappers Run-DMC for a 1986 video duet/duel on "Walk This Way." What the hell was going on? Soon the phenomenon was so widespread, Oprah would have to do a whole show on kids' racial cross-trafficking. MTV and market research firms were sending pierced and black-clad pods of spies into the mosh pits to try and buy some edge.

But Madonna had no need of their weird science. After all, she'd lived the downtown life, lugging a heavy synthesizer up six flights to her Soho loft, ooohing over the vogueing Spanish boys in the clubs who wore Claude Montana better than Cindy or Iman. Given the fierceness of competition between the vying "houses," some called the posing competitions the lavender equivalent of gang warfare. These gay hothouse flowers were gorgeous, and their catwalk insouciance could be downright contagious.

Attending a vogueing ball hosted by the nonpareil House of Africa in the late eighties, I found myself an instant if unwitting partisan, clapping deliriously during category events like "Butch Realness." It was like *Spartacus* in Maude Frizon pumps. During one intense pose-a-thon overseen by the imposing Pepper LaBeja, a Japanese photographer near me screamed and fainted; a couple of contestants pulled out Evian facial misters to revive him. Imperious deejays and drag divas all claimed vocal retinues as sound and style vamped in perfect, tongue-in-chic sync. When he came to, the Japanese gentleman explained his swoon: "The *signifying* knocks me out." Only in the best Kabuki had he seen a tiny finger gesture so codify a culture.

Already, of course, there were agents provocateur in the crowd who could appreciate the theatrical values. Toward decade's end, Jennie Livingston was filming Manhattan drag queens and vogueing balls for her documentary *Paris Is Burning.* And Madonna, ever the quick study, was learning the boys' studied runway mimesis for her single and video *Vogue.* It went multi-platinum. "Celebutantes"—club kids with high Attitude— were booked for the afternoon talk shows, delighted, in their vintage Pucci prints and creaking rubber, to *épater* the Barcalounger bourgeoisie. It's no accident that many of the tour dancers Madonna mothers in *Truth or Dare* are untested club kids, pinching themselves in the glitzy Neverland of their Gaultier-corseted Tinkerbell.

Say what you will about her diva mien. At bottom, Madonna's is an egalitarian impulse, much as disco was. A vast cross-section, from teeny-boppers to gay men to smitten soccer moms, heeded her call to "Express Yourself." And no pop star, male or female, has ever managed her own autocracy with greater sangfroid. Who else could have looked up at a helicopter siege straight out of *Apocalypse Now* during her wedding to Sean Penn and, after a few bad moments, laughed at the sky?

Yes, it took a village to create Madonna—a canny manager, stylists, video directors, fashion designers, panting magazine editors, two record companies (Warner Brothers/Sire and her own Maverick label), hair and makeup swamis, platoons of challenging and worshipful photographers. But there's never been any question as to who's the head memsahib. What Colonel Parker did for Elvis, Madonna has done for herself. By 1991, she was so merger-savvy, she won a $60 million advance for her company, Maverick, in a joint venture with Time/Warner. The bigger company was only too happy to oblige—the eighties Madonna had sold over 70 million records and earned over a billion dollars for her bosses. Oh, and please—might they bump their gratitude up to a 20 percent royalty rate?

Does she feel like the Control Queen she's perceived to be? I asked her, and she laughed out loud: "Oh, *please*. Who's in total control? As soon as you're famous, you're out of control. You can't control what anybody says about you, so that's an absurd notion."

Maybe. But so ingrained are Madonna's instincts for media counter-offensives, even her unconscious works the trades. Consider the dream she describes in the "private diaries" she published in *Vanity Fair* during the filming of *Evita*. The entry for February 2, 1996 is a lulu:

Dreamt last night that Sharon Stone invited me to her house because she wanted to know me better. I went, with some suspicion, and when I arrived she was taking a bath with a red dress on and all her makeup . . . the doorbell rang and Sharon immediately submerged her face . . . to prove to me that she didn't care if people saw her looking bad. When I opened the door Courtney Love was standing there in a torn dress, waving a gun at me and slurring her words: "I know you guys are in there—I'm going to shoot you both." Then she burst out laughing, saying it was only a joke.

Did Susan B. Anthony dream of doing shots-and-beers with Carrie Nation? Only Madonna's teeming uplink subconscious could come up with such a swell multimedia romp: bad girls who have come to know the press value of occasionally playing unplugged and unretouched . . . of using old tricks to win new prizes and yes, r-e-s-p-e-c-t. From Stone's journey (pantyless infamy in *Basic Instinct* to Oscar-nominated *Casino* star) to Madonna's well-chosen path from "Material Girl" through "Blond Ambition" to the queenly centerpiece of a $60 million production of *Evita*, the speed and the stakes were amazing.

James Brown got at the heart of this determined transit with his knowing subtitle to "Hot Pants"—"She's Got to Use What She's Got To Get What She Wants." But it's a modus operandi as old as Salome. The twist of today's multimedia titillation: Madonna has more veils than there are Internet sites and no need—ever—to tear away the last one and bare her True Self.

Playing with the video form worked best for those who strode into the studio with a strong sense of self. Hard-headed Annie Lennox was raised in Aberdeen, Scotland, a port city once famous for its top-grade granite. She stuck resolutely to her plan for a classical career, attending London's Royal Academy of Music until she grew unaccountably restless. She left, knocked around London, playing with shifting aggregations of rock musicians, until she met Dave Stewart, who, she said, "looked like he'd been dragged through a hedge backward."

Their collaboration and, for a time, their romantic partnership, formed the duo called Eurythmics. Annie's voice, a roaring alto, was as strong as her will. It was a gutsy update of Dusty Springfield's affecting blue-eyed soul. Her visuals were equally striking: from punky, buzzed redhead to platinum siren to the black-suited, slick-haired Elvisoid Annie who appeared at the '84 Grammys. "When I started wearing mannish clothes onstage, it was to detract from what people had come to expect from women singers," she explained. "The height of which was Debbie Harry, who I loved. But I felt I couldn't be a sex symbol. . . I tried a way to transcend that emphasis on sexualilty. . . I simply wanted to get away from wearing cutesy-pie miniskirts and tacky cutaway pushups."

Performance artist Laurie Anderson wasn't able to compress her witty sprawl into compelling MTV fodder and quickly gave it up, declaring in

1984 that "I'm not real interested in that kind of image making. In general, I think it's some kind of washed-out sort of soft-core porn and soft-core violence and it doesn't interest me at all." Anderson found plenty of lively alternatives: theater pieces, long-form videos, installations. But other artists found their options badly hedged as style spoke more loudly than ever and carried a huge price tag. By the mid-eighties, video was fast becoming a tough, voracious and rather sexist master—one that wouldn't particularly favor a singer/songwriter like Joan Armatrading, who eschewed makeup and dressed in a crisp white shirt and black jeans. No matter; video directors were never short on willing talent. L.A. casting offices were besieged by lines of young and tasty things eager to tie on a thong as set decoration for Billy Idol or Van Halen.

The nadir—an example MTV executives hasten to point out did not air on their network but on their cable imitators—was the late comedian Sam Kinison's little passion play. Cameras lingered on him roughing up a scantily clad Jessica Hahn (she of the Jim Bakker PTL sex scandal) in a wrestling pit as leering males looked on. Prince seemed to fancy himself an impresario with a Frederick's of Hollywood mind-set. His female band protégés, Wendy and Lisa, could play; so could drummer Sheila E. But his other ingenues, Appollonia and Vanity, were better suited to the mercifully silent posing of a lingerie catalog. The C-cup, babes-'n'-bondage efforts of boy bands like Aerosmith, Van Halen and Guns N' Roses contributed to a post-feminist lapse that set even committed sirens' teeth on edge. Tina Turner, no slouch in the steam-heat department, told me that she had to just say no to one panting video director. "They wanted me in a red satin bed," she said. "With some fire or something. And I'm not getting in bed— I'm not a bed person anyway. I don't like doing sexy parts in those videos."

Long Island, New York-born Pat Benatar was a glam belter with a tiny body built for spandex. Benatar played the corporate rock game and played it well, delivering a well-calibrated mix of knee-jerk power chords and melody—on time, in the pocket, one album every twelve months. She filled huge arenas and scored respectable hits like "Hit Me with Your Best Shot," "Love Is a Battlefield" and "Invincible" in the mid-eighties. But even the tractable Benatar dug in her heels when her record company, Chrysalis, removed some of her clothing—via airbrush—for an ad in *Billboard*. "They were abusive and disgusting," she declared later. "It took me two years and one record that went in the dumper before I said, 'Give me whatever I'm owed and let me go.'" Benatar chopped her hair short, deglammed her stage presence and turned to a bluesier sound.

"You know what I hate?" grumped Ann Wilson of Heart in 1977. "I hate being asked what it's like to be a woman in the rock business." The Woman Question was tiresome, but it never slowed the Wilson sisters, Nancy and Ann, a pair of West Coast military brats who managed to front Heart for a decade's worth of big hair, humongous guitar chords and sizable hits between 1976 and 1990. Their first label's sexist ad campaign (HEART'S WILSON SISTERS CONFESS: "IT WAS ONLY OUR FIRST TIME!") was just part of the reason they left the company. But they dealt and got on with it. Instead of bemoaning woman's place onstage, Ann voiced a sisterly concern for female fans: "It's really maddening to us, as women, to see young girls just lay themselves at the feet of any male who happens to be involved with rock and roll. It's really a sad sight, like sheep to the slaughter."

"I'm with the band" could be a feminist statement if it came from a young woman like Joan Jett, who stood and delivered the black leather bombast of "Cherry Bomb" amped to ear-bleed levels. Damn-the-gender-and-dig-the-music was certainly the driving force behind Joan Jett's classic "I Love Rock 'n' Roll." And the song's sentiment was heartfelt, since Jett's career has touched all the hot buttons of gender issues. Her first group, the Runaways—which she joined at fifteen—was laughed off as a novelty all-girl band of party-hearty L.A. teenagers. (Another of the quartet was guitarist Lita Ford, who later managed a modest solo career.) They did keg parties—anything. And they took a lot of flak. Women hated them, Jett has said. Men tossed beer cans and insults: *whoredykeslut!*

Joan Jett was never about pretty-girl rock; her personal heroine was the fierce, guitar-slinging Suzi "Can the Can" Quatro. After the Runaways, no label would have Jett, and she put out "I Love" on Boardwalk, an indie outfit. Her eighties incarnation with her second band, the Blackhearts, reeked of leather and punk, a result of Jett's sojourn in England and working with a pair of ex-Sex Pistols. The band's 1981 album, *I Love Rock 'N' Roll*, was a hit, and its title single reached number one in 1982. Jett's guttersnipe humor produced another brat manifesto, *Glorious Results of a Misspent Youth*, in 1984. But by that year, Jett found taking her act on the road was no less painful than those grotty keggers, as she told interviewer Evelyn

McDonnell: "We were playing in Italy and Spain. The audience, it was all guys, and they were like worked up into this frothy frenzy. They wanted to kill me—'you fucking cunt!' Violently trying to get to me, hawking loogies. I was covered in spit, and it was hanging off of me, and I would sit there, and I wouldn't leave the stage. . . . I cried every night because I couldn't understand why they hated me so much."

When she asked them directly, they told her: "Girls playing rock and roll—you shouldn't be doing this."

Wisely—and perhaps a bit in self-defense—Jett joined up with the wailing tribes of riot grrls in the early nineties, working with L7, Bikini Kill and Babes in Toyland. Recently, a peroxided, buzz-cut Jett came out happily as a lesbian. And as leather jackets made a big comeback on runways and in Gap ads, Jett posed for *The New York Times Magazine* in a $1,200 motorcycle jacket—by Calvin Klein. Of her new look, Jett told writer S. S. Fair, "That heavy-makeup, black-hair thing, I was becoming a parody of myself." Elsewhere, Jett offered this tart observation on the changes she's seen: "I read a piece on L7 the other day, and it didn't mention they were all women until the last sentence. With the Runaways, it would have been the first."

Things are not going well on the set of Tina Turner's video, set for release in the summer of 1984. It's for a new single, "What's Love Got to Do With It?," a tough-but-soulful look at love in the age of sanctioned greed, AIDS and post-modern irony. Tina has just made her life-changing album, Private Dancer, *and she knows it. But do these people know her? Ms. TNT, normally a placid Buddhist, is about to explode. The fussy stylist they hired has arrived with an armful of those torn-looking rag-dresses, the Clan of the Cave Bear stuff that was tired even in the seventies.*

Tina is thinking of the men that have dressed her with so much more care. How Bob Mackie understood her needs and made tough, glittery things that worked. How, at seventeen, gangly Anna Mae Bullock opened the door to bandleader Ike Turner who brushed past her bearing a blue-sequined dress, long gloves, costume jewelry, a little fur wrap. Ike wanted to make her pretty, make her a star. He tossed the rest of the stuff on the bed: two more grown-up dresses. Sling-back shoes! Stockings with seams up the back! And how proudly Ike displayed her in his big pink Cadillac. She rode beside him, chin up, gaze forward, the big boat taking wide turns through the narrow opportunities of tumbledown East St. Louis. She was feeling so doggone Bette Davis . . .

*Oh, Lord. Forty-five now and WHAT HAVE THEY DONE? Tina looks
in the mirror at the drama-queen mask the video makeup guy has spackled on. She
has always found doing her own pre-show makeup to be . . . meditative. This fool
has made a mess. She rises, stalks past the racks of distressed designer nightmares
and toward her own bags.*

*"Ughhhh," she tells her director. "I'm not wearing this. Here's a little
something I brought along."*

How does a middle-aged woman step into the light as a solo act in
a twenty-year-old's game? What presentation of self will secure her de-
cent rotation amid the nubile Go-Gos, those pouty Bangles? That day,
Tina unpacked a tiny leather skirt, a standard-issue denim jacket. Any
10th-grader could have put together her signature look in the finished
video. She dead-eyed the camera, planted her legs and sounded the soul
of Experience. She says she would not have predicted the three Grammys
that tough, torn-voice song brought her. But she knew that day what felt
"totally Tina."

Tina Turner, she will tell you over and over, is a *working* woman..
Always has been. And her stage clothes have always been all business. Just
as she used to have the Ikettes' minis made out of wash-and-wear Quiana
("great for the road"), she says she dressed herself for maximum overdrive:
"I don't think much about looking fabulous," she told me. "I need my
clothes to work. The short skirts let me move, the leather doesn't show
perspiration. People thought I wore the fishnet stockings 'cause they were
sexy. Well, they don't run, they're a lot cooler, and they also give great
support."

The first time I met Tina, visiting backstage in the late seventies, she
was swathed in a white terry robe and turbaned with a thirsty Turkish
towel. Perspiration still streamed down her temples and collarbones. That
night she had generated amazing heat in one of those tired theaters-in-
the-round on Long Island. Fifteen minutes after she left the stage, we could
still hear folks wahooing in the lobby.

"Is it always this way?" I asked her.

"Yes, darling. I make sure of that."

She's always worked hard for her money. Tina had been solo for a
couple of years by then. But I had been getting myself to her live shows,

those with and without Ike, for years. A hour with Tina was always better—and cheaper—than an entire spa weekend. Ike and Tina didn't have many big hits, but her voice had always leapt out of them. In 1960, she ripped some wild, hormonal screams across the demure girl group backup of those shoop-shoop times with "A Fool in Love." The song's punch line would prove eerily prescient:

You know you love him and you can't understand
Why he treat you like he do when he's such a good man.

Onstage, Tina was never dirty, but she was hot. Her mike technique was eye-popping; her stance alone could drop a deacon. That Tina—the wild R&B thang—makes her uncomfortable now sometimes, when she looks back. But she's too smart to try and shove that sizzling karma under a rug. When I asked her if the old image disturbed her, she said, "The raunchy, the wild, sexy—it was uncomplimentary. But I understood it. I still see photographs, and my stance and my body form is very much like that. I have to stand like that to hit high notes, and high heels will give you a certain body form. So I never liked [being thought of that way], but I thought, Well, that's what you've done, Tina. I mean, you have stood there with crotch open, ripped at the seams. It was only after I started chanting that I realized, Well, that's what you've put out there. That's what people see. And as soon as I started accepting it, that's when it all started to change—where the knowledge of who and how I am became public and people accepted me differently."

But it would be a long time before the *60 Minutes* cameras would film Tina chanting amid the tasteful landscaping of her home in southern France. Ike and Tina remained a raucous R&B roadshow, largely unknown to rock and pop audiences, before the couple—married in 1962—met up with producer Phil Spector. Legend has it that Spector paid Ike to stay out of the studio while the producer wrapped his mammoth Wall of Sound around Tina's vocal firepower, torqued up the tempo and came up with "River Deep, Mountain High." In 1966, it stiffed in the U.S. but was a huge hit in England, which led to the Rolling Stones inviting Ike and Tina to open for a tour there.

This proved a mutually advantageous exchange program: Mick Jagger got some much-needed dance tips, and Tina cozied up to rock and roll, cutting a successful cover of "Honky Tonk Women" in 1969. "Proud Mary," a supercharged remake of a Creedence Clearwater Revival hit, is still a setpiece of any grand Tina tour. Watching her stage exhortations over the years, seeing her make screaming testifiers of even the most sedate suburban audience, it did not surprise me, when I finally got the chance to ask her, that Tina's earliest inspiration was some full-tilt boogie gospel: Sister Rosetta Tharpe.

Live, Tina has always presented the fullest conjugation of the verb "to rock." And even in the video age, live performance remains the key to her legend and her success. Despite some decidedly Vegas trappings, her shows had the clamor and immediacy of a great soul revue. Orbited by that changing galaxy of Ikettes, a big band churning behind it all, Tina could pop out of the wings like James Brown—eeeeeyahhh!—a power pinball shooting off the spring, stuttering across the stage on one leg, spinning, thrashing, the body language telegraphing instantly that it could be no one else but She, Tina! Her spike heels could pierce a hubcap, her voice always hit the rigging and cracked, exquisitely, in half. And the gams—those rock-solid limbs. Long, strong, planted slightly apart, Tina Turner's legs bracket rock and roll imagery. They straddle decades and styles, from the roughest R&B of her early St. Louis gigs with Ike, to the creamiest contemporary pop. In fact, if there is one photo icon that fairly screams "Rock and Roll is here to stay," it's Steven Meisel's miles-o'-leg jump shot of Turner wearing just a silk shirt, black patent stiletto heels and fishnet stockings. Airborne, leering from under all that haystack hair, she's as vital and ferocious a rocker as has ever growled into a mike, "Sometimes, we like to do things nice . . . and *rough*."

Nobody knew how savage the game was until 1986 when her autobiography, *I, Tina*, thudded onto bookshelves. She says "the world was shocked" by her accounts of the beatings and other, more creative abuse meted out by her former husband and stage partner. Ike's mash notes to his wife included busted ribs, a fractured jaw and swollen eyes, nose, lips. Drive-by shootings. Firebombs. The sorrow and the pity in the book came from witnesses interviewed by co-author Kurt Loder. But there was nothing lachrymose about Turner's own first-person testimony, not even in the stories of being left behind by both parents in poor, rural Nut Bush, Tennessee. Given the revelations in *I, Tina*, a hindsight listen to "What's Love Got to Do with It" made her breakthrough song seem the modern survivor's *cri de coeur*. The tracks were contemporary, but the lyrics were adult and experienced.

Private Dancer's title cut was an update on an old transaction—the resigned dime-a-dance girl for whom "any old music will do." It was dark, slow, shot with cynicism and resignation—and a reasonable metaphor for the modern pop star. Madonna would take it further, would play a peep-show dancer in her "Open Your Heart" video—and close it out in studied Chaplinesque, walking hand-in-hand with a child. Tina closed her four minute passion play alone—but strikingly, defiantly so. The resultant Grammys raised a profile that grew fifty feet high with Tina's movie appearance as the fierce, chain-mailed Aunty Entity with Mel Gibson in *Beyond Thunderdome*. There was also a Rock Event—a global showcase—to amplify the sizzle.

Backstage at Live Aid, July 1985. Mick Jagger and Tina Turner, clotheshorses extraordinaire, are discussing togs for their show-stopping duet. Tina will be wearing a little something by Azzedine Alaia. Azzedine is a minimalist when it comes to fasteners.

"One snap," Tina tells Mick, "and that skirt is gone."

Mick wants to know what's underneath and is told that it's just fishnets and a leather corset. Now Mick is brooding. With just days to go, he had called up Stephen Sprouse and asked for something yellow. Sprouse pulled together an outfit using, oddly enough, something he'd been calling his Rolling Stone jacket—modeled after an old Stones outfit. Now His Dandyness tells Tina he plans to change clothes for the finale.

"Oh, yeah?" says Tina. "You do, and my skirt comes off."

And so it was that Jagger reached out and Azzedine's creation bit the dust in the Live Aid finale beamed around the world. "It was fun," Tina told me shortly afterward. "'Cause Mick is a bad boy. You tell Mick Jagger something snaps away, forget it."

To the millions watching, it seemed one of those impetuous rock moments. But it was also a glimpse at the control Tina had begun to wield as a Woman to Be Reckoned With. She had also found a tough, canny strategist in Englishman Roger Davies, who has managed her to her current Olympus of corporate sponsorships and live, VH1 divaship. Rock divadom, in its current multiplatinum, megatour, sweeping-retinue incarnation, coalesced in the late eighties; its practitioners began to settle into predictable archetypes: the protean Provocateur (Madonna, Annie Lennox), the Difficult Diva (Aretha Franklin, Whitney Houston) and the stalwart Survivor (Tina Turner).

As the latter, Tina had credibility on all counts: major adversity, the strength to overcome, and triumphant box-office and record sales. The plucky dame has long been a popular American sweetheart, from *The Unsinkable Molly Brown* through *Funny Girl* and *Hello Dolly*. It wasn't until Hollywood had decided to lionize Tina's life that I understood her to be a bit of an unwitting heroine. We talked in 1993 just before the film version of her life and book, *What's Love Got to Do with It?*, was about to be released. As stunt experts choreographed Ike's violence against her, as she pondered how many millions would be seeing and hearing those blows, Tina said she had been doing a lot of thinking. It was certainly the most animated conversation we've had.

The suite at Manhattan's St. Regis Hotel is plush and quiet as a country chapel. Tina is dressed for a flight to L.A.: fuzzy white sweater, loose charcoal knit pants, thick wool socks, clunky black lace-up boots. She is cheerful this day after turning Carnegie Hall upside down at a Rainforest Foundation benefit. Skittering across stage in a black leather catsuit, she had reduced the likes of Sting, George Michael, Dustin Hoffman, James Taylor, Tom Jones and Sir Ian McKellan to goofy, adoring, tambourine-banging backup boys. *TEEEENAAAAAH!* The well-heeled crowd had leapt to its feet, screamed her name; even the squad of face-lift detectives seated around me— the tabloid gossips—had gasped, "Oh, my God, she looks *faaaabulous.*"

And she does, through the steam of a cup of herbal tea. Tina says she was delighted with the choice of Angela Bassett to play her, but unhappy with certain aspects of the film. People had laid so much on her since The Book. They had their own ideas about her motives. She says she didn't tell all for sympathy over the hand life dealt her. She wasn't moping. She was just good and mad.

"I wrote the book because I was so tired of people being really upset that I left Ike," she says. "Like, '*How could you?*' When I went out on my own, I had a hit record and people were still in my ear about Ike and 'our music.' Music? We couldn't get a hit record in those days. We didn't draw people, and he was freaking out, doing more drugs."

At that point, Ike's most creative output was demolition. He especially liked to rearrange his wife's face. The director re-enacting those years was fretting aloud about how to age Angela Bassett through the film when Tina whirled on him:

"YOU THINK I'VE HAD WORK DONE!"

Photos of Tina's late mother, Zelma, in her seventies attest to the genetic durability of the Bullock clan, its smooth, high cheekbones and wellspring collagen. When the film director, Brian Gibson, caviled, "Well, Tina, you *have* to have a sag here and there," the diva pulled her hair back to show him the absence of clip marks or scars. Still, people must *talk* . . .

"I had a little nose work because there was so much cartilage floating," Tina tells me. "I had been hit so much, this stuff was floating around and it got worse as I started to fly more. My sinuses got blocked. So, yes, they changed my nose some. But there's no plastic in my body."

This engenders a lively little aside on the fine points of singing onstage after a beating, when hitting the right note brings on an unsightly nosebleed. "I went home, put on an ice pack, found a way to sing the next few days," she says. "Just kept going."

Heck, Oprah wouldn't let that one slide. I have to ask her: Given the current vogue for celeb shrinkage, and facing the rehash of these traumas on the silver screen, are we talking some kind of long-term syndrome here? Does she see herself as some textbook victim of domestic violence? Tina responds with a yelp worthy of the harrowing Acid Queen she played in Ken Russell's *Tommy*.

"VICTIM? *VICTIM!* GIMME A BREAK!"

She narrows those hazel lioness peepers. "Did I say something funny?"

Reeling in my grin, I confess to her that my question is loaded, that I've been cranky as a wet cat lately about the high tide of public casualties. Tina's autobiography seemed to have loosed a floodgate. And we're deep, deep into the Age of the Victim, when you can off-load boring family fights on live TV with Sally Jessy clucking, "I hear you." Canny Oprah got

Michael Jackson to confess "regurgitating" at the very sight of his abusive dad—nailed it right on the cusp of the first commercial break! Don't get me wrong—solidarity is well. Victims' rights, victims' support groups. Absolutely. Just spare me all this victim chic.

Tina has been patient, even enthusiastic throughout my harangue. I guess I'm giddy in the rarefied presence of One Who Will Not Whine.

"Oh, I'm with you about that victim thing," she says. "It's put into our heads. It's everywhere. And I don't think it does anybody any good."

We giggle about some of the jargon the victimologists might toss at her own grim dossier. What would they say about a mother to four boys trapped in a loveless, all but sexless marriage with a paranoid, womanizing drug fiend?

"Enabler?" Tina squeaks. "What is that, anyhow? 'Dysfunction?' You'll never hear that out of this mouth. Maybe it's because I'm naive, maybe because I was brought up a country girl—I didn't get into all that."

But "victim" isn't a fancy, new-age term. It's as old as poor, put-upon Job.

"Never!" she says. "Some people want that title. It's an excuse. I never needed it and I don't want it, would never use it to describe what went on."

She says she reaches her flash point when well-meaning folks try to cast her as some domestic-trauma poster girl. She quietly contributes to an organization her friend Ann-Margret sponsors for battered women. But she refuses to assume that mantle herself. And don't you dare call that Denial.

"Someone tells me I was a victim, I become *angry!*" she says. "I was *not* a victim. I want to talk about that. Because, okay, yes, if you tell my story to somebody who knows nothing about Tina Turner, they would label me a victim. But I was in control of everything I was doing."

She senses the next question, says she always sees it forming above people's frowns with the subtlety of a runaway freight train.

"WHY, WHY, WHY?" she yells at the ritzy chandelier.

Why did she stay so long? Okay, here it is, once and for all, not from Hollywood but straight from the woman warrior. By her reckoning, this trial by Ike was her chosen Path to Enlightenment. Besides, she *liked* the man. He was a big cheese on the St. Louis club scene, with his own popular band, the Kings of Rhythm. He gave her a chance to sing and she took it, took his friendship, too, without romance or sex at first.

"This man was very nice and very generous to me. Way before our relationship started, I promised him that I wouldn't leave him."

Not until he had what he so desperately wanted. The producer wanted to be a star. But despite his serious musical chops and his snazzy revue, Ike Turner seemed destined to remain a background player. Tina says she convinced him that he could sing, literally hauled him out front with her. She made a deal with him: "After I help you get where you want to," she told Ike, "I'm not going to stay."

She says they "weren't each other's type." She was dressing her Ikettes by studying *Vogue* fashion spreads; to this day, she says, Ike can't make a restaurant reservation. He loved cocaine; her biggest vice was coffee. "Everyone says to me now, 'Why did you stay with him so long?' There were tons of things involved. Where was I going to go? Was I going to leave my children there? There was a *mother* there," she fairly bellows. "To Ike, to the children. Not this sniveling, crying, little weak woman. They had me crying in the film script, and I said, 'I never cried that much in my life.' Maybe from anger, sometimes."

She says that even the judge in divorce court acted as if she was feebleminded. When she made it clear she'd walk away from the real estate, the money, the jewels, rather than prolong the agony, he called her into his chambers and asked, "Young lady, are you sure?" By then she was deep into Buddhism, chanting daily. Security lay within her own thrumming rib cage—not with a Neiman Marcus charge card.

"Give me a break—it's not about leaving with *money*," she says. "You leave with knowledge. Inner strength. All the discipline I have to have now came from being with that man. I know that when I looked in the mirror with this horrible, swollen face that it was taking strength to stay there. I knew what I was doing and I knew why, and I got out. You don't step out and do what I did with my life if you don't have some control there. I *know* I was strong then."

And now, at play in the fields of the rich and famous, with a villa on the Mediterranean and a luxe ex-pat life, how is the view?

"I know what I've done. Sometimes I'm a little blown away by it. What is this I've done? I can sing and dance better than I can do anything else. I care about myself, my health, how I look. I never did drugs, drank alcohol. There's nothing I did that's so extraordinary. But people don't expect rock and roll people to care about themselves."

Tina is up pacing now. She stops, looks out at the pricey midtown view.

"You know, I wonder when the day will come that I don't have to talk about Ike Turner anymore. I wonder . . ."

She's musing out loud, pondering whether she ought to rewrite her book, make it clearer why she stayed. She admits a thorough Ike-orcism would be tough, considering the film, the material on record, the strength of pop/cult mythology.

"Will that day come? A totally Ike-less future? Lord, *what decade?*"

Tina stops herself and smiles.

"Of course it will. Of course. I can wait."

Her laugh is light and easy, the timbre of temple bells.

For younger, less secure women, the atmosphere that elevated a Madonna, a Tina, an Annie Lennox, could prove problematic. Given the eighties' breathless pace—already viewers were complaining about too much repetition in the MTV rotations—few took the time to measure the quieter tyrannies of style. Scan the video oeuvre of Janet Jackson, for example, and you can see a woman fighting for mastery over her career and her body, from the tough, slightly chunky dancer in "Control" to the sexy sylph in "That's the Way Love Goes" to the hollow-cheeked, intentionally spooky Michael doppelgänger in their joint performance, "Scream."

The first time I watched "Scream," it brought to mind a visit I'd had with both Janet and Michael Jackson in 1982, as Michael was recording *Thriller.* The family manse was being renovated and we were at the Encino condo the two were temporarily sharing—along with their pet snakes. Janet was showing us proofs for the cover of her debut album, *Janet Jackson.* It was a pretty portrait of her face as it emerged from a pool. As Janet leaned into the refrigerator to get a drink, her brother opined that a head shot was wise because, *"Lookit that butt!"*

Seeing the look on her face, I wanted to thump him one. Nice talk from a buttless wonder who kept only lettuce leaves and Hawaiian Punch on hand for a snack attack—a man whose body-image fixations would soon fuel a global debate. The truth is, Janet recognized the double standard: She knew what she had to do. There is no female Meatloaf, no tubby-girl Ozzy. Cass Elliot of the Mamas and the Papas had to endure a barrage of fat jokes from deejays and lounge comics. Zaftig Ann Wilson of Heart suffered humiliating comments and pressure to reduce for years, until it led to a self-consciousness so intense the band could no longer perform. When Belinda Carlisle put on twenty pounds, she said, "It was awful to be in a band and hear people say, 'Uh-oh, she's been hitting too many deli trays.'"

Body-fat percentage would even distinguish the eighties from the nineties Madonna. By the time she launched her Blond Ambition tour in 1990, the early post-adolescent roundness had been honed and sweated off; huffing around the roadways of Central Park myself, I'd see Madonna and bodyguard running on the vilest of mornings. By the time she slipped into those custom Gaultier corsets, her arms were cut, the abs positively sculptural. It was another of Madonna's amazing acts of will. But whose will? some might ask.

Twenty years before Karen Carpenter died of heart failure induced by anorexia nervosa in 1983, Dinah Washington's long dependence on diet pills collided fatally with a night of drinking. At their deaths, both women weighed about 75 pounds. Cass Elliott seesawed wildly during her career, losing up to 110 pounds at once; her embattled heart gave out at age thirty. Florence Ballard's growing inability to fit into the Supremes' slinky gowns was one of the contributing factors to her being asked to leave the group. By the late nineties, Faith Evans's tour preparations for the release of a new album included a $6,000 bill for liposuction sent to her record company, Bad Boy.

It's an obsession present on both sides of the footlights as I found when I asked Ronnie Spector what all those clamoring sixties teenettes wanted to know from her. "It was the weirdest thing," she said. "They wanted to know what we *ate*."

The Ronettes were *skinny*, vacuum-packed into short, tight skirts and slacks. Having started as Murray the K dancers, they had taut glutes and supercharged metabolisms. One shudders to think of the high-cholesterol ripple effect as teen mags printed the Ronettes' road-food "diet" of burgers, dogs and fries.

There have been holdouts amid all these diet derbies. To wit: All hail (as her first album title commands) the Queen. When New Jersey–born Dana Owens rechristened herself as Queen Latifah, she summoned all the firepower of queen-size opera and gospel divas behind her bold, satisfied rap—some "ample sample," in her own terms. She strutted her stuff in cuts like "Princess of the Posse," declaring herself "Queen of Royal Badness" with a bravado that harks back to the imperious proclamations of the Empress, Bessie Smith.

The Queen has said that she is not so much about pan-feminism as about "getting mine." And sometimes, a straight-up shot of such self-possession can feel awfully good. The boss a pain? Boyfriend *too* bad? Slide your furrowed brow beneath the headphones, girlfriend, and punch up Latifah's "Ladies First" (with the able assist of Ms. Monie Love). It's the ultimate answer to James Brown's "It's a Man's Man's Man's World," an estrogen-fueled diatribe spoken atop funky horn riffs pioneered by Mr. Brown's JBs.

As ever, black female groups were a bit more . . . fierce. En Vogue preened with soigné self assurance. They were self-declared Funky Divas vamping in stylized videos shot by photographer Matthew Rolston. In terms of style, substance and straight-at-you delivery, Salt 'n' Pepa (Cheryl Jones and Sandy Denton) were a lot more barbecue than bubblegum when they loosed their debut album, *Hot, Cool & Vicious,* in 1987. Their tough talk went gold immediately. Like so many girl groups that went before them, S 'n' P—a pair of cashiers at Sears—were also the creation of a strong male producer (Hurby "Love Bug" Azor) with an eye for the main chance ("Girl rappers are a gold mine," he confided to writer Lucy O'Brien in *She Bop,* her history of women in popular music).

Azor was right, to a degree. Female MCs did find an immediate following; pioneers Roxanne Shante, Sweet Tee and DJ Jazzy Joyce, fierce West Coast mackette Yo Yo, MC Lyte. But their sales would not explode until the late nineties. Wisely, Queen Latifah knew to expand her royal domain, leaving pioneer rap label Tommy Boy for a mammoth Motown contract and her own varied franchises. In the spirit of Dinah Washington and Sam Cooke, she founded a record label and management company, Flavor Unit. Like male rapper Fresh Prince, a.k.a. Will Smith, Latifah would go on to films—a tiny shot in Spike Lee's *Jungle Fever*, a lesbian bank-robber role in the bad-girl flick *Set It Off* and a standout performance as a worldly-wise cabaret singer in *Living Out Loud*—and television, anchoring the long-running Fox sitcom *Living Single.* In 1999, her straight-from-the-hip style earned her an afternoon talk show. Along with B-boy impresario

Russell Simmons, who is busily marketing his Phat Farm threads, the Queen is hip to the latest rapper's delight: Be fly—diversify.

Upstairs in this small Manhattan club, Cissy Houston, soul survivor, has just finished rattling the ice cubes with a love song. And now she is reaching out of the spotlight, gathering in a pretty, slim teenager who is dressed, rather primly, in a white middy-style blouse. Now Cissy's daughter Whitney will sing us a little tune.

Good God, it's "Tomorrow," that cloying anthem from "Annie"—favored fodder of countless stage mamas and their tapping, twirling brats. But hold it . . . three bars in, the child has planted her feet, is lifting and holding huge notes, bending them, blasting the confines of this clichéd show tune with a fiery melisma that has left us gaping in the dark. At a front table, R&B veteran Maxine Brown is on her feet, clapping, hollering, "Sing it, girl. Carry it on."

For me, no subsequent video, no Oscar-nominated soundtrack or multi-Grammy triumph since scored by Whitney Houston has eclipsed that live, unvarnished demonstration of vocal firepower, circa 1983. Cissy's girl went on to become a $45 million woman in 1988 when *Whitney*, her second album, spun off four consecutive number-one singles. Signed to Arista in '83, she had been a diva-in-waiting since she was seven, watching her mother and her aunt Dionne (Warwick) back up Aretha Franklin behind studio glass.

The circle remains unbroken: "When I used to watch my mother sing," Whitney says, "which was usually in church, that feeling, that soul, that thing—it's like electricity rolling through you—that's what I wanted. When I watched Aretha sing . . . the way she closed her eyes, and that riveting thing just came out. People just . . . *oooh*, it could stop you in your tracks."

Whitney had the genes, the pipes, the looks, the connections and the iron will that have since sustained her through countless trials-by-tabloid (most having to do with her marriage to bad boy Bobby Brown, his numerous arrests, Houston's rumored "gal pals" and the couples' alleged drug problems). And despite her ability to upend flatware with the strength of her instrument, she opted for a more mainstream pop sound—a decision that has made her one of the most powerful black female entertainers ever, extremely rich and predictably susceptible to accusations of selling out her soulful side. The truth is, any time she chooses, Whitney Houston can sing

the bejesus out of the Yellow Pages. It is the mark—and the prerogative—
of the true diva to do exactly as she pleases. Striding off briskly to a film
career (*The Bodyguard, Waiting to Exhale, The Preacher's Wife*), the girl in the
middy blouse has not looked back.

There was room alongside the Whitney phenomenon for vocalists with diverse updates on classic soul. Sleek and exotic, Sade arrived in 1985 as a rare
soul import from the U.K. An Anglo-Nigerian fashion student, she tailored
her sound—soulful ballads, a dusting of jazz lite, Europop—with an icy
aplomb. The lyrics and the VIP-lounge cool of her first single, "Smooth
Operator" (from her debut album, *Diamond Life*) had an international appeal.
And her stylized beauty, part Billie Holiday, part Lena Horne, was a
welcome sophistication amid MTV's lathered-image extremes.

Warmer, and far more emotionally accessible, was the silky retooled
R&B of Anita Baker. This soul veteran had been working, chiefly in Los
Angeles, for nearly a decade before she found the right fit: a big label
(Elektra) and a set of lush ballads that resulted in her album *Rapture* in 1986.
Baker's strong, controlled voice smoldered through hits like "Caught Up
in the Rapture" and "Sweet Love." This was pour-the-chardonnay-and-
light-the-candles music—what record sellers would begin calling "adult-
oriented" soul.

Straight-ahead earnestness did not get totally lost in the eighties' leather-
and-tulle whirlwind. The singer/songwriter stream was quiet but wider,
heading inexorably toward today's musical delta of Venus. At the beginning of the eighties, Joan Armatrading, a West Indies–born island girl who
grew up in Britain, put out two strong albums *(Me, Myself, I* and *Walking
Under Ladders)* that seesawed smartly between the warmth of romantic love
and the cool observations of a stranger in a strange land. In her plain, sensible clothes, face scrubbed, hair uncompromisingly natural, Armatrading
was decidedly, bracingly "alternative."

From Dublin came Sinead O'Connor. Her Bambi eyes looked even
larger for her shorn head. Her lyrics were raw and prickly with the pain
and deep defensiveness of the abused child, which O'Connor has since
revealed she was. As a teenager, shoplifting sent her to reform school, where

she received her first guitar from a sympathetic nun. Beginning in the late eighties, her music would be a shifting amalgam of the ancient and the avant-garde, of mournful Celtic tunes and didactic dance beats. The strength of her otherworldly pipes—a voice that conjures clear streams and peat smoke—was too soon beside the point. Fiercely anti-British and anti-Catholic, O'Connor made headlines for, among other things, tearing up the Pope's photo on *Saturday Night Live*. By 1992, appearing at a tribute concert for Bob Dylan, she was booed off the stage. It was only after a near-breakdown and a suicide attempt that she told the horrific, sickening tale of her mother's abuse, sexual and otherwise—that had spun her into the world such an angry young thing. Since then, O'Connor's spent several years underground—the only press reports involving domestic turmoil and custody issues over her own children and her successive religious journeys. Recently she re-emerged with a new album, dark hair and a slick new video.

Like Madonna, Suzanne Vega was a former dance student. But musically, she came up hard on the lean New York folkie scene, rather than the clubs. She sang at Carnegie Hall with Pete Seeger as a child. And in that moralist's tradition, Vega infused basic human issues with a literary sensibility. Her videos would feature no jiggles, no baubles—just the muted, non-exploitive sadness of the abused child who was the subject of her 1987 hit, "Luka." The theme wasn't exactly Top 10, but A&R departments took note: Vega was selling. Her self-titled debut album sold more than 400,000 units, far exceeding the expectations for an "art" record. Two years later, the reception of *Solitude Standing* proved Vega to be a portent of things to come.

Signings picked up for thoughtful types with an acoustic guitar on their shoulders and a stack of poems in a battered leather carry-on bag: Tracy Chapman, Edie Brickell, Melissa Etheridge, Sam Phillips and Shawn Colvin got record deals in the late eighties that would bear fruit in the nineties. So, too, did Natalie Merchant, along with her already successful band, 10,000 Maniacs. So many of these discoveries were wayward troubadours—women who had to leave home or country—or the company of men.

Gotta go . . .

Writing their own words and music, traveling light, they'd prove a dream for an industry that had already begun a quiet downsizing of its mad, fleet-of-eighteen-wheelers, 24-hour-stylists and shiatsu-lounge excesses.

One of the biggest "overnight" successes had already logged more time on the road than she cared to think about. Bonnie Raitt had had been an accomplished slide-guitar player since her early twenties; red-haired, freckled and pale as 2 percent milk, she learned to hold her own with her blues heroes, from Sippie Wallace to Buddy Guy. She released two albums of smart, capable blues, country and rock in the seventies that went largely unnoticed. Playing with the big boys, Raitt would note later, set her to drinking with them as well. She told *Rolling Stone* in 1990, "There was a romance about drinking and doing blues . . . I bought in to that whole lifestyle. I thought Keith Richards was cool, that he was really dangerous."

It would take another decade to sober up and marshal her forces behind the 1989 album, *Nick of Time,* that brought Raitt three Grammys and some overdue recognition. The title cut was perfectly in-the-pocket for the times. The singer's single girlfriend cries at night, longs for a baby as that infernal clock ticks. But there is hope; Raitt herself had found love— love in the nick of time.

She hit a long, throbbing nerve. Baby blues were everywhere by the late eighties as baby-boomer eggs were reaching the end of their shelf life; I'd discussed the subject with Bonnie myself in the few quiet moments when she wasn't passionately arguing some neglected blues singer's medical hardship case as a fellow board member of the Rhythm and Blues Foundation. As an activist—in this case for the appreciation of rock's originals, the retrieval of their lost royalties and the maintenance of their health— Raitt is formidable. I've watched her face down record moguls, unblinking, from beneath that hedge of red hair. Twenty years past her apprenticeship to slide-guitar wizards and blues mamas, her allegiance to the blues— and the industry's unpaid dues—is undiminished. Raitt came by her own blues honestly, tearing through the seventies with a slide guitar, a bottle and, by her own reckoning, no road map at all. But always, she's careful to make a distinction between her own somewhat tortured journey and those of the blueswomen who came before her. "Let's not presume," I heard her tell a bespoke-clad boardroom one day, "that we know *anything* about paying dues . . ."

As the eighties screeched and sighed to a close, as Bonnie Raitt blasted from the dashes of countless soccer-mom minivans, as Madonna was outfitting another big tour, in rode a true low-overhead Alternative. From Canada, yet. She was, in her own words, "a big-boned gal from southern

Alberta," with a sackful of her own torchy, country-infused songs. Her voice was expressive enough to cover Patsy Cline classics, strong enough to make an audience scream for her lambent reading of Roy Orbison's "Crying." Astride a motorcycle, hair cut in a sleek cap—lesbian, vegetarian and heavenly singer—low-key, lowercase k. d. lang would roar onto the scene—and the cover of *Vanity Fair*—as a Woman for the Nineties.

THE NINETIES

riot grrls and

mack mamas,
troubadours and
pissed-off
hippie
spawn

Ever since my daughter was born, I feel the fleetingness of time. And I don't want to waste it on getting the perfect lip color.

—Madonna, 1997

My mom's like, "Want me to tell my daughter to stop cursing? Would you like a ride in my Mercedes?"

—Lil' Kim, 1999

B*rowsing amid the huge overalls and tiny tops at a suburban Old Navy store, I fall into conversation with a cute teenage clerk named Tawatha. We're talking topstitching, but I find myself staring at her mouth. It's been painted in an opalescent coat of light mauve, rimmed deftly with something that borders on sienna. The color is contoured with a photorealist's precision, and it works.*

"The best," I tell her.

"Mary J. Blige," tattles her uniformed, headset-wearing colleague. And I step back to get the total picture: the blue acrylic nails, the high, plucked brows, the sculpted flatness of the hair . . . Sure enough, it is She—part B-girl, part Cleopatra and utterly BET.

"The 'I Can Love You' video?" I venture.

"Yeah," she says. "But this weekend I'm going to try the hair streaking on the Share My World *cover."*

It's that favorite girl sport—the one that kept the Ronettes at their grandma's mirror trying to get their hair HIGHER!, their eyeliner out to their ears. That impulse toward refracted rock cool still flops girls belly-down on flowered bedspreads to decode 16 magazine (now over forty years old!).

I feel duty-bound to warn Tawatha of the high school weekend I tried to streak, pulled the strands through a rubber cap with a crochet hook and came out looking like a half-platinum poodle. Her look is pitying. She says she's not worried; her aunt, a beautician, is in charge. And if things go badly, she can always chop it off for a short Lil' Kim thing.

"Just don't tell me," Tawatha says, "that you had this many choices."

Touché and word up, Ms. T. The nineties was an era of alternatives—some of them as diverse as Valvoline and honey when it comes to female rockers. And it would serve us well to note here that the restless, impulsive choices of the very young (and not those contract-wielding record geezers) are what really move this market. Children reared in a 200-channel, multiplex universe can switch allegiances in a nanosecond. Malled and bar-coded since infancy, they're mad for something different.

By the early to mid-nineties, that something was female voices—sounds that range from a whisper to a shriek, from the lyric-driven lilt of singer/songwriters to the stark, slashing guitar chords of queercore bands. There was also a lively, lucrative middle ground; artists like Alanis Morissette, Sheryl Crow and Melissa Etheridge could make depression and desire rock. Echoes of Pure Patsy (Cline) surfaced, uplifting and updated in the voices of k. d. lang and that seventeen-year-old phenom, LeAnn Rimes. Slicker country crossover arrived in the leopard-skin packaging of Shania Twain and her slick "Feel Like a Woman" Revlon campaign, of the aggressively marketed Faith Hill and the relievedly antic Dixie Chicks. Good-natured comic relief was also available in the cartoony Spice Girls, the Village People of our time.

Of course there were—and will always be—divas and their fabled competitiveness. Overwrought media handicappers had been hyping the sales-and-sensationalism derby among Madonna, Whitney, Janet and Mariah. In 1995, all four released product within the same nine days in October, something one press report called "the great pop-diva pileup." Sales lived up to the considerable hype—or vice versa—as the cult of the diva became an industry in itself.

On the fringes, edginess played well: Liz Phair and Polly Jean Harvey flirted brilliantly with punk athleticism and frank erotica—what I'd call inverse power vamping. For the most stubbornly introspective, perserverance had begun to pay: In 1996, at twenty-six, having run her own label for six years, folk/punk alternative Ani DiFranco hit solidly with *Dilate*, the eighth album she'd cranked out of her shoestring operation in Buffalo. Queried about her "overnight" success on CNN, DiFranco offered a swell home-shopping metaphor: Her career was exploding like a Chia pet.

On the West Coast, other sisters doing it for themselves created a chiefly indie, load-in-your-own-amp scene that required far more grit than glamour. Backstage at clubs featuring all-female bands in the early nineties, the greatest perk one could hope for was a flushable toilet. But one thing was ear-splittingly clear: Never before had girls with guitars been quite so LOUD. Los Angeles, that occidental beacon of extremes, had nurtured a pierced and studded daisy chain of hard-rocking female bands. As children, these girls were driven to dance classes and orthodontists beneath those lubricious billboards on Sunset Boulevard. How many singers blown up 50 feet high in their underwear had they peered up at?

By junior high, standard-issue electronics for white L.A. kids (beeper, cell phone and trust-fund Stratocaster) were widely available in the garish teals and fuchsias that also rule girls' bikes. From Encino to Santa Monica, girls were bickering with their brothers over garage rehearsal time, rattling the neighbors' Weber kettles with their over-amped passions. By the time Mattel released a pert Baywatch Barbie in 1995, L.A. had already seen a roaring wave of sweet young things in torn slips and smeared, sanguinary lipstick, the best known of whom were L7 and Hole (the latter a West Coast combo platter). Seattle, Olympia and Portland had a rumbling new thunder to go with all that rain.

The music called for nothing less than "a revolution, girl style." Riot grrls, they proclaimed themselves, papering the country with militant fanzines like *Riot Grrl*, *Girl Germs* and *Bikini Kill*. They offered one another support in networks, concerts and other femtastic forums comprising what one trend-conscious teen magazine called "the angry girl scene." Not that the music hied to some monolithic PMS perspective; there seemed to be a band for every nuance, area code and sexual orientation. Among the better known: Vancouver's Mecca Normal, England's Huggy Bear, New York's witty, acerbic Luscious Jackson and San Francisco's militantly lesbian Tribe 8, whose stage show often featured the ritual castration of a rubber penis.

Should they emerge from beneath their own fierce din, this generation of satellite vidkids could zap into a full menu of mainstream female assertiveness: the quiet dignity of Anita Hill facing that roomful of Congressional Suits on the 6:00 news, the laugh-track feminism of that doyenne of dyspepsia, Murphy Brown, the cool self-containment of sax-blowing toon Lisa Simpson, the shrieking outrage of "domestic goddess" Roseanne. What was a girl to think? Just how do they process all the crazy mixed signals about growing up female in the age of Princess Di and Paula Jones?

Get angry, get even, have fun—or all of the above—is the rowdy M.O. of the smart slut set. Cuisinart your femininity: Dress like a baby doll and cuss like a stevedore. How else to explain the cheerful anomie of female-dominated Veruca Salt's EP, *Blow It Out Your Ass, It's Veruca Salt*? Of Hole's "Teenage Whore"? Or the penchant of Bikini Kill's lead singer, Kathleen Hanna, for stalking the stage topless with the word "slut" scrawled across her midriff? Plenty of the unwashed and unenlightened—mainly punk boys—misinterpreted Hanna's sexual semaphore as a hard-core come-hither. At the center of the girl-band scene in Olympia, Washington, Hanna had long been an inveterate activist. But with the tummy art she had something quite pointed in mind, as she explained in an interview with Andrea Juno collected in *Angry Women in Rock*:

> I did mailings to hundreds of women, with suggestions like, "Write on your hands with Magic Marker," because punks used to write words on themselves with Magic Marker so that when they were photographed, there would be a text or message. Photographs don't have sound, so I felt that if I wrote "slut" or "whore" or "incest victim" on my stomach, then I wouldn't just be silent. I thought a lot of guys might be thinking this anyway when they looked at my picture, so this would be like holding up a mirror to what they were thinking.

"CUNT!" the predictable oi boys yelled back. "Fuckin' bitch! Rock star fuckin' cunt!" And the spittle-soaked coup de grâce: "GIRL POWER IS BAD!"

Certainly, a boy amped up on beer, hormones and crystal meth might miss the irony of Hanna's self-published grrlzine, *Fuck Me Blind*.

But there was nothing ambiguous or accidental about the assaults that Hanna and her bandmates Kathi Wilcox, Tobi Vail and Billy Karren fended off from mosh-pit neanderthals. Hanna's accounts of the onstage scuffles, the stageside and back alley stompings she both endured and meted out in self-defense are strikingly similar to the workaday brutality that Henry Rollins describes in numbing, viscous detail in *Get in the Van*, a journal about low-rent touring with neo-punkers Black Flag. For Bikini Kill, sexual violence was an unwelcome add-on to the customary butt-kicking. In printed flyers, Hanna pleaded to at least move the mosh activity to the back of clubs to protect women dancing up front. This proved about as effective as leafleting Attila. Here's Hanna again, on one especially nasty evening:

"It really sucks when you have a 'flashback' onstage. Once some guy spat a mouthful of beer in my face—he was *this* close—and it reminded me of when I was fifteen and being raped, and the guy came in my face. All of a sudden I had a flashback of this guy coming in my face, and I wondered, 'Does Tommy Tutone ever have something like this happen to him? I don't think so.'"

More than most suburban girls in the northwest, Hanna had plenty to be angry about. Let her count the ways: 1) The mainstream media sucks. Hanna said that the *Washington Post* wrote that she claimed her father had raped her because she wrote a song ("Daddy's Little Girl") about incest. She says this is untrue and that she got her subject from her work at a domestic violence shelter. 2) Radical feminism can be a bitch, too. Hanna was publicly harangued and humiliated by anti-porn activist Andrea Dworkin for having worked in the "sex industry" as a dancer. 3) The club scene can really suck. As a recovering drug abuser and alcoholic, Hanna says she loathes playing for roomsful of unruly drunks. 4) Rock stardom can and does kill. As the band's popularity grew beyond the Pacific Northwest, *Newsweek* outed Hanna as an exotic dancer by printing an unapproved band photo—in bikinis. She claimed that her dance clientele recognized her by the tattoos and learned her real name. She complained that it cost her a "private" life—and a second income. When Hanna accepted $250 and a trip to L.A. to be in a video for a well-known band, Sonic Youth, she endured the hisses of those who accused her of selling out:

ROCK SSSSSTAR!

Worse, few seemed to realize that beneath all the snarling, Hanna did jokes. "It's important to highlight that a lot of what we do is *humorous*," she complained to Andrea Juno, "a lot of our music is really funny."

It was an alternative comedy, rather Andy Kaufmanesque in its willingness to tweak and goad a crowd, to go beyond joke-joke-rim shot and into a certain theater of cruelty. This can be a strange and terrifying place, if energizing and addictive to the committed provocateur. I was with Kaufman one night when he decided to insult and wrestle women on the stage of a small Manhattan club; watching him push the vibe from goofy to homicidal inside of five minutes, I found myself wrestling Andy's date for the lethal cut-glass ashtray she proposed to defend him with. She was big and drunk; I was small and stunned to be in . . . *gawd,* a bar brawl. The faces that swirled above us showed equal parts amusement and rage. Afterward, Andy was hugging himself with glee. His eyes were unnaturally bright; he was bleeding here and there, but he seemed immensely satsified. As the rest of us embarrassedly daubed at scratches and tucked our inner beasts back into their secret pockets, Andy smiled.

"Hey, kids, let's get some ice cream."

Was it that way for Hanna? What might Bikini Kill's willful, nightly, steel-toe-to-steel-toe performances be but the most volatile form of catharsis? How more direct could one be than leaping into the mosh pit to head-butt pustular misogyny aside so that a pierced, esctatic sisterhood of girl fans can swoop in beneath the beat and dance? And how perfect a moment it was to be militant and *damned mad.*

Thirty years past the publication of *The Feminine Mystique,* the public expression of female rage was nothing new. But given the ferocity and speedy flaring of the so-called angry grrl scene that raged like late-night brushfires in L.A., in London and the Pacific Northwest, one has to consider its larger context—that is, a rising national whirlwind of publicly vented rage. One of the Seven Deadlies was gaining ground as a legit mode of personal expression, as a victims' and consumers' movement and, in no small way, as the latest and most lucrative subgenre of entertainment.

As it happened, the riot grrl scene was just heating up as Americans were confronted with a grisly, gothic ballad of the ultimate Angry Woman. In the early hours of June 23, 1993, Lorena Bobbitt, a Venezuelan-born manicurist in Manassas, Virginia, was raped by her club-bouncer husband, John Wayne Bobbitt. Afterward, as he slept, she took a sturdy butcher's knife from the marital kitchen and hacked off two thirds of his penis, then fled, taking the hated object with her. In a panic, she flung it out the car window and later directed emergency services there, whereupon the penis was retrieved and miraculously reattached by microsurgery.

In the circus that followed—a *20/20* camera crew drove Lorena's route and panned the roadside penis repository and even *The New York Times* ran a long reattachment story with diagrams—I found myself working on a column that sought to track the commodification of Lorena's mad moment and John Wayne's habitual abuse. I had been curious about the rising tide of cultural anger, domestic and otherwise. Anger argot had just christened Internet spamming. Road rage. M.A.D.D. (Mothers Against Drunk Driving) acryonyms. Anger-management courses were gaining on diversity training as the new management-tool franchises. The growing use of "victims' statements" was unleashing shock waves of anguish and purgation in criminal courtrooms.

Thus, if greed greased the eighties, outrage—be it righteous or perverse—electrified the nineties. Religious, political and sexual anger reached critical flash points: Witness the mass rapes and genocide in Bosnia, the racial troubles in South Central L.A., Crown Heights, the Golan Heights, the neo-Nazi murders and tortures in Germany. The Rev. Martin Luther King's peace marches had hardened into Al Sharpton's "Days of Rage" demonstrations. Against the backdrop of such incendiary headlines, Everyman conducted his ceaseless skirmish with the daily outrages of living in this world—the computer snafus, the health-care boondoggle, the car, food and drug recalls. Madison Avenue caught the zeit with ads that featured motorists screaming, "I'M NOT GONNA PAY A LOT FOR THIS MUFFLER!" Pouty supermodels were slapping faces in Calvin Klein Obsession ads.

Given this anger-accepting atmosphere, the question was, Who would manage—and stage-manage—the Bobbitts' domestic fury? John Wayne's plastic surgeon found his patient an agent. And Lorena's nail-salon employer helped her find . . . representation. This was the rather mysterious Alan Hauge, a hedgy operator I had to track through blind fax addresses. When I finally reached him by phone, he told me their entertainment-related plans were extensive: "I think that Lorena's show will be done as a movie of the week or maybe an HBO exclusive, and then it will go to television and to videocassette and may even go theatrical overseas." He pointed out that

Farah Fawcett's battered-wife TV film, *The Burning Bed*, did very well with video sales "because it was a very hot subject."

Hauge was right; anger in America had gone very high-yield. Was it any wonder, then, that a few high-profile Rage Queens seized the headlines and the public imagination? Teenage Amy Fisher, a.k.a. the Long Island Lolita, fired point-blank into the obdurate skull of her lover's wife, Mary Jo Buttafuoco. Lorena Bobbitt committed the most primal of domestic crimes in retaliation for another. As I looked further into the story, I found that though penis hacking in Thailand was much more commonplace—a 1985 medical journal reported cases of 100 women having severed the units of their philandering husbands during the seventies—news reports were sparse and only eighteen reattachments were attempted, "with mostly poor results."

More to the point, few or none of those Thai avengers had agents. Or as many media outlets. Amy and Joey, Lorena and John Wayne were swell bundles of dynamite for increasingly explosive talk radio. On AM and FM, on network and cable, you could hear America losing it. Here was my cabdriver, yelling back at best-selling wrathmeister Rush Limbaugh, who was blustering about those despicable "feminazis." Even once-soporific Sunday political chat shows were all but Jell-O-wrestling over the finer points of NAFTA. *The New York Times*'s Thomas Friedman bellowed, "SHUT UP!" at his press corps colleague, the admittedly pesky septuagenarian Sarah McClendon. George Bush snarled live at Dan Rather. Controlling one's anger was no longer expected in the highest office or the most public forums. There arose a new ethic, born of our post-war, over-shrunk tendency to ventilate, not sublimate. I'm not OK. You're not OK. Let's rumble.

And let's sell tickets. If Hollywood produced its male cadre of Terminators and Demolition Men, if Michael Douglas ranted and gutshot his way to a $41 million payday as the geeky L.A. rampage killer who had-just-had-enough-dammit in *Falling Down*, there was also a spate of babes-with-a-mad-on flicks: *Fatal Attraction, The Hand That Rocks the Cradle*. Even the more PC *Thelma & Louise*, with the understandable motivations of rape trauma and abuse, did not shy away from making murderous anger sexy. And on the small screen, women hosts joined the Maurys, Geraldos, Montels and Phils as network enablers to tap boundless reserve of domestic rage amid the hoi polloi.

Amid all this arguing and adrenalin, what more perfect manifesta-
tion of female rage than a roiling, topless, thrashing clutch of loud girls
with big axes? As male gangsta rap snarled about bitches and hos and
accessorized with scowls and Rottweilers, Bikini Kill stormily evicted all
the chromosomally impaired (i.e., males) from in front of the stage. But
non-righteous babes were fair game as well: In a tour film that mocked some
scenes in *Truth or Dare,* and with her "splinter" group Ciccone Youth, Kim
Gordon (and Sonic Youth) gleeflully flamed Madonna as an immaterial
girl. The direst mosh-pit grossout came from L7's Donita Sparks, who left
off strumming her guitar, reached under her skirt and produced a used
tampon that she lobbed into the crowd.

Song titles strutted the take-no-prisoners mien: "No Fuckin Way,"
by 7 Year Bitch, Bikini Kill's "I Like Fucking/I Hate Danger," "Pussy
Whipped" and—with Joan Jett—"Rebel Girl." Screaming antecedents—
from Poly Styrene to Yoko Ono—were acknowledged and appreciated.
After all, punk itself had barely reached twenty-one and was still to be
trusted by the young. And given the video excesses of the eighties and the
bloated corporate drift of the music industry, there was a fresh wave of
admiration for the stripped-down guerrilla rock of punk's progenitors. Kids
applauded the fact that Iggy Pop had merely crawled upright again and
survived his addictions and stage mutilations; L.A. garage-band kid Jakob
Dylan, staggering through endless one-nighters with his Wallflowers, told
me he still treasured a bloodied vest once belonging to the Clash's Joe
Strummer, and had it framed for his wall.

Many a riot grrl revered Kim Gordon, who had fled her native Cali-
fornia for the Manhattan alternative scene at the outset of the eighties.
Gordon had been making noisy avant-rock with her quartet Sonic Youth
for nearly a decade, earning her the honorific "godmother of grunge."
Though her bandmates were male, she was vocal about the locker-room
stink of rock's longtime male hierarchy. In 1990, on Sonic Youth's album
Goo, Gordon wrote a song, "Tunic (Song for Karen)," about the late Karen
Carpenter and her struggle with body-image issues. She explained to Bar-
bara O'Dair in *Rolling Stone:*

"I wanted to put Karen Carpenter up in heaven playing drums and
being happy. This whole thing about teenage girls cutting themselves and
that being associated with anorexia and girls being conditioned to having
such a big desire to please—I'm just curious . . . At what point do girls start

getting their sense of self-worth and [need to please] people, and why don't they have anything else?"

Younger grrls heard her loud and clear; Julie Cafritz (formerly of Pussy Galore) joined Gordon's "girl bonding" offshoot band, Free Kitten. Over forty, married to Sonic Youth's Thurston Moore and mother of a toddler girl, Gordon was also a muse to Seattle's primo grunge band, Nirvana. Its front man, Kurt Cobain, had no problems with forthright, aggressive women. He was such a vocal fan of the Raincoats, a late seventies, early eighties British art school band, that they, too, became known as "the godmothers of grunge" for the nineties Pacific Northwest girl-band scene. The Raincoats were never known for their vocal or instrumental prowess; founding member Gina Birch has admitted that the band virtually learned to play onstage. Their performances were more like art happenings; the band's appeal was a certain Fender fauvism born of a purely experimental verve. In early 1994, Cobain wrote a rather sweet tribute for the Rough Trade reissue of their 1979 debut album, *The Raincoats*. He explained their influence on his own music this way: "Rather than listening to them I feel like I'm listening in on them. We're together in the same old house and I have to be completely still or they will hear me spying from above and, if I get caught—everything will be ruined because it's their thing."

These cool older sisters were set to tour with Cobain's band on Nirvana's British tour in 1994; his death in April intervened. And it produced a new rock widow—a very angry grrl with a canny eye for the main chance. Given the times, it was no surprise that this latest hard-core musical hiccup produced a bankable star—a woman who could dress the part, articulate the prevailing sentiment (FUCK YOU!) and play the game well enough to totally transcend the genre.

The ascension of Courtney Love, Hole's lead singer, seemed inevitable. Even her pedigree was perfect: Love Michelle Harrison is the daughter of a feminist therapist and a committed Deadhead whose marriage was short-lived; Mother renamed Courtney once she was awarded custody. The little girl was forced to sing Joni Mitchell's "Both Sides Now" in the family Volvo (a torture she eventually forgave once Mitchell's masterful album *Blue* proved an invaluable balm). Courtney was swathed in asexual flannel and denim, and raised in a Eugene, Oregon, commune that deemed Barbie the devil and Cap'n Crunch the Antichrist.

Revolutionaries can be the most merciless of domestic tyrants. Besides Love, a clutch of current rock poetesses have drawn some of their churning oeuvre from waftily uncertain upbringings. Icelandic rocker Bjork, born to hippie parents in Rekjyavik, had freedom forced upon her at the age of five in the form of a latchkey around her neck and a vigorously laissez-faire parenting style. Bjork's parents may have left her too much alone, she's speculated in interviews. But she does not rue the self-sufficiency she zipped herself into at an early age. Once a punky pixie for the Sugarcubes, she arrived from Iceland as a solo act in a haze of disarming boho grace and technopop as ethereal and upbeat as the Northern Lights. Her mascara was green, her undies orange. She could write very personal lyrics to detached, booming house beats and displayed an instant comfort with video—the perfect multimedia muse.

Jewel, while proud of her itinerant Alaskan heritage, suffered humiliations and medical consquences when the family's let-it-be lifestyle precluded expensive treatment for her kidney disease. As these hippie progeny reach adulthood, we're only now hearing some of the long-term reverb of once-beatified freak family life. It's a cultural contretemps so ripe for parody, ABC launched a successful sitcom about the backlash of hippie spawn. Sweet kooky Dharma—of *Dharma and Greg*—defies her parents and gets married to a straight WASP lawyer. Her drug-fried dad rues the day they allowed her to have an Easy Bake Oven.

Little Courtney tore the heads off her baby dolls. And once puberty body-slammed her with acne and puppy fat, she acted out in those time-honored teen ways: shoplifting. Drugs. Running away. In a juvenile home with other misfits of parental science, Love says she pricked up her ears to the rebel yells of the Sex Pistols and Chrissie Hynde's Pretenders. She listened to "the seminals"—Patsy Cline, Tammy Wynette, Loretta Lynn and Joni Mitchell. But, she says, the rowdy, messy rockers made her ache for guitar-callused fingers: "When I heard my first Patti Smith record, *Horses*, it was like, the ticket's right here in my hand. I can write it. It's a free zone." Love took wholeheartedly to the rock and roll life: As she bounced around punk and sleazoid corners of L.A., London and the South Pacific, she'd turn up as an extra in the punk biopic *Sid and Nancy* and in an L.A. girl band, Sugar Baby Doll.

Hole's name came not from the obvious anatomical association, but from a reference to a quote from that hip ancient Greek, Euripides. "It's about the abyss that's inside," says Love. A commited online yatterer, she is smart and reasonably well read. But onstage, she opted for body language, with writhing a specialty. Band members quickly learned to sidestep thrashing limbs as Courtney hit the boards with the speed and flexibility of a swamp gator. This is also a very basic band: Where Madonna thrust forward a pricey, steel-tipped designer nipple, Ms. Love made do with flashing a bare one. But dressing in the distressed dolly style of her trashed toys was not, she insisted later, a sexual ploy: "I didn't do the kinderwhore thing because I thought it was so hot. My angle was irony."

Though there was a quarter century between Love's 1992 marriage to Nirvana singer Kurt Cobain and Yoko Ono's union with John Lennon, the comparisons were inevitable, if unwelcome. First were the accusations of riding Cobain's flannel shirttails. Then, when he shot himself to death at their Seattle home in April of 1994—leaving behind his wife and their 18-month-old daughter—the mantle of Rock Widowhood fell heavily on Love's admittedly unstable shoulders.

Live Through This was a prophetic title for Hole's second album. It was scheduled for release just days after Cobain's suicide—which was followed in short order by bassist Kristen Pfaff's overdose death. All plans—promotional, tour and otherwise—were smashed. The record started slowly, charted modestly (reaching only 52) but ended up platinum. And on the '95 Lollapalooza tour, though Courtney carped ("Rock is really about dick and testoterone"), Hole proved to be the best-selling act on the festival's main stage.

In the ensuing year, Love would also undertake a media-savvy makeover. She hired Jodie Foster's publicists, began lining her lips instead of smearing them. She straightened her nose, wore Versace in place of those torn slips and called herself an Actress, playing an out-of-control, drug-addicted porn star in *The People vs. Larry Flynt*. Already at odds with some more committed—and less Tinseltown-minded—grrl bands, Love sparred with the likes of Bikini Kill, whom she derided as "Kathleen and her little pack of estrogen terrorists . . . well, estrogen lemmings." But Love was no more sisterly to Liz Phair ("a potato") and Hanna's glam antipode, Madonna: "Her music has always sucked; I don't dislike her, I respect her. But I can't stand her *art*."

As for her own recent runs at eclipsing the Material Clotheshorse in shocking designer deshabille, Love maintains she's always enjoyed bein' a girl. Nonetheless, in September of 1997, when Love, Madonna and Tina Turner convened in Los Angeles for a joint cover shoot for *Rolling Stone*, I politely—and hastily—declined the invitation to hang out amid the garment bags. I knew that the negotiations alone had taken over three months, that an entire studio was rented to contain the clothing options. Later, both Madonna and Tina described the day as a hell equivalent to the 10th ring of Loehmann's gang fitting room, with dueling stylists and one exalted makeup genius—Kevyn Aucoin—to paint this rock Rushmore. Over the arduous day-into-night, the photo editor recommended smoking; Tina stayed in her dressing room and chanted.

Afterward, Love's fashion assertiveness—she ended up in icepick stillettos and a nearly transparent tube dress—was much remarked upon. Her physical exhibitionism—now played out on velvet-roped runways instead of beer-soaked clubs—has reinvigorated paparazzi from Brentwood to Cannes. "This has never been about butch to me," she told Katherine Dunn. "I can be as much of a woman as I want, and bring as much elegance and grace and sexuality that is from my womanhood to this form. . . . One of the tools and energies that I used was rage—sexual rage. And sometimes that would be misconstrued: 'Oh, people give her shit, but all she's really doing is acting like Jim Morrison.' *No!* I'm not acting like a male rock star. . . . I'm following something that hasn't really occurred. Deal with it, because it is not coming from the collective of images of masculinity."

December 1999. Late night in Los Angeles Coliseum, on a rain-soaked field. A video crew and a clutch of burly men dressed as football players surround a tiny bright figure in a blue dress. Courtney Love is filming the video for Hole's song, "Be a Man," set for inclusion in Oliver Stone's football film, Any Given Sunday. *Love's hair is tinted blue; so is the air, cobalt with the lusty roar of male shouting.*

Love has dropped her dress top, stalks past the cameras grinning, breasts jouncing. The night is freezing, the money men outraged. No time for such unusable and expensive footage. Love is packed off to her trailer with a hot toddy and a gentle admonition.

But what's this? Seconds into the next take—SHE'S DROPPED THE WHOLE DRESS! Men bay with astonishment and delight as she stands in the bright lights naked, save for a tiny G-string.

Love's headstrong and budget-chomping dalliance lasted until nearly 2 A.M. Scolded gossipeuse Liz Smith: "Courtney in the near-nude might make her significant other happy. Or her fans. But moneymen don't want to know from Love's hubris or pubis." Love's now-legendary lack of self-control—or its crafty, calculated opposite—is a Hollywood attraction reaching back past Carole Lombard. Misbehave with humor, and you can get away with a bit more. Like Lucille Ball playing the perennially dizzy redhead, Love seems stagily commited to her PMS-queen rep. At last glance, she was accusing the Rock and Roll Hall of Fame of misappropriating her family grunge memorabilia.

More removed from the mosh pits, modulated rage would have its market as well. Rape may have rocked the house as a male fantasy for the Rolling Stones in "Midnight Rambler." But few real victims had put violation to a beat before Tori Amos, a woman who is part of the singer/songwriter vanguard now turning pain into platinum. Amos went public with her trauma as a rape victim in "Me and a Gun," a cut from her *Little Earthquakes* album. It was, she maintained, a true and powerful statement. But she had this to say about the overall Gen-X compulsion for existential hand wringing: "I think our generation loves our pain and if you dare fucking take it away from us we'll kill you. We like our pain. And we're packaging and selling it."

Amos's wry assessment—coinciding with the rising Prozac Nation—might help explain the roaring success of *Jagged Little Pill*, Alanis Morissette's collection of danceable diatribes, most notably "You Oughta Know," the poison—and profane—valentine to an ex-lover which was a huge hit in 1995. The singer wonders if her replacement can match her own special perversities. The ugly little fantasies of the jilted (is the Betrayer thinking of Alanis as he fucks that new bitch?) are laid out, naked and squirming. And howling the f-word created a noisy little radioplay controversy. Morissette's stage delivery seems to have taken a page from Liz Taylor in *Who's Afraid of Virginia Woolf*, reeling, snarling, hair whipping. But femme rage, not gin, fuels her high-test histrionics.

Given Morissette's first rock outing in 1990 as a mall rat-with-mike and a serious hair volumizer habit, it's understandable that many critics viewed her brand-new-angsty-me with a certain amount of cynicism. Damaging tapes had surfaced; she'd first tried out her chops on *Star Search*. But her mass appeal seemed undeniable. *Pill* sold over 24 million copies and won four Grammys—ample testament to the current lively market for the well-amped kvetch. After all, Alanis arrived on the scuffed heels of the dismal, rains-on-my-pain worldview of boy grunge bands like Nirvana. Her sophomore album, *Supposed Former Infatuation Junkie*, was less of a whine, with one actually joyous dance cut ("So Pure"). Romantic dirty laundry—Morissette's specialty—was still heaped in scornful and nasty, chiding little heaps. But her relaxed, confident peformance on *MTV Unplugged*—and that resulting album—revealed a mercifully reduced angst index.

The general condition—pissed off, pushed around and not about to take it anymore—persists in at least 57 varieties. Angry "answer music" between the sexes is a time-honored tradition; at the outset of female MCism, squeaky fourteen-year-old Roxanne Shante scored a bull's-eye with "Roxanne's Revenge," an answer to UTFO's most disrespectful "Roxanne, Roxanne." Painfully thin, seething just inches from the camera lens, Fiona Apple spits out her own alto vitriol. Listen to Ani DiFranco, a writer of considerable depth, and even she is reduced to snarling, "Well FUCK YOU" repeatedly on a cut from *Dilate*.

Liz Phair's *Exile in Guyville* was a powerhouse riposte to the Stones' bad-boy classic *Exile on Main Street*, right down to its attention-getting, rent-me-by-the-hour sexual braggadocio. Later, discomfort with the siren-in-lingerie image and the onset of motherhood would move Phair to temper that unbridled raunch. She recorded the demos for its eighteen songs on a 4-track system in her Chicago bedroom; it was a kick-ass, attention-getting debut.

"I'll make you lick my wounds!" roared PJ Harvey. And whoa—what new strain of rock and roll DNA has spun out Polly Jean Harvey? There she is, stomping across the stage in trousers and a dour, don't-mess-with-me mien. This diminutive Brit with the sensibilities and lung capacity of a Willie Dixon is perhaps the decade's most exhilarating anomaly. Appearing as PJ Harvey (herself and a two-man rhythm section), she shows the same reverence for root American blues that animates an Eric Clapton or a Keith Richards. But Harvey's is not a slavish fealty; she takes the passion from the form and dresses it in her own, very female concerns in songs like "Long Snake Moan." Her mother, a sculptor, organized blues shows, and little Polly played beneath the very adult noise. Harvey explained her singular education: "I was brought up to listen to John Lee Hooker, to Howlin' Wolf, to Robert Johnson, a lot of Hendrix and Beefheart. . . . My mum makes me listen to Bob Dylan interviews. He was really clever the way he controlled things. When I try to do that, I fall flat on my face."

Like so many British rockers of legend, Harvey went to art school and in 1992 released a small album, *Dry,* on an independent label. Bluesy and hard-core, rocking and vulnerable, it shrieks into a room like a dense meteor of Catharsis. The critical hosannas and resultant industry hoo-ha nearly shut her down. Harvey wisely opted for rest and retreat and returned with the roaring *Rid of Me,* all sex and arson. Like many of her blues heroes, Harvey has proved herself an able poet of myth and menace. Her sexual landscapes are both dreamily familiar and scary as hell, making her a masterful erotic impressionist. Her public persona has been breathtakingly mercurial, from stomping guitar jockey to red-lipped wraith in a cocktail dress to electronic priestess. Like the best pop shamans, she conjures the irresistible need to know: *What's she gonna do next?*

Anger was just one of the stormy emotions shaking the miserable junior high student in Halifax, Nova Scotia, whose classmates kicked her and pulled her thick black hair while screeching, "Medusa!" By her own reckoning, Sarah McLachlan was the kind of girl who invited the unspeakable cruelties only adolescents can administer. She was a conservatory nerd, studying classical guitar from the age of seven. "I was terribly unpopular," she told writer Ann Powers. "I had curly hair and really bad teeth—pre-braces.... You know that movie *Welcome to the Dollhouse?* That was me. I was the Weiner Dog."

Singing, she added, "was my security blanket. I would sing to myself, just for fear, for comfort, for joy, for whatever reason. It was a constant best friend."

Real pals materialized in high school, when the punk and New Wave kids found that Sarah could really play guitar. By the time she was nineteen, she was recording her own music; the breakthrough was her third album, *Fumbling Towards Ecstasy,* made when she was twenty-six. Its angry cut, "Possession," about an obsessed fan, brought a lawsuit by her longtime tormentor, Uwe Vandrei, who claimed that the song came from his letters. McLachlan found herself in a nineties absurdist hell—sued by her stalker. She was freed from the terror, the rage and the lawsuit by Vandrei's suicide. Her next album: *Surfacing.* It won a pair of Grammys and sold over 6 million copies.

Like Carole King's *Tapestry* before it and *The Miseducation of Lauryn Hill* to come, *Surfacing* was another woman's journey record that reached women where they thought they lived. Men were just as smitten with the nineties incarnations of Ronstadts and Kings. Tiny Sheryl Crow fronted big ideas and a muscular band. Melissa Etheridge, Joan Osborne, Tori Amos—everyone hit the road hard. No one was afraid to sweat in modest-sized venues. And audiences still suffering flashbacks from too many over-wrought, big-screen stadium shows responded in kind.

As chief architect of the all-female Lilith Fair tour, which ran for three summers ('97 through '99), Sarah McLachlan seemed to relish her role as troubador/tour guide. Lilith was a huge success, grossing over $28 million in its middle year. McLachlan wisely timed the release of *Mirrorball*, her fifth album, for the end of the '99 fair, which by then had begun to split a few seams in its gauzy sisterhood. There were rumblings of star shenanigans. Picking up credentials to cover one leg of the tour, I found a pair of photographers in spasms at a thick stack of photo release forms and astonishingly petty prohibitions.

"Great," a female photographer honked. "We're all here to worship these women. But God help you if you try and shoot a goddess in a forbidden right profile."

Black American women have long danced across wavy tectonic plates of anger; it's always been part of the landscape. And while white riot grrls mustered in the Valley and the scenic Cascades, Los Angeles's other urban sounds came from the 'hood, that downscale grid crossed by chain-linked and Rottweiler-patrolled avenues of Compton and Crenshaw. Like white rock, black female music had its own great divide, between the smooth, silky ultra-femme sounds of Brandy, Toni Braxton, Monica, Whitney Houston, Mariah Carey and En Vogue, and the hot 'n' nasty hard-core snarl of South Central gangsta girls like Yo Yo.

It was Yo Yo (Yolanda Whittaker) who stood toe-to-Niked-toe with Ice Cube in a battle of the sexes duet, "It's a Man's World." Their give-and-go had none of the good-natured breeze that leavened Otis Redding and Carla Thomas "Tramp," in 1967. This was war. Standing firm, blond braids snapping with the steely force of her rap, Yo Yo delivered semi-automatic bursts of merciless drive-by dis. She followed with the bratty single, "You Can't Play with My Yo Yo."

Out of the spotlight, Yo Yo has been a community activist, working with a national coalition on issues that range from battered women to teen pregnancy. But hard-core was selling; ever a practical mack mama, Yo Yo's been as in-your-face as the market would bear. It was the same on the East Coast; Brooklyn's MC Lyte (Lana Moorer) got in a yowling cat fight with Roxanne Shante; she scratched and slashed at her rival MC in the vicious cut "Steady F—king," and later acknowledged it was just showbiz.

New Yorker Lil' Kim has staked her claim as Empress of the Explicit; her pride has been in telling any male dog where to put it, for how long— and at exactly what r.p.m. Kimberly Jones was working in Bloomingdale's before she became a protégé of rap artist Biggie Smalls (a.k.a. The Notorious B.I.G.), a huge, ham-fisted producer who suggested, among other things, that Kim sing and rap about "Aunt Dot," the black female euphemism for one's menstrual period. "You need to do a song called 'Your Aunt Dot,'" he told her, "and you just need to freak it."

Freak it she did, with a 1996 platinum album, *Hard Core*, white and blond wigs, XXX-rated talk and an estrogen-overload style. She was such a cartoony presence, some voiced opinions that she was a composite, a creation of Smalls and his corporate collaborators. Kim addressed the charges in *Interview*: "I admit, there were a lot of people telling me what to do. A lot of people's hands were in the pot. I didn't understand back then, so I let them. But I was also being myself, and that shines through."

She, too, has seized more control, aided and abetted by lectures from her good girlfriend Mary J. Blige. Kim had enough flash and sales to start her own record company, Queen Bee Entertainment. Her market position was solid. But tiny, foul-mouthed Kim, teetering on those absurd platforms, says she was knocked seriously off balance when Smalls, whom she adored, married R&B swallow Faith Evans. And she was devastated when he was killed in a drive-by shooting credited to the long-simmering East Coast/ West Coast rap rivalries. As she was gearing up for her second album at the end of 1999, she said that she had no romance in her life "and I don't even look anymore." Content to run with her "queen bitch" girlfriends Mary J. Blige and Missy Elliott, she declared, "Biggie's the only person I will ever love and have ever loved, period. And whoever I marry will have to know that when I get to heaven, I will be with Biggie." Her devotion did not stop there: Kim titled her second album *The Notorious K.I.M.*

Most successful—and for a time, the most troubled by success—is TLC, a trio of Atlanta women with stagey handles (Rozonda "Chilli" Thomas, Tionne "T-Boz" Watkins and Lisa "Left Eye" Lopes) and the Supremes-drubbing distinction of becoming the world's all-time best-selling female group. This happened in 1996, when their second album, *Crazysexycool*, sold over 8 million copies. But the smooth, rather restrained R&B of their smash single "Waterfall," and its pretty, tranquil video belied the group's personal turmoil: management troubles, bankruptcy, and Lopes's alcoholism and arson arrest (she set her abusive lover's mansion afire). That same boyfriend, a professional football player, forgave Lopes and lent all three women money to hire a bankruptcy lawyer. Later, after treatment for alcoholism, Lopes would work the whole mess into a darkly introspective B-side—more salve than salable.

The group's 1999 comeback, *Fanmail*, was stunning, given their recent disarray. "No Scrubs," a song about loser guys trying to make some time, set the women—dressed crazysexyFuturecool, but smoldering—in a flashy, big-budget video. The second single, "Unpretty," took on all the female body-image insecurities and pathologies—from breast enlargement to bulimia—in a graphic, visceral video that belied the gentle, melodic song itself. Its visuals: a female chest marked for surgery, a cast-aside plastic implant bouncing to the floor, a stout overeater running to the toilet to vomit. The images were decidedly unpretty; the cease-and-desist message was clear in the same way that Lauryn Hill's "Zion" celebrated her decision to bear her son at twenty-two, at a most inconvenient time in her career, against all advice—and out of wedlock. Singing STOP! in the name of love, motherhood and common sense was a growing expression of Control. The better news: It was selling, very well.

Standing comfortably astride the tough/tender divide is Mary J. Blige, a smooth operator in pin-striped suits and Fendi shades. She began her career as the rather pliant protégé of then up-and-coming Puffy Combs, who gets the credit as "stylist" on her debut album, *What's the 411?* But, having lived the kind of gritty urban life Mariah Carey would hire rappers to describe, Blige turned inward, began writing her own material and re-emerged as a smart, sad-eyed survivor.

In many ways, not the least her looks, Blige brings to mind the early Mary Wells, who never had to reach far to get ache and sorrow into a song. Watch Blige in repose—backstage at a rehearsal, on the fringes of an industry party—and there is a wariness visible, a self-containment that seems to say, "Don't trust all this." Trouble began to crackle like a live wire around

Blige's press encounters, her private life, her public partying with chemical aids. But there would be no tragic end; she grew out of it and made
better, stronger music. "Love Is All We Need," she insisted on a cut from
Share My World, an airy but substantial soufflé produced by Jimmy Jam and
Terry Lewis, the team that helped Janet Jackson get her groove. The sweetness is cut by a rap from Nas and an assist from ex-funkster Rick James.

In 1999, seven years into her career, the twenty-eight-year-old Mary
was being worshipped—rightfully—as an ageless ghetto madonna. She still
rarely smiles in photographs; her interviews are clipped and distracted. But
on record, the voice has a range of expression that makes any promotional
chat expendable. Admirers—from Aretha Franklin to Eric Clapton and Sir
Elton John were happy to work on her album, *Mary*. Less hip-hop, more
adventurous, *Mary* served notice that Blige could mix it up with anyone,
could cross over market niches and touch deep soul—on the beat, and at
will.

Such savvy sampling—the ability to mix genres, grooves and generations in totally new permutations—has long been the hallmark of the
best black music. But when the sampling grew social, visual—when rappers and real estate moguls started trading cell-phone numbers and bull-
market tips, when socialites saw coyote-ruffed rap queens flouncing into
couture fitting rooms—the party got loud. And delicious.

*Will someone get a glass of champagne for the gentleman in the leather camouflage
suit?*

*Dispatched by an anxious-looking captain, waiters scurry to reach rapper
Treach, of Naughty By Nature, who stands dead center, clad in full custom Fubu,
in the cavernous Cipriani party space on 42nd Street. This converted bank, once
the hushed temple of Brahmin bankers and white-shoed lawyers, is host to Arista
Records president Clive Davis's massive party for Whitney Houston. Tony
"Taxi" Danza is here. Donald Trump, arm around his rhinestone-clad model-
du-moment, is craning to see the object of a photographic frenzy by the door.*

*It's Mary J. Blige, in cowboy hat and couture jeans, fur tails exploding off
the denim beneath her knees like millionaire mukluks. Shorter, stumpy fur tails
fly from her chest. On either side of her, large black men talk into tiny mouthpieces,
securing perimeters unseen. Two Lil' Kim–like drag queens sip Bellinis while,
over at the head table, Cissy Houston, the stalwart who backed up Elvis for his
Vegas comeback, shakes her graying head, smiles and intones, "God bless."*

Whitney Houston's husband, Bobby Brown—jaunty as a racing tout in checked vest and cap—wraps his pretty wife in one arm. He is here by the grace of a Florida judge, having squeaked through another probation-violation hearing stemming from old drug charges. Brown kisses his wife, grins and lights a very large cigar.

"Mary," a male admirer in orange leather shrieks in the direction of the bobbing fur tails. "Mary J. Blige! This world is YOURS. You da bomb!"

Soon after, Mary would be the toast of Milan, where her appearances at the runway shows draped the mantle of hip on the Continent's smitten minimalist tailors. More and more design houses were hand delivering invites imploring Mary and her uptown sisters to take their places amid the desiccated couture hags, the overripe actresses, the imperious magazine arbiters who could make a show an Event. Many of the fashionistas detested the music itself or, at best, were indifferent to it. No matter when the lure was the Look. Rumors of large payments, in cash and goods, made the young, hot and hungry prick up their ears—and settle down on those rickety runway-side chairs.

It was a transverse that would see rapper Foxy Brown on huge billboards wearing Calvin Klein jeans, Dolce and Gabbana designing Whitney Houston's tour wardrobe. Hip-hop fashion would reach its dizziest heights in the last month of the century, as Sean "Puffy" Combs, a.k.a. Puff Daddy, presided over a *Vogue*-sponsored Rock and Style costume exhibit at Manhattan's Metropolitan Museum of Art. There, the rap mogul sauntered over to Oscar de la Renta, addressing him as "Mr. D." Nan Kempner, the ultimate "social X-ray," in Tom Wolfe parlance, was seen flapping bony wrists above her head as Puffy exhorted, "Get yo ass up!"

"Did you ever think you'd see a scene like this?" *Vogue* editor André Leon Talley asked a *New York Times* reporter. "Annette de la Renta in her billowy couture silks and Lil' Kim in her Versace bikini. They are the sum of the evening." To bring it all home, Puff Daddy's boom-boom girls shook bikini-clad booties where pharoahs were trying to slumber. A blowup photo of a young Mick Jagger grinned wickedly over it all.

The last party of such heady, headline-worthy mix was the Stones' legendary café society brawl at the St. Regis Roof in 1972, when *Vogue* editrix of legend Diana Vreeland graced Mick Jagger's birthday, end-of-tour bash for one boogaloo good time. Her fellow revelers: Zsa Zsa Gabor, George Plimpton, Woody Allen. There was the majestic Count Basie leading the band beneath the Stones' lascivious tongue logo, Mrs. Jacob Javits, Dick Cavett. A naked girl leapt from the cake as Andy Warhol Polaroided it all. That night, when the *Times* asked Bob Dylan for a description, he offered, "It's encompassing."

A quarter century later, the Met's A-list was conspicuously, consciously more diverse. African-American style currency had never been higher against old money and the Peter Duchin way of life. But this was no spontaneous happening. The fact that hip-hop artists—especially women—could achieve this rare nexus was due to some serious work behind the scenes. New faces need to be seen in the right places. When I asked him about his own ascent, Mick Jagger had a clear-eyed recall of the Stones' early days, when photographers like Norman Parkinson and Cecil Beaton looked up from their Balenciagas and saw fit to immortalize the boys. "All these people worked with us—the Rolling Stones, the Beatles," Jagger told me. "Everyone wanted to photograph you because you were young and fashionable."

Even in England, stylish clamor had begun to erode the barriers of class consciousness. Photographer David Baily, a Cockney upstart himself, was glad to play Professor Higgins to Jagger's Eliza Doolittle, steering him to the right clubs, teaching him to tip properly. "I took Mick," Bailey told me, "and soon, like a fifties debutante, he came out, with a little help from his friends." And if fashion and art photography helped the scruffy Stones onto the cover of the blueblood *Town & Country* in 1966— in the company of a real, gowned debutante!—hip-hop kids have had their skilled facilitators as well.

Another troop of rock and roll women—for most stylists hired by artists and record companies are female—stepped up in much the same way as Berry Gordy's Mrs. Paul and Mrs. Johnson undertook makeup, hair, clothes and etiquette instruction for Motown's raw recruits. Once again, many of the artists were from the projects. But if Motown kids took eagerly to a sequined, showbiz look, hip-hop presented a visual perplex that challenged the very nature of its street roots.

By 1997, hip-hop was riding high on MTV, but its visual impact was drooping lower than the baggy shorts and oversize jeans that hung on every rapper's hips. For male stars, the Mack Daddy requisites prevailed: brand-name sweats and sneaks, accessorized with pager-sized jewelry, unclad women—and the occasional foaming Rottweiler. It went worse for female extras, who were vacuum-packed into tiny sheaths that displayed big assets. Directors draped them over car fenders like trophy deer. Palettes were murky army/navy, props were predictable: cars, Cristal and chain-link fence. Streetwear, which had seemed new and fresh in the late eighties, had calcified into cliché.

Into this drive-by disaster zone rode a pair of style subversives who believed that despite rap's gritty urban reality bites, music video should be about escape. They felt the Look should signify as boldly as the lyrics. Rap would never catch up with rock, they reasoned, without killer visuals. Stylist June Ambrose and director Hype Williams—a couple of New York kids who had begun in the video industry as a dancer and gofer, respectively—lobbed their first, phantasmagoric, primary-color grenade in the person of Missy "Misdemeanor" Elliott, an artist whose wit, sensibility and plus-size presence fit no known marketing category.

"The record company didn't know what to do with her," recalls Ambrose. "We thought, 'She's cute and funny—let's make her a cartoon.'" This is how Missy remembers it: "Hype said 'I want to put you in a big blowup suit.' I said, 'Hype, I'm too *big*—are you trying to destroy me?' And he said, 'Trust me, it's going to be like the Michelin man.' It was so cool because I had to go to the service station . . ."

Sitting on the set of another Missy photo shoot at a retooled beauty shop on 14th Street, June Ambrose is laughing about that day she tugged and guided their star—all but helpless in that shiny black inflatable suit— into a Queens gas station to pump her up: "I had to take a bicycle pump to the set because she kept losing air." The video "Supa Dupa Fly (The Rain)" was a smash, and Ambrose and Williams had made their mark with a video that snapped bored, lolling heads back toward the small screen.

Over the last three years, the pair has accrued a solid platinum clientele: R. Kelly, Puffy Combs, Busta Rhymes, TLC, Janet Jackson, Will Smith. Along with Williams's director protégé Paul Hunter, they have created an oeuvre of big-budget, high-impact videos that hark back to the rainbow-sequined days of George Clinton/Parliament Funkadelic space Kabuki—and into the future of digital special effects. Two years before the Pokémon craze, they flew Missy Elliott like a Japanimated cartoon figure in "Sock It 2 Me." They have put Busta "Woo Hah" Rhymes in primitive bushman scenes—with a neon face; they have morphed his sabre-toothed grin and signature dreads into a metallic droid akin to the creepy crawler that plagues Sigourney Weaver in all those *Alien* flicks.

Their successes sparked the current rap renaissance that finds TLC floating like Hindu goddesses in "Unpretty," and a pair of Lauryn Hills in split-screen street parties ("Doo Wop") that match her contrapuntal song style with the flavors of sixties soul and nineties urban cool. Even habitual drama queens are reaching deeper; witness Whitney Houston in shiny dominatrix-wear, reading out her cheating boyfriend with the help of an all-girl army clad in various shades of Dress for Success; the sisters belt out the title chorus: "It's Not Right but It's Okay!" (She's gonna make it anyway). It reads very *Norma Rae* by way of *Working Girl*, cinematic and slick.

Staying ahead of the pack, Ambrose concedes, often leaves her limp at the end of a sixteen-hour day, even at a spry twenty-nine. It's always easy to identify her on a soundstage or a photo shoot. She's the ponytailed blur, the buzzy one in shrink-wrapped Gucci zebra-print pants. Her yellow tape measure flutters in the wake of a major Walk, dancer's derriere swaying *badda-bing!* above syncopated stiletto Blahniks. Her white Lincoln Navigator—the SUV of choice for the velvet-rope crowd—is a swank mobile office, careering around Manhattan crammed with swatches, sketches and a few takeout tins of West Indian food.

Clients do trust Ambrose, who often steps in where record companies tread less and less these days—that critical grooming period known as Artist Development. Kids who get record deals at seventeen can be blindsided by the lush life. As a young black woman born in Antigua and raised in Brooklyn, Ambrose is sensitive to the warp speed and the culture shock of her clients' journeys; she knows how far these kids have to travel in a single zip code. And she understands her role in this multiplatinum version of Pygmalion. Day to day, hip-hop style must be fluid enough to take one from the 'hood to Amagansett, from Sylvia's rib joint in Harlem to Soho's Moomba. And despite hip-hop style's deep brand dependencies, it must be knowingly tweaked to become one-of-a-kind for its wearer.

These days, "custom" is a word that can set Ambrose to twitching. Her impetuous urban poets will call at noon wheedling for a fawn suede and leather motorcycle jackets—custom!—with contrasting panels!—for Puffy's birthday party! Tonight! But as the business gets more competitive and the shooting schedules more absurd, Ambrose is trying to wean some of her clients of their bratty custom habits. She has been trying to turn all these manic mannequins out—and into the playing fields of Prada and Gucci. Until recently, Missy Elliott shopped only at Foot Locker.

Ambrose says she has seen her branch out—small European labels, a little D&G, a seat at this week's Versace show. And she had to holler at Busta: "Go to Gucci! *Buy the coyote coat!*"

The hip-hop tribes have long been wise to the two-way traffic between street and haute. Rather than becoming slaves to fashion, they play with it. They tend to accessorize the designer kicks with silver spiderweb Nikes, vibrating Nokias and megakarat, platinum and diamond Jacob Arabo ankhs and crucifixes—custom, of course. Hip-hop clothing lines like Russell Simmons's Phat Farm and Fubu are so successful, Busta Rhymes is developing his own, edgier line, Bushie.

Afrocentric style has made inroads beyond clothing. Mad manicures—rainbow colors, rhinestone accents, moons and palmtrees deftly airbrushed—have long created a boom industry in inner-city salons; now they are showing up in established fashion and beauty magazines and designer ads. I had been particularly struck by the new, luscious-and-lingering emphasis on the full, well-painted woman's mouth, especially in music videos. Missy Elliott's high-gloss smile lingers like the Cheshire cat's grin. She is so comfortable with the shiny signifying of her lips that she actually falls asleep while makeup artist Billy B. lines and daubs. Many black female artists—Lauryn Hill, Mary J. Blige, Lil' Kim, among others—rely on Billy to accentuate the full, sexy lips that shape their art and their image. And he couldn't be happier with the trend. "I really *love* mouths," Billy tells me. "I rarely do a middle-of-the-road mouth." He does, however, customize according to musical style and personal temperament: "For Lauryn Hill we do a beautiful brown, burgundy natural thing. She's clearly spiritual. Lauryn never wears lip gloss. She's not wanting to be overtly sexual and doesn't like a wet, sexy mouth. Missy is almost like a caricature—and big. We have always done really shiny mouths—say, a pearlized peach with MAC Lip Glass."

That product, he says, is the secret to the current sepia flair: "It gives like a shiny plastic coat, very thick—like melted plastic. Lip gloss is here to stay. Anybody looks good, looks sexy—and really young." Billy is an astute cosmetic anthropologist; he can trace the evolution of the lip-liner craze from photographer George Hurrell's Hollywood portraits on up through black model Naomi Campbell's eighties influences to where it trickled into the street ("that Bronx look of the darkest pencil lip liner filled in with light") and, says Billy, "lost all purpose, really."

For his artists, he softens such street trends with contouring worthy of Vermeer. Watch him paint a full, lovely African-American mouth and it's clear Billy appreciates the sculptural requisites of his craft. On so many video sets, cameras zoom and linger on his moist moving targets. The over-due appreciation for the charms of beautiful black women, he says, have all but made his career.

"Hip-hop is so much more exciting visually than the pop genre," Billy concludes. "It causes me to stretch, especially as a white person. What's going on with these hip-hop women makes people rethink stereotypical beauty. How do I know it's sticking? Look at the glossy magazines. When you see ghetto nails in Gucci ads, you see what these girls have brought from the street."

The bottom line of all this crosstown traffic? There hasn't been such a tasty style watch since the days one encountered Chuck Berry—in a fake fur sportcoat!—boogying pass the minimalist Halston at Studio 54. Industry parties are fin de siècle spectacles as rappers used to trading verses get equally competitive with their closets. Unbound from all that gold-chain tyranny of yore, hip-hop artists will test new limits and plunder the clos-ets of countless eras and cultures looking for the right fit.

If there is a downside to all this style swapping, it is creeping com-mercial control. One exasperated record executive dubbed it LogoLock. Monica Lynch—a white Irish girl from Chicago—was the unlikely red-headed president of rap label Tommy Boy Records for seventeen years. Lynch was one of a strong corps of female record executives who got their toeholds in rap, which was such an outcast genre at first it knew no corpo-rate glass ceilings and old-boy networks. I have known her since rap's lean years in Manhattan in the early eighties, when she was hustling a James Brown/Afrika Bambaataa collaboration. In those days, the designated "styl-ist" would have been Lynch running a skinny, nervous ingenue into the nearest Wings store for a serviceable pair of Adidas and a clean shirt.

Now a consultant to Tommy Boy and a late-night deejay, Lynch told me that yes, she felt a bit crisped around the edges and disillusioned with the scene. And what did she mean by LogoLock? Wearily, Lynch outlined the intense corporate skirmishes over hot young things; record company scouts vie for time with shoe and soft drink makers, rag merchants and fragrance czars who now court inner-city talent with the same voracity and big checkbooks proffered to talented black athletes. Lynch agrees that no one can blame the artists for cashing in; rides are notoriously short in the rock and rap rodeo. But she was wistful for rap's early improv, for a time when product placement wasn't a prime video requisite:

"Now you're nobody till somebody endorses you. As soon as a young MC off the porch in New Orleans has a hit record, Donatella Versace wants him sitting in the first row at the Versus show. And he's gonna get Andy Hilfiger, Tommy's brother, all over him like a cheap suit, getting him geared up. Sprite will be looking at him for their next ad campaign. It's a major commodification of these kids."

Even June Ambrose says she is feeling the breath on her neck. Hungry stylists are trying to poach her clients. And so many things are so . . . *over*. "I'm over futuristic," she declares now. "I did that two, three years ago. I want to go back to Queen Elizabeth and make *that* futuristic. Metal cuffs. Make that the trip."

Missy in a ruff of aluminum Alençon? Busta in a Mylar frock coat? Why not? When it comes to muses, Ambrose's clients are the ablest fashion juxtaposeurs, mixing periods and modalities in ways that Sex Pistols svengali Malcolm McLaren never dreamed of. As they stretch their shiny selves into the next century, Ambrose plans on being a few paces ahead "if it kills me." She'll be shopping, swatching—and diversifying. She's planning to expand her business to marketing, consulting and more extensive artist development. And when she gets a second, she'll stop and smell the roses. She is smiling, thinking about Busta's face when he dove into a rack of clothes she had pulled for him at a photo shoot a few days earlier. He fingered the edgiest offerings of Helmut Lang, Gaultier, Vivienne Westwood. And Busta knew.

"This is some ill shit," he told her.

Translation: *Faaaaaabulous.*

Costume—Afrocentric, elegant and bright as a savannah sunrise—is also central to the lambent R&B of Erykah Badu, an art and drama student from Dallas whose depth-charged emotional readings and divaesque vibe have invited comparisons from Sarah Vaughan to Billie Holiday. On record, her strong, flexible vocals spring from jazz to hip-hop to out-and-out blues; her debut album *Baduizm* pops with jokey references to Wu Tang—then rocks jauntily above the mighty bass anchor of Ron Carter, who earned his chops keeping up with Miles Davis. Onstage, Badu is her own Lilith Fair, spinning an alluring female ambience with incense, candles and a stunning high-priestess look: long dress, the glint and shiver of countless bangles, a tall, dignified head wrap that gives her tiny figure a sculptural height and heft.

A proud few new artists defy any sort of categorization beyond their being female and black. In 1999, Les Nubians—two sisters of a French father and Cameroonian mother raised partially in Chad—turned heads with their hybrid smooth Euro-hip-hop and African roots accents. Madonna's Maverick label—which also records Alanis Morissette—had wisely invested in the future of Me'Shell Ndegeocello. Her debut, *Plantation Lullabies*, was as eclectic as the artist, a bisexual single mom who poses in black leather tutus and good-naturedly fends off flak from gay magazines for "not being gay enough." A crack addiction nearly killed her. She credits her work in music with the big save. Living with dualities, she explained to writer Touré, is a natural thing: "My anger is always staring me in the face; my love is always staring me in my face." Blessed with a healthy recording contract and an eight-year-old son, she's not about to blink.

If the nineties were a fine time to be female, feisty and independent, they were also an era of weighty responsibilities for the big label Arena-Diva. With the possible exceptions of the Cher/Diana Ross Vegas throw-downs, stage shows had never been more elaborate, nor road companies more unwieldy. And amazingly, at the center of one of the biggest touring franchises was a shy, soft-voiced young woman who had sat beside her brother Michael Jackson and gentled him through our interview in 1982.

By 1995—that year of the vaunted Diva Derby—Janet Jackson's entry was, amazingly, a 10-year retrospective, *Design of a Decade*. She had turned twenty-nine, and was four years into her $32 million deal with Virgin Records. Besides chiseling her physique, Janet had learned to maximize her small voice with big but edgy production and fiercely executed choreography. Having come through a brief failed marriage and the legendary repressions of her wacky showbiz clan, Janet had also discovered sex. She appeared in *Rolling Stone* topless, with a man's hands—allegedly those of her boyfriend—covering her breasts. On record and on videotape, her libidinous epiphanies rang joyous and true. With her 1997 album, *The Velvet*

Rope, Janet may have been venturing toward Barry White massage-oil ooze (especially in the groany phone-sex cut, "Speaker Phone"). But so far, her personal eroticon has held fans rapt.

Control was the title of Jackson's late-eighties album, but it serves well as the female rocker's mantra for the following decade. Control—of one's music, finances, publishing and public image—was a central issue for many women, as TLC filed for bankruptcy after a debut album that sold over 8 million copies, as Madonna's sexual odysseys—on video and between hard covers—engendered vicious, unexpected backlash and über-diva Barbra Streisand built herself a new website with a "Truth Alert" feature to systematically deflect media "untruths." Control was also the issue when the decade's most consistent hit machine, Mariah Carey, took a long and scary walk . . .

Delighted ripeness is Carey's latest essence. Like Janet Jackson, she recorded and packaged her own sensual awakening. Carey was born in 1970, the daughter of a black Venezuelan engineer father and an Irish-American opera-singer mother. Sleek, compact and ambitious, she tossed her caramel mane, married the boss twenty years her senior (Sony Records president Tommy Mottola) and, by 1996, was able to bring a fat $250 million purse to the company with sales of her album *Daydream.*

Carey is possessed of a genuinely strong instrument; press releases and profiles have belabored her alleged eight-octave range. But her style is much like that of fellow vocal contortionists Michael Bolton and Celine Dion. Their delivery is hyperbolic, the arrangements bombastic, the body language all flailing arms and straining throat tendons. In the sixties, they called the syndrome "oversouling"—holding and bending notes until alarmed audiences call 911; Patti LaBelle was its most thrombosis-inducing practitioner. But since the days of Al Jolson, American music audiences have shown a weakness for canned ham. In the nineties, amid all the grungy and teenyboppy boy bands, the tough gangstas and too-proud-to-beg rappers, unabashedly emotional singers enjoyed a surging market share. In delivering what became the number-one signifier for love and longing— a drawn-out, ululating *ahhwoahwoahooooowhoah*—Mariah Carey's lips could assume more pouty poses than the *Kama Sutra* has positions.

This smooth, pliant pop made Carey very rich—so well off that when Barbra Streisand's sixteen-room Central Park co-op went up for sale at $7.5 million (beauty salon included), she put in a bid. Carey was still waiting for a verdict from the co-op board when I talked to her in 1999. Calling from L.A., where she was taking acting lessons and "praying over a stalled film deal," she was frank, funny and decidedly tired of being considered a lightweight. She was annoyed, particularly, that she was not often credited as singer/songwriter, since she has written so many of her huge hits and—"thank God"—retained ownership of her songs.

"At eighteen, I almost sold my publishing for five thousand dollars," she said. "I was broke and five thousand seemed like five million to someone who didn't have enough to buy a bagel for lunch. I was living on my own, I was a backup singer but I really only had my demo tape with songs on it—songs that actually did become number-one records. This person heard it and he liked it. I considered [selling] it but I had heard a bunch of horror stories about people selling their publishing."

A beat of silence. A sigh.

"I don't think a lot of people even realize that I *do* write. I write most of what I sing. A lot of people who are divas don't write and have to rely on that ballad by a songwriter that you have to battle with another diva to get."

She would also like people to know just how hard she has worked. "I've put an album out every single year since I first came out. I've never had any break, basically since right out of high school. Every year, *no matter what.*"

Having also endured serious domestic stress—she and Mottola separated in 1997 and then divorced—she says she is learning to relax a bit. "I'm feeling a little bit okay about having some time to take a couple little vacations and enjoy my life, which I haven't had a chance to do. " In fact, Carey's post-separation nightlife revels have kept Manhattan and L.A. paparazzi in a state of frantic preparedness and pursuit. But she realized that being photographed almost nightly in the company of men with names like Puffy, Snoop Dogg and Q-Tip could have its downside for a rich diva arriviste seeking R-E-S-P-E-C-T and prime real estate. "Sometimes," she told me, "I'm in the paper every other day in New York. It's not cute when you're trying to get approved by a board."

Hers had become a strange privileged-gypsy life, she said. She was still living mostly in hotels and didn't own a car except for a limo she would not tool around in herself. How did she get here? she mused aloud. When I hauled out my trusty inquisition—Why *did* she leave home and go do this crazy thing?—Carey added her voice to the rock refugee chorus: "I just had to get *out.*"

She says that her childhood was marred by her parents' divorce, countless moves, little money and the schoolyard cruelties that beset a daughter of mixed race. "What drove me was *lack* of things—lack of money, stability," Carey said. "I didn't feel safe growing up. We moved around so much, I really had a feeling that I wanted to grow up and feel safe, that I didn't have to worry that the rug's going to be pulled out from under me. And the lack of acceptance is another thing that drove me. Being of mixed race always made me feel I didn't belong or I wasn't good enough to just be myself. Singing was the one thing that made me feel special. It was the one thing that made me feel okay."

Carey's marriage to Mottola may have cosseted her in a multimillion-dollar Westchester mansion and wrapped her in a snug multiyear contract. But it didn't get her to that longed-for comfortable place. "I thought it was what I wanted but it wasn't," Carey says of the marriage. "I had that home, that stability, that safety and it was stifling." And walking out on the boss with plenty of time left on her contract has since put her in platinum handcuffs that clearly chafe.

Her voice is quiet and guarded when she discusses her situation. Clearly, she has been well briefed in what she can say publicly; it's just as apparent that she is very tired of the charade: "I think about that just about every day. I can't think of a day when it doesn't come up, and I'm really being honest with you. It's just *difficult*. My situation is highly unique. That's the only way I can describe it without getting into specifics. You can't fight the system. You do your best and work your hardest and that's what I try to do. I try to not give anybody the opportunity to say, 'Well, she wouldn't support it [an album]' or 'She wouldn't work hard for this.' I try to stay on top of every detail because for so long I didn't."

She has found that full control is a wearying business. It was pleasant, she says, to have her interests guarded by someone else and just concentrate on the music. But once the boss became her ex and legal lines were drawn, "I just had to make sure I was fully aware of what I was supposed to have, on every level. It's like well, get the *Billboard* numbers, get the Soundscan, be *equipped*. I'd rather not deal with all the business stuff, 'cause it does stifle you a little bit creatively. But you have to today."

Regardless of personal feelings, Sony could hardly afford to part with a star who took under a decade to amass 14 number-one hits (Elvis got his 16 over as many years). She released an album's worth, *Number Ones,* in 1999.

Like Bob Dylan, who poured vitriol and tenderness into *Blood on the Tracks*, Carey also made her divorce album—*Butterfly*. Compared to Dylan's dark masterwork, the poetry was Hallmark Lite, all fluttery wings and urgings to fly abandonedly into the sun, but the record—which sold nearly 5 million copies—did move Carey down the highway.

Her post-divorce video image is all tube tops, thigh and wet rubber, skipping through dripping tunnels, tantalizing shifting constellations of panting male rappers in urban-cool videos. In a remix video of her chicks-scrapping-over-a-no-good-guy hit "Heartbreaker," she appears in a tiny shiny bikini, draped across the hood of a convertible driven by a leering Snoop Dogg. Vying with another tough babe for his smirking charms, Carey wrestles her in a scene that makes those old *Dynasty* catfights between Joan Collins and Linda Evans look like the teddy bears' picnic.

In her estimation, this is progress. This is one woman's control. Over and over, she tells inteviewers, "This is the *real* me." She says her steamy new stance is purposely different from the cloying album art and the safe-as-Sprite tone of her first several records. That was what she calls "the non-threatening image—the girl on the swing with the curls. That was easy to digest. It worked once and it worked twice. When it started to be like the seventh time, I was like, okay, can I straighten my hair? Can I put on a pair of pumps? *Work* with me, boys."

The boys would not—at least not while she was still married to Mottola. They kept her barefoot, in cutoff jeans, emoting in meadows. Makeup artist Billy B., who worked with Carey from '93 to '98, was in on some of her frustrating stormy sessions with company management. "She was completely like a puppet," Billy says. "They dictated her look, everything—right down to her makeup."

Of her liberated new look, Carey says, "I guess people thought, where did *this* come from? But I guess that's 'cause nobody was in the room when I was trying on the outfits that got nixed." Finally, she says, "I just did what I wanted." In making the change to ripe nymphet, Carey did prefigure a hugely successful retro phenom that would, by decade's end, spawn platinum-selling jailbait like Britney Spears and Christina Aguilera, as well as the older-and-hotter Puffy protégé Jennifer Lopez. Spears's canny improv—she decided to tie the top of her school uniform white blouse over her pert little bra in the video for "Baby One More Time"—played well to fourteen-year-old boys and older male fans hip to the Humbert Humbert leer of the old blues classic "Good Mornin' Little Schoolgirl." In the wake of Spears's phenomenal sales, it's probably no accident that, soon after, Mariah Carey taped a Fox TV special in her old junior high on Long Island and appeared in a tight green satin cheerleader outfit.

Given her abrupt switch to videos populated with so much hip-hop macho, Carey has also faced accusations that she acquired her deeper and darker R&B roots overnight—once rap had achieved its mighty late-nineties stronghold. This she has vigorously denied, even to a puzzled-looking Charlie Rose on public TV. Carey reeled off what she said were longstanding hip-hop props. And certainly, she may have long loved the genre. But in working with Snoop Dogg and Da Brat, Carey is part of a general trend by pop divas—everyone from Aretha Franklin to Whitney Houston—to buy a little nineties currency with booming contemporary tracks and nasty boyz—and girlz—dripping hot sauce into what were standard pop confections.

Carey was philosophical when the show that heavily promoted her in 1998—VH1's *Divas Live*—lampooned her the following year in a skit that featured a Mariah Careyesque diva too ditzy, too queenly to order a pizza. She pronounced it "pretty funny," and reasoned that her position would always be somewhat embattled, by critics, corporate boogie men, the ravening tabs. "I always have to look over my shoulder," she said. "It's just the reality of my life."

She does enjoy the perks of multiplatinum divahood. Her late-nineties list of backstage musts would make Janis Joplin slap a panné-velvet knee and whisper, "*Sheee*-it!" Among Carey's essentials: two bottles Cristal champagne, chilled properly . . . Guiltless Gourmet Baked Not Fried tortilla chips . . . honey served in plastic honey bears. Shortly after our talk, Streisand's co-op board turned Carey down, but she kept shopping. She had bought Marilyn Monroe's grand piano at auction, and it needed a worthy home.

When it all gets too much, Carey told me, she relaxes by riding the "Tower of Terror," a Disney World ride that drops the unsuspecting reveler thirteen stories in an elevator shaft. She's done it so much she's not scared anymore. But she and her friends have great fun collecting the souvenir photos the theme park snaps at the moment of descent. Having mastered the terror, she just nails the poses.

* * *

Whither the nineties Madonna amid all these self-declared sirens, Valkyries and sluts? Her own Hot 100 question—"Who's That Girl?" — remained tantalizingly unanswered. Could a real Rock Star—the kind of Kathleen Hanna's worst nightmare—find and claim some edge? Madonna decided to try something borrowed—hadn't Mae West scandalized in 1926 with a Broadway show called *Sex?*—and something blue.

Long past midnight on a muggy Miami night in 1992. A caravan of naughty children drives through the darkness in battered seventies Rent-A-Wrecks, incognito cruisers crammed with camera bags, friends, lingerie and ooh-la-la props. Designer water bottles roll on the stained floor mats as they take the corners, laughing. Madonna is in the convertible's backseat, hair blowing in the backdraft, voice bouncing over the trunk as she shrieks directions to the car behind. The procession halts at all all-night gas station. She leaps out, breasts jutting from a frontless black lace body stocking, nipples at attention in the drive-by breeze. She bends, straddles the gas hose, starts to pump. Alabaster skin and oil stains.

Click. Whirrrr. A film crew is making the making of.

Traffic hisses by, unmindful.

Then, as quickly as they arrived, they are gone, piled back into the big American heaps. Taillights wink around a corner and disappear. There is only laughter. Fade out . . .

So great was her puissance after a decade's adulation that Madonna may have thought she could make a clean getaway when her photo book, *Sex,* was published. For the book, she adopted an alter ego, Dita Pardo, who wrote its text in letter form; she had celebrity co-conspirators in the photos: Isabella Rossellini, Naomi Campbell, Vanilla Ice, Big Daddy Kane. After all, she had the vaunted "full creative control." And this was the woman who shrugged off the huge Pepsi endorsement lost when religious leaders took loud issue with "Like a Prayer," a video that featured Our Lady lustily embracing a black man before God, crucifixes and candles. An actress willing to drip hot candle wax on bondage boy toy Willem Dafoe in the regrettable *Body of Evidence.* When tabs published naked photos of Madonna taken when she was a model for art students, she shrugged and said, "So what?" So why couldn't she shoot, crop and package her deepest erotic fantasies for all the world to see (and buy)? Just after the *Sex* shoots were completed, Madonna told me that she was exhilarated by the experience. She said that it felt as liberating as she had meant it to be:

"We were out of New York, away from the usual environment. We were doing this very documentary style of photographing, and for the first time we [she and photographer Steven Meisel] were both kind of free of the constraints of lighting and all. We basically just ran around in cars. When we would find a place we liked, a pizza parlor or a burlesque club, we'd just run out. We had so much fun. I remember spending the entire night laughing."

Their exercise in guerilla exhibitionism was unreal—but delicious.

"It was like were were in a Fellini movie or something," Madonna recalled. "I just had the best time, and I know Steven did, too. Free from everything. We could do what we wanted. Nobody was watching."

Here Madonna heaved a wee, weary sigh.

"Nobody knew that I was me."

Then she put it all out there, in a shiny silver cover, for $49.95.

Five years past the fiasco, after a rolling tsunami of condemnation, scorn and stinko reviews, I asked Madonna if perhaps, even in this age of insatiable celebrity curiosity, she may have upset people by giving them *more* than they thought they wanted.

"People couldn't take having the mirrors turned on them like that, absolutely," she told me. "Sexuality has always been forced down our throats, but it's always been from a male point of view. The woman is always objectified. And in this circumstance it was the opposite. I think that not only men but women responded in a really hostile way. . . .

"People didn't attack me in a personal way before the book. After the book, they did. I'm talking about criticizing everything from my choice of men to my body—things that have nothing to do with my work. I also found myself the subject of almost any interview anyone did with a female. Writers used to just throw my name up there just to get six paragraphs of sensationalist journalism."

Madonna turned on her heel and did the only thing that made sense to her: She became a Single Working Mother. She said she gained a few pounds and some much-needed perspective when her daughter Lourdes was born in 1996.

"I don't take it [the criticism] as personally as I used to. I'm a more forgiving person now. I'm sure my daughter has a lot to do with it. But I feel much more compassion toward people who have hostile feelings toward me. Because I know that it's coming from the opposite place that it appears to be coming from. And once you accept that format and learn to forgive people . . . it's just been a lot easier for me. Being famous has been a lot easier."

I asked her when she made that turn, and she traced it to the filming of *Evita,* during which she was pregnant, scared and besieged on location where outraged Eva Peron lovers loudly condemned her casting outside her hotel windows. Being alternately and passionately loved and loathed, she says she was "sort of living vicariously through what had happened to Eva Peron—then finding myself pregnant. Going from the depths of despair and then coming out on the other side . . . you know, becoming a mother, I just have a whole new outlook on life. I see the world as a much more hopeful place."

She did deliver an angry diatribe at the 1997 MTV Video Awards, chastising the media's hounding of the recently killed Princess of Wales. She elaborated on it a bit at my urging: "We've chosen technological advancement over spiritual involvement. There's a huge gap, and I think that has a lot to do with it. I think because of TV and the Internet, people have forgotten how to be resourceful. So they're just living vicariously like leeches through other people. And they become spectators. They don't inhabit their own bodies anymore."

Strangely, though, Madonna has found fans somewhat better behaved in the presence of a mother. She said she and Lourdes had just had some great outings in the big city: "I do enjoy going to the park with her, and when I do, people inevitably concentrate on her. It's fantastic— I love it. You know, since Princess Diana's death, I have to say I've had a lot more freedom. I spent two weeks in New York right after it happened and I haven't had so much freedom in, like, ten years. I went to the park almost every day with my daughter and pushed her in the stroller and nobody bothered me. And I was in shock. Except for one day, I never saw paparazzi."

We laughed about what motherhood can do to glamour, and the frightening conditions—sweatpantsed and sandy-eyed—we have found ourselves in on the street. I wondered if this acknowledged master of glamour and deception regarded her professional image-making as a challenge or a burden.

"Ultimately," she said, "it's a burden. I want my music to be reviewed, not whether my rib cage is too small or not. You want be thought of as attractive, but it's a very competitive world, and there's always going to be another beautiful girl around the corner. Even though people don't admit it in the music business, people are very looks-conscious. And just like in the movie business, men are allowed to not meet the conventional standards of beauty and still be celebrated. It's much harder for women."

Still. But she wouldn't deny that bold visual presentation of self has been a huge part of her success . . .

"Yeah, it's been part of the attraction, but ultimately it's delusional. And it's only one percent of what I am. And what everybody is."

So can she envision a day when she'd just stand there with a mike?

"Holding a flashlight under my face? I've threatened it." She laughed. "I just might. Doing the *Rolling Stone* photo shoot yesterday was really difficult for me."

Here it was my turn to laugh. I could recall one instance when that magazine scrapped a whole Madonna story—I had been set to do the interview—after she rejected *seventeen* proposed photographers, all of them A-list. Brace her on it and she says, simply, that the thrill is gone.

"I used to enjoy doing video shoots. I don't have patience for it anymore. I feel like I've done it all a billion gazillion times. There isn't the thrill of turning myself into something else and creating something else. It's just not as fun as it used to be." And then she added: "I'm feeling very un-divaish right now."

All this duly noted, I tuned into the next Grammy telecast at which Madonna performed. There she was opening the show in full geisha gear: rice-powdered face, kimono, black wig, full teahouse set design. The smile was too inscrutable, too controlled to interpret.

We're at the hottest traveling show of 1997. A band composed of tall and lanky men is vamping in gauzy long dresses and wool caps. Wearing tight pants and a midriff-baring shirt, fiddling with a navel ring on a chain, Fiona Apple is introducing them each with the surname Spice, a naughty little knock of those made-for-MTV creatures, the Spice Girls. Now Fiona is getting serious:

"I'm a girl. So to put that [Spice] on my name would mean I had no talent
and no integrity."

Up front, the little girls—average age about fourteen—are screaming their
approval, braces glinting in the night. Fiona asks:

"Will you help when they come beat me up?"

They squeak back their fealty.

Eeeeeeeeeeeee.

She's got her own hell to raise, does Fiona. And, it seems, her own
devoted underage following on this stop of that summer's Lilith Fair. She
played to them gratefully, cannily, raising the decibel level simply by
wringing her frail Morticia wrists. As women rock deeper and more con-
fidently into their art, they are learning what Bessie Smith knew, jouncing through the dangerous southland in her well-appointed railcar; what
Patsy Cline had to believe as she flung herself headlong between the music and the kids. They knew that standing pat just won't do. That the best,
truest popular music is one born of journeys and arrivals, of long odysseys
and lightning epiphanies. That lyrics and careers can turn on unanticipated
moments. And that to keep moving is the sanest thing to do . . .

Despite the solidarities claimed by Sarah McLachlan's much-bally-
hooed traveling show, one dark and stormy night I caught the tour I was
surprised by the distinct, vocal pockets of partisans for each flavor—those
alternatives again. If the little girls squealed and hugged one another as
Fiona Apple fingered her navel ring and indulged in her antic, mighty-
Aphrodite hair whipping, the deeper voices of men hollered for McLachlan's
pretty stylings and the athletic, primal drum-thumping of the spirited
Paula Cole. Different audiences seemed to file into the seats around us,
depending on who was on. The single act that roused the entire crowd
was the magnificent Tracy Chapman, whose extended rave-up on her
hit "Give Me One Reason" was the only interlude that truly rocked the
house-at-large.

Lilith's success and its fragmented fairgoers proved two things about
female artists. First, there is a lively market for competent, thoughtful music
performed in a kinder, gentler venue. Apart from the stubborn tyrannies
of ladies' room lines, there were no physical impediments to enjoying the
music. No one seemed to miss the hurtling bodies and projectile vomiting
of all those macho summerfests of yore.

Second, and most important, there is no such thing as monolithic Women's Music. There never was—nor will there ever be. By the late nineties, despite the categoric tyrannies of the big charts, there was a richer, fuller menu of fare, from the thrilling, immediate harmonies of the Indigo Girls to smart-waif revelations of Michelle Shocked. Voice over affect, interpretation over production catagorized the infectious stylings of Shawn Colvin. Toshi Reagon came across with the heart of a woman and the heft and power of Big Joe Turner.

Women of Other Appetites either kept their counsel or came out as it suited them. And when they did, lesbian rockers proved as diverse as any other "genre." Certainly, big stars like Whitney Houston may be perpetually pressed and nipped at by "lesbian rumors." But they will not be victims of the nasty, dogged inquisitions that pursued Dusty Springfield almost until her death. Times have changed, and some big stars, owning their own labels and production companies, are simply too powerful an economic force to alienate.

So-called lipstick lesbian stars—notably the sublimely gifted k. d. lang—are encouraged to vamp in today's mad celebrathon. *Vanity Fair* was clearly convinced that lesbian louche had some sales potential when it posed lang on its cover being "shaved" by a grinning Cindy Crawford. And for other tastes there is a Phranc—née Susie Gottlieb— rangy, butch and pleased to call herself "a Jewish lesbian folksinger." Melissa Etheridge and her lover chose dissolute rock royalty—David Crosby—as the father of their children, celebrating their commingled bloodlines on the cover of *Rolling Stone*. Gossip columns covered the subsequent split and spats between comic Sandra Bernhard and Madonna as they would any other velvet-rope dalliance. All this lesbian chic—and a few Anne Heche–produced HBO movies—has hardly turned the historical tide of anti-gay sentiment. But it has afforded lesbian artists some of that essential ether: airtime.

In fact, if the current high-water mark of women in rock has afforded anything to future generations of artists, it's the chance to venture even farther afield. Theirs will be a wider range of choices, from available venues to basic tools. That venerable American institution, Martin guitars, just made a limited edition of smaller instruments designed for the arms and hands of women; when the whole collection sold out in 48 hours, Martin decided to get into the business of making women's guitars—permanently.

Commerce is the ultimate pop arbiter; so it was that record companies noted the disparity between the huge promotional budgets and the disappointing recent sales of male supergroups from U2 to R.E.M. and Hootie and the Blowfish. Like those quirky, low-budget indie films that go on to kick studio butt at the box office, new female acts can be low-risk, high-yield investments for the cost-conscious A&R department. And for the struggling singer/songwriter or all-girl band, there may be safe haven in punk-friendly record companies like Kill Rock Stars and the new woman-owned shops: Madonna's Maverick, Queen Latifah's Flavor Unit, Missy Elliott's The Gold Mind, Inc., and Ani DiFranco's Righteous Babe.

Empires—Amazonian or otherwise—can be built on that timeless impulse to open one's mouth and *git*. Touring over the summer of '97 with Bob Dylan and enjoying equal billing, worshipped in a global tangle of websites now as the "Ani Lama," DiFranco was cautionary about the cult of personality ("I'm No Heroine," declares one song). Like Dylan, a fabulously rich man who opted to spend much of his summer playing college auditoriums, she'll probably stay a solid, committed road warrior. To an interviewer's question about why she's been doggedly plying the clubs since age eleven, Ani offered this simple answer:

"I just had to get out of the house."

DAY OF THE DIVAS

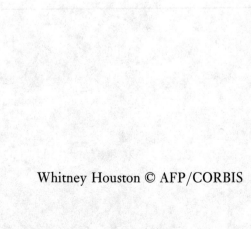

Whitney Houston © AFP/CORBIS

As a singer, she appears to me of the first order; as a specimen of womankind, a little more. She is enough to counterbalance, of herself, all the evil that the world is threatened with by the great convention of women. So God save Jenny Lind!

—Washington Irving, 1850

A breast can be as proud as the prow of a racing boat, or it can droop, pallid and sad. Madonna, by this purview, was obviously depressed.

—Norman Mailer, 1996

C her, are you *sure* you want to do this?"

"Yes, Tina."

"Because I can bring the moves down some. The girls . . ." (Here, Tina Turner points to a pair of backup singers.) "The girls are doing a . . . *quieter* version of my regular steps."

Cher and Tina Turner are standing arm in arm on the stage at Manhattan's Beacon Theater. We are at Diva Ground Zero, peeking at rehearsal fuss and fabulousness millions of viewers didn't see on VH1's *Divas Live '99*, which aired in April of that year. I have gone deep diva here for nearly a week, the better to parse the diva fever that has dominated the charts, the box office—even infected certain tough men of letters— over the century's last decade. Pop divas have emerged as the most worshipped and sought-after of celestial bodies; in their ability to be all things to so many people, they fall into their own goddess archetypes. Three species are on the bill here: the Survivor Diva (Tina Turner, Chaka Khan). The Vegas Diva (Cher). And the Difficult Diva (Whitney Houston). A live show such as this can ill afford the shenanigans or demands of a class we'll call Divas Provocateurs (Madonna, Courtney Love). But a brace of more tractable Divas-in-Waiting (Brandy, Faith Evans, Mary J. Blige, LeAnn

Rimes) fill out the bill after some spirited handling by their marketing cadres. And for a touch o' camp, there will be an appearance by that "honorary diva," Sir Elton John.

The D-zone boasts a full block of double-parked "talent" trailers and semis rumbling serious entitlement on West 75th Street. Here, anxious men bearing small Kate Spade makeup bags are heard to bark at much bigger men: "Let me through NOW—her lip liner is RAGGED!" Over the three days of rehearsal, even the air suffers diva buildup: free-floating maribou fluff and hair-extension fuzz in the wake of Whitney Houston's dancers has one security guard hitting his asthma inhaler.

Onstage we have a quiet, off-mike game of Diva Double Dare. For it is one thing to share a verse of "Proud Mary" with Tina Turner—but quite another to dance with her. This is Tina! whose Tilt-a-Whirl choreography has sent a couple of generations of spent Ikettes limping home to Mama.

"Am I *insane* to do this, Tina?"

Cher has dressed down for such strenuous work: a black jumpsuit with strappy bustier top, boots and a black wig with so many silvery baubles woven into the top it resembles a battle helmet for the Knights Templar. Tina is in a slim Armani suit. No makeup. No fooling.

"You want to *work* it?" she asks again, a touch wickedly. Cher looks straight into her eyes and says evenly, "You know I do. Gimme a chance. I'll get it."

The band vamps, and Cher tries Tina's trademark backwards stutter step into a forward crouch but flies out prematurely, once, twice. On the third attempt, the women fold into perfect twin forward flops. They rise out of them simultaneously with eyes locked, arms up, and the duet ends in full frontal vibration. Breasts, hips, thighs, chins—nothing's jiggling that shouldn't be, despite their combined age of 114. *Badoooom!* On the last rim shot, they fall into a victory hug. "There's your million-dollar shot," says a cameraman. "Divas ascending."

Elsewhere in the darkened house, John Sykes, president of VH1, is jubilant. He is thinking Yes, we've got a *moment* here: classic, telegenic, iconic. It's just the kind of high-beam promo and programming that has helped transform VH1 from MTV's dowdy stepsister into a small-screen siren that's finally attracting those gentlemen callers from the ad agencies.

Backstage, Cher is hiking up her bustier and extracting a tiny earphone from beneath her wig. When congratulated on her fortitude, she grins and cites the Diva Credo, a mantra I've heard chorused, amplified and shoop-shooped over nearly two decades of interviewing pop stars, male and female. "Hey, you've gotta *go* for it," Cher says. "No matter what."

Why do they burn so brightly, so fiercely? And why are we so mad for these loud and leggy provocateurs? We fall in thrall with their voices and their vamping, with their artful distillation of human emotion or their most out-rageous expression of whim. But whether you seek your divinity in a per-fect, sustained high C or the moist red lips that send it heavenward, the bottom line is the same: On the charts, the concert stage—even in current fiction—by the dawn of 2000, diva fever was raging as never before. And it is very big business.

When the marabou settled and the numbers came in, it would be clear the divas delivered. The week after the broadcast, Cher's album *Believe* won *Billboard's* Greatest Gainer award, jumping from number 12 to 5; a compi-lation of her greatest hits rose 57 spots. And Whitney Houston would score a 13-place jump for her album, *My Love Is Your Love*. *Divas Live '99* got rat-ings higher than anything in VH1's fourteen-year history—nearly double the viewership for 1998's first record-shattering diva event (starring Aretha Franklin and Celine Dion, among others)—and enough to give that net-work its first showing ever in the number-one spot for a primetime cable show.

I asked VH1 Executive Vice President Wayne Isaak, who came up with the concept, just why he settled on flamboyant, platinum-faceted women. He told me it was a no-brainer: "We had always put together a big concert every year, but it always kind of underperformed. Okay, here's a thousand stars, what is the unifying concept? We were sitting around trying to figure out how to make it more enjoyable and more watched. Divas was something that was easy to market—that you could explain with a photo and one word."

Such is the iconic might of the standout pop chanteuse. Isaak ac-knowledges that it wouldn't have been as successful five or ten years ago. He thinks women's strengths play well in these rather affectless times: "To me, the reason is they're a bit more emotional as singers. I think they feel more at ease in front of people, showing off the sexy side, showing off a variety of emotions from anger and sassiness to love and seductiveness.

There are very few men who can do that. Mick Jagger. Elton John—on a really good night."

Though VH1's demographics are generally evenly split between the sexes, 63 percent of the *Diva* audience was female. "It was clearly driven by women," Sykes told me. He and his staff have paid close attention to focus groups, both male and female, who have responded strongly in recent years to programming featuring strong female performers. The channel has added half-hour "Women First" video blocks and a five-part series, "100 Greatest Women in Rock & Roll."

In Sykes's view, his station, and the music industry in general, are simply playing catch-up to the seismic changes feminism has brought to other fields. The pressure to change came from without; the most chauvinist record man is not going to argue the booming sales figures of female pop artists. Says Sykes, "I think the entertainment business was the last men's club holdout. It's finally responded to the power women have in the marketplace. There have always been powerful women artists, but it seemed they were coming one every year or every few years. Or they were women who were supposed to act like men—those tough female rockers of the seventies or eighties. These divas are women who are worshipped for being women, not for being guitar goddesses or grunge queens."

Their record sales are staggering—nearly 200 million units between Mariah Carey and Whitney Houston alone, another 100 million for Celine Dion. (In 1998, Dion earned a reported $55.5 million, having sold 28 million records that year.) But nothing underscored the diva's cultural entrenchment like the little farewell party in the final hours of the 20th century. Only one modern diva could have pulled it off. And even so, it had the precision and forethought of Charlemagne's campaign in Saxony.

In late spring of 1999, Barbra Streisand was in Italy, on one of the languorous vacations she has been enjoying with her new husband, when she got the news: RIAA, the record sales certification organization, confirmed that she has finally surpassed the Beatles in the number of gold albums, with 40 certified. Only Elvis had more (62). And, as one of Streisand's publicists pointed out, the King is gone, but "*she's* still going."

Is she ever. The gawky naif of the 1965's *My Name Is Barbra* is now the powerful fifty-eight-year-old director/producer/politico Barbra in

Love. In late June, she released a single, "I've Dreamed of You," a love song she commissioned then sang to actor James Brolin at their wedding reception in the summer of 1998. A soft-focus, beach-at-sunset portrait of the embracing pair graced the CD sleeve. Shrink-wrapping and selling this *billet-doux* is just the opening salvo in an escalating campaign: Streisand's record company, Columbia, was hoping the nuptial-specific ballad about a couple holding hands on "This blessed day" would catch the dewy-eyed fancy of that summer's brides in much the way that Celine Dion's *Titanic* weeper "My Heart Will Go On" has become the top song requested at funerals.

Riding this anticipated romantic swell, Streisand plotted a fall album launch (*A Love Like Ours*) with liner notes that coo: "I've usually thought of love as a private matter. . . . Yet once you've found love . . . you somehow want to share that joy." Streisand controlled all pre-release publicity by insisting interviews be conducted in a Malibu location she rented for the purpose—miked and lit to her specifications. Additional sales heat came from her aggressively publicized millennial Event on New Year's Eve. That night Streisand performed one show in the 13,000-seat MGM Grand Garden in Las Vegas. Her deal took nearly a year to negotiate, resulting in a payday reportedly between $15 and $20 million. This one mad Diva Moment should be weighed for its startling economic *gravitas*.

Streisand's MGM ticket prices ranged from $2,500 to $500 (with the majority at the $1,500 and up level). When tickets went on sale on May 2, the show set a one-day, single-performance record in dollar sales for any sports or entertainment event ever handled by the thirty-three-year-old brokerage Ticketmaster. And as Streisand devotees were funneled through MGM's high-impulse maze, the casino hotel take also included special room packages (*starting* at $3,999), restaurant and souvenir sales and heady fin de siècle gambling revenues. The concert was taped "at the very least for archival purposes," according to the Streisand camp—rights owned by the artist. Revelers were offered this reassuring guarantee: When the clock strikes midnight, Ms. Streisand *will* still be onstage.

It took an überdiva to stand up to the unreasonable expectations of New Year's Eve 2000. Only Sinatra or Elvis would have been an equal draw. And Streisand took a drama queen's approach to hyping the event. Just before tickets went on sale, her spokesman announced that this *may* be the last live concert by the woman with a voice "like buttah." *Evah*.

Injecting personal drama into the performance arena has long been a diva trait, from Maria Callas's Hellenic tantrums to Madonna's visiting her mother's grave with cameras in tow in her documentary, *Truth or Dare.* But Streisand's millennial chutzpah and her decision to get so personal on CD evince a deep understanding of the cultural forces that have made these such Diva Days.

The ageless appeal of the diva—talent, emotional delivery, flamboyance—has now crossed streams with the newer, more intense cult of celebrity and its powerful digital delivery system. Lifestyles of the female and fabulous, in book, movie, TV bio and CD formats, have created an infotainment juggernaut. Even men of letters have fallen hard for the pop diva: Norman Mailer's breathless enounter with Madonna for *Esquire* revealed the big lug gone just gaga. Elmore Leonard's *Be Cool* resurrects reformed loan shark Chili Palmer from *Get Shorty* as the manager of a headstrong female rocker. Salman Rushdie's 1999 novel, *The Ground Beneath Her Feet,* is a hymn to the galvanic powers of the pop siren. Vina, its heroine, has a compulsion to publicly dissect every intimate aspect of her bodice-ripping life. Rushdie told me he wrote her that way because "She's a kind of confessional creature—somewhere between Princess Diana and Germaine Greer—people who make the kind of narcissistic assumption that everything that happens in their lives defines the meaning of the culture they live in. I've been noticing just in the last decade this incredible growth of our need for confession. We seem to have a *culture* of confession."

And in this relentlessly full-disclosure culture (confessional lit, confessional daytime TV, excruciatingly confessional Congressional hearings) women are historically more willing and able to *talk*—witness the female-dominated memoir boom. The women's movement itself took a confessional route to self-knowledge via consciousness-raising groups and cauterizing tracts like *My Mother/My Self.* All of this helped set the stage for the best-seller reception of that landmark diva confessional *I, Tina.* In the wake of its success, book editors continue to toss fat advances at the likes of Cher, Diana Ross, Aretha Franklin, Gladys Knight, Grace Slick, Patti LaBelle. And on record, women's songwriting has become far more autobiographical and purgative—from Tori Amos's tale of her own teenage rape ("Me and a Gun") to *The Miseducation of Lauryn Hill*, an extremely personal odyssey that bops between sex, God and the intimate joys of motherhood.

Add this inherent frankness to the pop diva's immense economic clout and the fiery, larger-than-life aspects of her character, and it's clear why she has become the perfect nineties meld of commerce and art. Surely Barbra Streisand *is* a happy woman in love. And just as surely, in these days of Ya-Ya sisterhoods and Oprah-inspired bookclubs, packaging the fairy-tale romantic triumph of a fifty-plus divorcee "who thought love had passed me by" is another marketing no-brainer. If Streisand does retire from the concert stage and into connubial bliss, she should easily be able to support her recent fun hobby: dabbling in the stock market.

It's diva-lock on the red carpet as the celebrity audience and presenters arrive on West 75th Street. Fans behind barricades bay recognition as women from all walks of fabulousness make their way past the camera crews in support of their sequined sisters: soap diva (Susan Lucci), home diva (Martha Stewart), fashion diva (Donatella Versace), chat-show diva (Starr Jones), model/slash/whatever diva (Claudia Schiffer). Trailing behind Elizabeth Hurley, actor Hugh Grant tosses a diva definition over his shoulder: "Glamour and the ability to induce fear in men." Grumps Donald Trump: "A diva is a very spoiled woman with a great voice."

Over a century and a half into its usage, the appellation "diva" has as many shadings as Madonna has video selves. Diva began as an Italian word first applied in the mid-nineteenth century to female operatic stars. (In Bellini's 1831 opera "Norma," the term meant "chaste goddess.") But since that time, it has been broadened into a loaded, contradictory term, overused and much abused. In this age of extremes, diva can be used as a verb, an accolade or an insult. Usage needn't even be music-related, nor does it distinguish between "high" and "low" art. Thus modern divahood in its widest interpretation can take in Dame Judi Dench and Roseanne, Toni Morrison and Jackie Susann.

What any divaship requires is a *mouth*—a stong female voice that, by dint of talent and/or will, makes itself heard. A diva is unafraid to express herself in song, word, deed and choice of foundation garment. A diva understands the role of passion in human life; in performance, she channels it for us more reserved mortals. Her powerful mystique is neatly summed in the experience of a man I know in his late thirties who screamed—involuntarily, and to his own deep shock—at a Madonna concert in the New

Jersey Meadowlands. "I don't know how she did that," he confided. "But I'm *so* glad she did."

Herein, we will confine ourselves to the pop diva, the woman with a voice capable of reaching and moving millions in a variety of popular genres: Top 40, hip-hop, jazz, country, soul. Though she is versatile enough to rock or croon, the biggest hit-maker in the modern diva's oeuvre is often the big, lush ballad. Thirty-five years after Streisand's "People," torchers still hold their own against the harsher, clipped realities of rap and hard rock. And just as there is a bull market now in inspirational tracts (all those *Chicken Soup for the Mother's/Couple's/Christian's/Teenager's/Golfer's Soul* tomes and Deepak Chopra tapes), record buyers are opting for the gooiest of vocal epoxies to make a fractured world whole.

Men can concoct this Top 40 emotional bombast—witness everything from Quincy Jones's "We Are the World" to R. Kelly's megahit "I Believe I Can Fly." But in sheer numbers and ease of delivery, divas rule. Whitney Houston's CD from *The Bodyguard*, anchored by "I Will Always Love You," has surpassed *Saturday Night Fever* to become the biggest selling soundtrack of all time. Celine Dion's *Titanic* effusions got her Oscar-night exposure and that diva-certifying Barbara Walters interview. When, in 1999, Dion's manager/husband Rene Agnelil was diagnosed with skin cancer, the diva announced a two-year hiatus to care for him, and an attempt to have a baby. She did not go quietly. During the big weepy ballads in Dion's televised farewell concert—one of several—cameras panned relentlessly between the wee emoter and her husband's beaming face in the audience. She also announced that yes, during her time off, she would be writing a "very intimate" book with a title to match her album, *All the Way*.

True divaship is conferred by one other essential: durability. Americans have long held a soft spot for the unsinkable gal, from Molly Brown up through Alice Kramden. And feminism heightened our thrall with women possessed of staying power and the moxy for inspired transformations. Young women cheer the I'll-get-my-own *puissance* of Madonna's public passage from Boy Toy to sexual provocateur to kabbala-studying single mom. For generations of women who have waited to exhale, the post-Ike Tina Turner is a heroine—while her pal Mick Jagger is just a likable old roué. Cher rose from Vegas and variety-show camp to win an Oscar. Bette Midler—that girl who sang in corsets in the gay baths—has become a huge movie star and front-page Lady Bountiful; with her charitable foundation,

Midler stepped forward to save imperiled community gardens in Manhattan. After her non-sectarian relief efforts on behalf of Hurricane Andrew victims in Florida, Gloria Estefan took to the barricades—and press briefings—on the side of Elian Gonzales' anti-Castro "Miami relatives." And as their power base increases, diva activism is on the rise: Madonna with AMFAR, Streisand as a primo Democratic fund raiser. Socially, politically, culturally, there is a lively cult of You Go, Girl—and the diva can stand and deliver.

It seems we have always known and worshipped pop divas in this century; from Florenz Ziegfeld's funny girl Fanny Brice, up through the Billie Holidays and Lena Hornes, the Miss Ellas and Mariahs. But who was the very first? I encountered her quite by accident, at a used book sale. My eye had been caught by a pair of textbooks clearly used for one of those sociology survey courses that began to characterize the rock and roll years of higher education. *The History of Popular Culture* was published by the Macmillan Company in 1968. This was at the outset of a brave new discipline that, twenty years later, would produce monographs on "Consuming k. d. lang: The Politics of Ambiguity" and symposium papers contrasting Madonna's and Bjork's approaches to narrowing the divisions between technology and nature.

The books went from the ancients to the tie-dyed tribes of my youth; I bore my treasures home and dove in, starting with couch etiquette at Roman banquets, prostitute fashions circa 40 A.D., culinary and entertainment uses for the French guillotine. The second volume ends with the dour pronouncement that acid heads are, in Marshal McLuhan's phrase, "post-literate," that hippies do not share our written, linear society and that "theirs is an esctatic, do-it-now culture, and rock and roll is their art form." Might this make the rock diva some sort of pre-literate priestess?

It was all great stuff, but I was astonished by a mid-nineteenth-century entry that described another public esctasy. It concerned a night in 1850, when the "Swedish Nightingale," Jenny Lind, was besieged at her rooms in Manhattan's Irving House hotel. The brief account was something out of *A Hard Day's Night:*

"The newspapers estimated these crowds milling about her hotel at thirty thousand. They reported a street fight growing out of a struggle to recover a peach-stone which [Lind] had supposedly dropped from the balcony; the enterprise of a speculator who had secured what was declared to be one of her gloves, charging twenty-five cents to kiss the outside of it, fifty cents the inside."

A century and a half ago, a single ticket to Lind's Boston concert was auctioned for $625—a price that might get you a fully loaded SUV in today's economy. The rest of the short entry on Lind raised some provocative questions: How, without the aid of incessant internet PR and MTV, in an age before voice recording and broadcast, might a young woman, even of prodigious talent, inspire such hysteria? As a cultural phenomenon, did Lind-mania set precedents for the pop diva worship that has characterized the end of the 20th century? What was going on in young, brawling post-Jacksonian America that encouraged such feverish effusions?

One thing was clear: Most of the answers lay with the singular talents of the man who brought Jenny Lind to America, P. T. Barnum. That great showman lived and schemed in Bridgeport, Connecticut. The Barnum Museum there has a Lind display, tucked just around the corner from his infamous "Fejee Mermaid"—a screamingly bogus naiad plainly stitched from fish and monkey parts. There were excerpts from Lind-related tracts by Thackeray, Carlyle, Emerson. And this cautionary verse by a poet of those times, William Allen Butler:

They'll welcome you with speeches and serenades and rockets
And you will touch their hearts and I will tap their pockets;
And if between us both the public isn't skinned
Why my name isn't Barnum, nor your name Jenny Lind.

When I settled down amid the Barnum archives in the Bridgeport library, the Lind scenarios seemed no less shocking than the Fejee maid. Colonel Parker couldn't have master-marketed his Elvis without the template cast by Barnum.

It is a sleepy Sunday morning in New York City on September 1, 1850 Yet as the packet Atlantic ties up at a lower Manhattan dock, 30,000 people jam the piers to welcome the "Swedish Nightingale." No one here has ever heard Lind sing a note, but they scream her name. Handsome young men, hired by an unseen force, rush to meet her with more bouquets and vocal near-swoons. Blossoms fly and and release their perfume in the crush.

Standing in the driver's box of Lind's carriage, urging its plunging pair of matched bays through the chaos toward her hotel is P. T. Barnum. He is beaming as he carries his prize through the imperial city; a year's lucrative odyssey has begun.

"I risked much, but I made more," Barnum wrote of his association with Lind. The assembled crowd was a result of his long and shrewd press campaign begun months before Lind's arrival. The king of Humbug had mortgaged everything he owned—more than he'd ever spend on Jumbo the elephant, the Bearded Lady of Genoa or Tom Thumb's wedding—in order to put up the breathtaking $187,000, paid in advance, for Lind's concert tour of America. (In today's currency, that would be between $1 and $2 million dollars.) Like the rest of the nation, Barnum had never heard Lind sing when he sent his agent to London to negotiate the deal. But the showman was banking on diva fever, which had already swept Europe.

The intelligentsia fell hardest: A smitten Mendelssohn accompanied Lind on piano; Chopin arranged his own works for her. Queen Victoria made the plain little coloratura soprano a court pet. Lind was no beauty, describing herself as having "little piggy eyes and a big, broad nose," yet Hans Christian Andersen proposed to her three times and wrote "The Ugly Duckling" in her honor. In Europe's capitals, the hoi polloi mobbed her. Something—the extraordinary voice? the radiant spirit?—was stirring both the masses and the high-culture snobs to an emotional fervor no freak show could match.

In his own memoirs, Barnum says that Lind's triumph in America was his greatest as well. To prepare the ground for her American tour, he arranged newspaper puffery and paid advertisements, persuaded dignitaries to attend her arrival. Just before she was set to sail west, he hired newsmen to plant glowing reviews of her last European concert in New York papers. When he felt the task completed he boasted, "She would be adored if she had the voice of a crow."

Besides the dizzying ticket auctions, the full houses, Lind had merchandising that rivaled the Spice Girls: Jenny Lind candle snuffers, pork sausages, calabash flasks, perfume bottles, pianos, poker chips, fishing flies, cigars, a Lind gooseberry, a muskmelon, a dahlia, trunks, beds, sofas—even Jenny Lind mule blinders in smitten Memphis; in 2000, both the Barnum Museum and the New York Historical Society mounted Lind-inspired retrospectives. Relics of Lindiania are still trading briskly on eBay.

The climate for such a wild embrace was an America three quarters of a century past its great revolution and just an uneasy decade away from a civil war. In 1829, the election of Andrew Jackson, the first western president, signaled the end of a government dominated by southern planter aristocracy and New England commerce nabobs. Despite his slave owning and loathsome treatment of Native Americans, Jackson was much heralded as a populist leader. In the wake of his two terms, he left a fractious, sprawling republic that placed much faith in the brain and breast of the common man. By the time of his death in 1845, Emerson's ideals of natural beauty and transcendentalism were gaining sway; when Jenny Lind arrived— much heralded and praised by Emerson—Thoreau was just three years from publishing *Walden*. The Hudson River School landscapists were lushly reasserting the purity of nature over the tainted artifice of portraiture and studio posings.

All these noble yearnings coalesced in Jenny Lind. Her voice was a natural wonder, ranging from high C to the B below middle C. Her background was humble. She was religious, viriginal and charitable to the extreme (she donated all of her $10,000 first New York concert fee and more to charities). She dressed in plain, purest white, never in makeup, and with minimal adornment—a nosegay, perhaps. She had begun as a successful soprano on European opera stages but turned to the concert stage, citing her abhorrence of opera's drama and contrivance. In concert, she offered some operatic pieces, notably the "Casta Diva" from *Norma*. When she performed in Washington, D.C., to an audience that included president Millard Fillmore, the fiery secretary of state Daniel Webster, also in attendance, listened politely to an operatic selection, then loudly requested a song of Lind's people. A nineteenth-century pop song. Breathless news accounts reported Webster's visible enchantment. ("The tone sped and lessened and Webster's broad chest grew erect and expanded . . . and foreward leaned the aroused statesman . . . the luminous caverns of his eyes opened wide upon the still lips of the singer . . .")

But what did Jenny do for Madonna, Mariah and Whitney and all those in between? Only this: For the first time in patriarchal Western civilization, she made the popular female singer a worthy object of admiration. When Lind sang "The Herdsman's Song," her voice could elevate barnyard sounds to the sublime. Men would throw themselves beneath her feet, but they'd never dream of drinking champagne from her shoe. She was not *that* kind of female entertainer.

Finally, there was a goddess who bestrode both high and low culture, whom anyone could be proud to love. And her willing collaboration with male-dominated commerce (though Barnum found her a tough negotiator) guaranteed her a stage. Neil Harris, Barnum's most astute biographer (*Humbug: The Art of Barnum*), sums up their groundbreaking partnership this way: "Every step of the way was prepared, every feature planned, every reception organized, every reaction nurtured. But his star was presented as the quintessence of spontaneity, lacking affectation or contrivance. Barnum labored long and well to bring together the various images—the modest girl, the benevolent philanthropist, the Nordic spellbinder, the shepherdess—but all were subordinated to the myth of simplicity, the image of innocence. It was the Spirit of Artlessness presided over by the Spirit of Artifice, and Americans loved it."

Barnum's diva would bring him his greatest financial gain, estimated at about $200,000. The extreme frenzy that surrounded Lind, a kind not seen until the Sinatra/Elvis/Beatles decades, would not find its equal with a female performer until Madonna. And Lind's ticket sales sagged once she and Barnum parted ways after some disagreements (he booked her into a pork butcher's shed in Madison, Indiana, quite redolent of its recent inhabitants). When, in 1852, Lind married her young German pianist Otto Goldschmidt in Boston, her popularity waned further. "Why is Madame Goldschmidt so much less than Jenny Lind?" wondered *Harper's Monthly*. Apparently, the popular audience preferred its earth angels untouched. Lind retired to domesticity in England, with occasional performances.

Soon after her departure, this country was plunged into the Civil War; when it emerged wounded and sobered, the most popular heroine—right through her work in the Johnstown Flood of 1889—was battlefield angel Clara Barton. Barnum had turned his energies to the big top; no showman arose to replace him when he died in 1891. Only technology, in amplifying and distributing the diva's voice, would come close to matching Barnum's achievement.

Certainly, we have traveled far from the chaste Nightingale to the accommodating tongue-in-chic of Madonna's Material Girl—or Britney Spears's sluttish schoolgirl. In this wide-open Information Age, we now celebrate Barnum's robust Spirit of Artifice (and its video goddess incarnations) for its own heady freedoms. The new "democracy" of Internet culture is certainly more specious than that of Emerson's Elysian America; today's realities are far more virtual than virginal.

Thus it makes sense to applaud the genius of a protean diva, such as Madonna, Annie Lennox or Missy Elliott, who can totally change her image with the release of each new video. The constancy that Americans revered in Jenny Lind has been replaced by the diva's ability to transform herself. And if, by now, the myth of innocence lies totally debunked, why not worship its shadow twin: irony. What was Madonna's breakthrough song? "*Like* a Virgin." The canniest of modern divas has been there and done it all; with the cosmetic sorcery of pixelation, she offers a full menu of iconic selves to click on.

An early rehearsal at the Beacon. A hyperkinetic publicity woman in a designer flak vest bustles down the center aisle; she tries to shoo the house photographer— her diva is NOT in full hair and makeup!

"I CANNOT HAVE THIS! SHOOT AT YOUR OWN PERIL!"

Whitney Houston is onstage, face turned upward, oblivious to the flap. She has asked that all voice-imperiling air-conditioning be turned off—didn't Aretha walk out of last year's Diva rehearsals when it kept blowing on those priceless pipes? And just now, Houston feels a breeze.

"I would appreciate your LOVE, while I'm here, to TURN IT OFF!"

She stops to listen again.

"I SAID I would appreciate your LOVE . . . "

Joining her onstage, awkwardly holding a vinyl tote bag and looking a bit ill at ease in her leather capris, is Mary J. Blige. She puts the bag down, faces Houston, inhales deeply and plants her feet like a middleweight challenger. The diva hugs her, whispers, "Baby, let's go."

Two bars into their a capella duet on Aretha Franklin's "Ain't No Way"— the program's tribute to The Ultimate Diva—gaffers are frozen to their ladders; chatty production assistants have clapped shut their cell phones and snapped their heads toward the stage. The singers are chasing each other up melismatic runs, moaning, then soaring, delivering the good bad news—Ain't no WAY there AIN'T no way, no wayay-ay!—in a mystical, reflexive lexicon that need not, cannot be rehearsed. Live, lambent and not-for-broadcast, it is the most soulful moment of the week. As the last notes die beneath screams and whistles from the crew, the women embrace. Both are visibly trembling, but after she towels off with a heather-hued chenille scarf, Houston has returned to herself.

"Dat's da TRUTH!" she declares from the stage. "My MARY! She know how to tell a STORY!"

Houston is still testifying when she flops into a seat beside me at the back of the theater. "We both came up on the bricks—you know what I'm sayin'? *On the bricks.* The streets that were—*not so nice.* Yessssss."

Ghetto realness is not a concept normally associated with Whitney Houston, who first skipped into the MTV universe in a prim polka-dot dress and cutesy taffeta head bow. Today, the lovely face is without makeup. Houston's nails are short, blunt and unpainted and her manner, despite worse press than Attila's, is relaxed and direct. A few rows back, a production assistant is clutching the current copy of *Redbook* which features Whitney on the cover, along with the umpteenth defense of her oft-stormy marriage to singer Bobby Brown. ("He is not a woman-beater," Houston insists in the article, "and I wish they would stop saying that about him." On her sometimes bizarrely effusive public behavior: "Sometimes people take it wrong. I'm out in public, and I'm really hamming it up, having a good time, and they are going, 'Hmm, what's wrong with her?'")

Sitting here now, Houston is secure in the knowledge that when she unleashes her live, take-no-prisoners version of Dolly Parton's "I Will Always Love You," people in this hall will stomp, cheer and sob. Handsome, volatile and vocally gifted, she is that classic diva—a creature of contradictions. She can blow the house down at will. But she cannot put out the tabloid brushfires that continue to flare up around her; within months national glossies would join the tabs with accounts of alleged drug "interventions" and entourage defections.

"Isn't diva a frame of mind, though?" Houston says. "This title worries me sometimes. It really worries me. It's the stigma that's put on diva that's not . . . cute."

If the stigma comes from without—the public, the press, "this trip they've laid on us"—Houston would like it known that there is such a thing as diva DNA, a natural woman gene, if you will. And no one has better bloodlines than Whitney Houston, who says her big eyes were trained wide on the divas who sailed through her childhood home.

"Diva means either a goddess, a prima donna or a very strangely insensitive overly bitchy person," says Houston. "I saw *all* these aspects." She laughs and admits that she got herself beaten up regularly in junior high for her ultra-nice clothes and the attitude she unconsciously zipped on with them. In the foreword to her mother's autobiography, she explained her early diva persecutions:

"The other girls were dressing down with their jeans and stuff and there I was with my plaid skirt, bucks and pigtails: my mother's version of Buffy from *Family Affair*. As you can imagine, in the mostly black East Orange neighborhood where I lived, my Buffy getup didn't play real well with the homegirls. At the age of ten, I was already a marked woman."

They chased her home, broke her glasses. After a failed attempt to mediate the problem through the school principal, Cissy Houston told her girl, "Whitney, sometimes you just have to be your own best friend. Sometimes you're better off just being by herself."

Concludes the adult Whitney: "My mother was right."

And in the Houston home, one was never alone. Women were there—fine, flamboyant, strong ones. Thank heaven, Whitney says, that the divas who raised her had one foot in the spotlight and the other in front of the stove. "Growing up with my mom and Dionne and with Aretha and Gladys [Knight] . . . it gave me the opportunity to see them at home, in the kitchen, with the children. Onstage and before they went onstage. So I got to see *all* aspects of these women. . . ."

Houston, who has a definite holiness strut to her dance steps and her delivery, is preaching now, arms flailing, head back. "AWRIGHT! WHAT MAKES A DIVA? She can bring the bacon home and cook it. Bring it on HOME, bring it onstage! And serve it up to a whole crowd of people. Those times were harder than they are now, there was a lot more pressure to succeed, to be number one. I saw a *graciousness* and a humility about these ladies that made them stand out. . . ."

Around little Whitney, the ladies dished—and cooked. "Gladys has cooked for me," Whitney Houston says. "Mahalia [Jackson] cooked for Aretha and Mahalia cooked for my mother also. It *does* go on . . . it does."

For the most soulful divas, the circle is unbroken and wide. When I ask her about the alleged contemporary diva wars—petty feuds fed and fanned by the media—she slaps a bony knee. "Oh, that Mariah business, you mean?" Before they met to record their Oscar-winning duet, Houston and Mariah Carey were rumored to dislike each other when, in fact, they had never met. They'd been in the same room at industry functions, darting glances over the icy perimeters of their respective entourages.

There is a tendency to view divas as purse-swinging gladiators. "Dueling divas" had been the VH1 promotional theme of the week as a captioned "pop-up" version of last year's diva show—larded with snarky detail about who borrowed more expensive jewelry, who wouldn't make eye contact with whom—ran in heavy rotation. Yet often the diva is hoisted by her own feather boa: Maintaining a secure perimeter can be perceived as aggression when viewed from outside the bunker.

"It keeps you alienated from people you might like to know," Houston says of the the pomp-and-posse that can attend divaship. "When Mariah and I finally met each other, we laughed so hard. We don't have to fight, we don't have to punch each other in the face—like some divas I know." She is referring to some recent industry catfights, drive-by disses between female hip-hop stars that could make a gangsta rapper like Ol' Dirty Bastard blush. "I've seen attitudes, *major* attitudes," she says. "I just laugh, though. I just figure, girl, you have *no idea.* I've been in and out of it."

She points out that she has been in it for fourteen years, long enough to conclude that maintaining one's diva status needn't be a blood sport. "We don't have to be *at* each other, constantly gnawing, like crabs in a barrel trying to get to the top." As she says this, a PR woman with Concern stamped on her forehead is still herding photographers like a border collie, barking peremptorily: *"Don't shoot!"*

The client rolls her eyes and laughs. "Have mercy," she says.

What does become a legend most? Arista Records president Clive Davis has cued up a contending Moment on the video monitor in his 57th Street office. He is still here, after hours, as he is most nights. "This is the part," he says. "People went *crazy* for this . . ." Onscreen, Whitney Houston, singing her woman-spurned hit "Heartbreak Hotel," is standing at the edge of the ocean; she takes off a white ermine coat and tosses it into the surf. *Why'dya do it?* the chorus moans. The coat sinks. *Ecce Diva!*

"Unforgettable," breathes Davis, who has more standout female stars in his stable than Barnum had elephants. A huge purple geode on his desk bears the message "Peace and Love, Whitney." His diva wall, an impressive expanse of black-and-white photos, features the bespectacled queen-maker with many of the female stars whose careers he's aided and abetted:

Janis Joplin (his first signing), Barbra Streisand, Dionne Warwick, Aretha Franklin, Patti Smith, Annie Lennox, Sarah McLachlan.

Davis has squired divas to the heights over the last four decades. There are other accomplished diva enablers—notably mega-mogul David Geffen, who walked Cher away from Sonny, Roger Davies, who guided Tina Turner's solo breakthrough and Jon Landau who predicted, then oversaw, Bruce Springsteen's ascension and has recently turned country ingenue Shania Twain into a leopard-caped crossover vixen. But no one can match Davis's depth of field and numbers. He is to the established artist what Sean "Puffy" Combs is to the waves of younger divas-in-training currently cruising the industry in fleets of big black Lincoln Navigators.

To be seen on Puffy's arm (as Mariah Carey has), to be produced by Puffy (as Aretha has), to be courted by Puffy's label (as Missy Elliott has) confers an automatic dollop of what Combs calls his Midas-like "floss." As a performer, Combs is hardly innovative, relying on heavy styling and sampling to get him through; in the same vein, he is far more of a packager than a producer—a committed, some say manic, detail guy. Gentling his protégé and girlfriend Jennifer Lopez through an early photo session, Combs reflexively put out his hand for her chewing gum; diva wannabes should pout, not pop 'n' chomp.

It was Davis who assured Combs of his corporate Daddy-ship, giving him creative control of his own label and a huge upfront payment. Though Davis is technically Combs's boss—Arista owns 50 percent of Combs's $130 million Bad Boy Records—Combs's aspirations go far beyond hit records to brand-building restaurants, fashions and talent agencies. ("I ain't foolin' around—I'm building assets" was the headline for Puffy's *Fortune* magazine cover story). With his straw boaters, his Hamptons parties and his Bentleys, Combs may be getting his name in more gossip columns; he may collect hip-hop ingenues like so many Amagansett polo ponies. But he cannot touch the boss's finesse with the most difficult and gifted of women.

Lady Soul herself called Davis years back when she needed a lift. Aretha Franklin was impressed with what Davis had done for Dionne Warwick, getting her hits like "I'll Never Love This Way Again" almost a decade after the storied Burt Bacharach/Hal David years. He found her "Freeway of Love," paired her with rock diva Annie Lennox ("Sisters Are Doing It for Themselves") and later, yes, with Puffy.

Davis has been criticized for the pop confections he's dressed some acts with—notably the early, ruffled and ruched Whitney Houston. But he is too smart a record man to interfere with an artist's inalienable rights to be edgy or extreme, be it Joplin's strident, unlovely blues or Patti Smith's Rimbaud-inspired stage trances. By his own admission, Davis is a nudge, a matchmaker, a collector of songs and talent, a tireless tummler. But talk to the artists like Hill, Franklin and Houston and it's clear they do not see him as an over-bearing Svengali. "He's a man who *listens* to women," says Lauryn Hill.

Then he goes out and sells them. Davis says that he has never met a diva—even the flower power–era Janis Joplin—who wasn't an avid chart watcher. And he is frank about his own Barnumesque aptitude for bang-ing the drum. Smiling broadly, he launches into one of his favorite war stories about the Making of Whitney. It was a two-year process so labori-ous, Cissy Houston told me, that she wondered what could possibly take so long.

Davis first saw Whitney sing when I did—during a set of her mother's at Sweetwater's. "I signed Whitney out of that set," he says. "I brought her on *The Merv Griffin Show* the week after I signed her. I introduced her for the next generation as someone—and don't forget I *had* Aretha and Dionne. So Merv had given me an open ticket to bring on anyone that I felt was special. And I brought on this nineteen-year-old girl. I said [on the air] 'If there's somebody for the next generation who would have the beauty, the lyric phrasing and the elegance of a Lena Horne and combine it with a fiery gospel church background of an Aretha Franklin, it would be Whitney Houston.' Those are my words—it's on tape! She did the song from *The Wiz*, "Home." Then we began the process of spending two years to find the right material and producers."

He is still hard at it, starting his own new label for Arista's German owner BMG after a much-publicized showdown with that company over its mandatory retirement. At sixty-six, he says he hardly feels finished. Now, Houston and Arista are at 105 million records—and rising. Davis has slipped a second video into the machine: miles of thigh behind a board-room table. Accusations. It's Whitney, scorned again but triumphant be-hind a squadron of approving sister survivors. The single "It's Not Right but It's Okay" is already "a monster" in Europe. Davis is waving the over-seas trades, rattling off numbers. "Give us a week's release here," he says. "We'll be chasing Cher."

A closed rehearsal—on orders of Sir Elton John. He has been the only diva to insist on them this week, the only headliner who ducks out of a limo without so much as a glance at the wind-chilled, cheering fans behind barricades on 75th Street. Now he is glowering at the keyboard; his single dangly earring shivers with visible irritation. Tina Turner has just tried to come back into their duet at the wrong point—for the second time. There is some miscue over a sax solo, and she looks exasperated.

"Fellas, I'm confused."

Sir Elton utters some less than noble eptithets. For a stout fellow given to waist-concealing tunics, he is up and gone in a huffy twinkling. Some moments later he returns, kisses Tina's hand and says that he wants to go on record as apologizing. He feigns a pinch to the iconic Turner behind. Aiiieeeeee! An unsettled mike shrieks beneath the tension of it all.

Troupers, the two plunge on, knowing in their hearts what will be announced shortly. No joint tour as previously planned; no promotional appearance on Oprah *tomorrow as scheduled. Apology bouquets will be sent to Ms. Winfrey and statements issued: musical differences. Jet lag. Facing each other, eyes flashing, they fall into the chorus of Sir Elton's old hit: "The bitch, the bitch, the bitch is back!"*

"Is 'diva' just a nice term for 'bitch?'" Whitney Houston had asked me earlier in the day. "Is that what we are?"

She whacked me on the knee and we both laughed. But digesting those record-company handouts, listening to the stories unspool into my Sony over the years, I have been struck not by bad behavior, but by long-term pathology clusters. Nearly every diva legend has some Identi-Kit heartache. Both Madonna and Aretha Franklin lost their mothers at early ages in Detroit; Bette Midler's estranged father would refuse to see her perform. Midler, like so many others, grew up an outsider—an eastern Jew in Hawaii; Janis Joplin had nothing but a zip code in common with the whole of Port Arthur, Texas. Drug and alcohol problems and faithless men dogged Bessie Smith, Billie Holiday, Judy Garland—and Janis. Ronnie Spector and Mariah Carey contended with mixed-race issues and the control of too-powerful spouses.

By simple virtue of her sex, the pop diva also comes from an historic underclass. And just as rock anointed mongrel male rebels—the poor-boy Elvis, the Jersey guttersnipe Springsteen—diva worship finds its idols in the least exalted neighborhoods. From coal miner's daughter Loretta Lynn to project dweller Diana Ross, most pop divas have populist, if not downright poor, roots. Celine Dion was one of thirteen children born in near-poverty. Dolly Parton was one of twelve; her parents paid the doctor for her birth with a sack of cornmeal. Shania Twain put all dreams of glory on hold to raise her younger siblings when her parents, Canadian loggers, were killed in a car accident.

The triple whammy of being born poor, black and female dogged even the most sophisticated ladies—the Billie Holidays, Lena Hornes and Ella Fitzgeralds. Their genius was unquestioned, but their market share was limited by both racism and cultural snobbery; artistically and socially, the black diva has always been a bit ahead of her times. It was rock, with its massive corporate airplay and crossover opportunity, that set the black diva at the glowing center of packed stadiums and Pepsi sponsorships. With rock, race and class began to take on an inverse cool: For the first time, being able to get *down* seemed preferable to movin' on up.

Thus voices from the wrong side of the tracks have delivered resonant diva anthems: Aretha Franklin's "Respect" thundering atop the tumultuous sixties, Tina Turner's "What's Love Got to Do with It?" eulogizing the desperately swinging Me Decade, Madonna's "Express Yourself" for the post-feminist nineties woman. Their wry truths, sung over steady bass lines, helped us navigate roaring social rapids. Diva democracy—the ethic that *anyone* can be fabulous—fueled disco, the most egalitarian of dance crazes. The music was synthetic and overwrought, and so were its queens, Donna Summer, Gloria Gaynor and those space vixens LaBelle. As drag culture flourished, from *La Cage aux Folles* to vogueing to RuPaul, every smart pop diva maintained a good-humored relationship with her loyal impersonators. It is no surprise that gay men should choose to burlesque their outsider position by preening in the gaudy plumage and haute mien of a Miss Ross— or a Barbra. Female, outrageous, loud-mouthed and very often black, the pop diva is the ultimate upstart heroine. And by virtue of that she is deeply, contrarily American.

Screams pierce 75th Street as the frozen, restive fans catch sight of Cher's headgear glistening at the stage door. She looks through an opening in the trailers, sees them and heads toward her admirers in what looks like sleepwalker's mode. Some are crying; some are holding copies of her CD Believe, *which, incredibly, has made Cher the artist with the longest span of hits in pop music history— thirty-three years between the platinum single "Believe" and "I Got You Babe." Earlier today she announced her huge supporting tour. She is telling a teenage boy,*

"Honey, it's gonna be plenty tacky, totally Cher. Giant lava lamps. Seventies shtick." She bends over an autograph, then looks up, grinning.
   "Anybody here think I can't pull it off?"

"Amazing, huh?" Moments later, curled in her diva-zone trailer with her pretty blond sister nearby, Cher volunteers that her outrageousness is often inversely proportional to her confidence. She's sure enough of her acting to appear onscreen looking like a nuke-poisoned dishrag, as she did in *Silkwood*. But she has never felt as secure about her voice. Feathers and leather G-strings can at least make it performance art. Hers is a very visual divahood. "I do it for myself," she says of the eye-popping displays. "I don't think of myself as a singer, I don't have that kind of confidence. I want to put on a *show*. I want to dazzle people. For me, everything goes through my eyes first. Even when I did 'The Star Spangled Banner,' I was wondering: *What should I wear?*"

She looks at me as though expecting some objection. But no—this is Cher.

"What am I going to do, stop being me?"

Being Cher has amassed a Q-factor I call the Cher Index. When a contemporary woman is about to slip the traces of convention, she can always ask herself, *"What did Cher do?"* Regardless of the "alternative" situation (plastic surgery? tattoos at forty-plus? much younger boyfriend? tattoo removal? lesbian daughter?), Cher has been there. And she's not apologetic: If unrelenting fabulousness also makes her a more conspicuous target, so be it.

"I am the perfect object; I'm a tabloid person's dream," she says. "Because I haven't lived a really nice neat tidy life. And because I seem so outrageous that anything you write about me seems like it could be true. If someone said Whitney Houston had her ribs removed, you'd go, 'That's ridiculous!' But if someone said Cher's had her ribs removed, everybody would go, 'Oh, you know I heard that, too.'"

More than most, Cher has tussled with the media-driven meld of public and private lives that now confronts the pop diva—and nearly any other celebrity. Inquiring minds want dish beyond the liner notes. Movies and musicals have probed the lives of Diana Ross, Tina Turner and soon, Janis Joplin. Cher was recently the subject of a campy miniseries (*The Sonny and Cher Story*) which she seemed to bear with good cheer. She says it's the day-to-day intrusions that have worn her down.

In a conversation we'd had several years ago, Cher told me that she'd just purchased the diva's essential kitchen appliance: a paper shredder. Those ravenous bottom feeders, celebrity garbologists, have long plagued her. Now she says it's only gotten worse. "I have to shred everything," she says now. And she acknowledges that both her mutations and her persistence may also give standup comics a reason to live. She is given to quoting a cartoon that asked what forms of life would survive after a nuclear holocaust. *Cockroaches and Cher.* But she's not necessarily laughing. "I still get really hurt by things," she says. "A couple of times I thought about stopping. And leaving this country. Just stopping completely."

The first time was over a mind-bending plastic-surgery item "about having everything from the cheekbones to my chin to my ass to my calves done. I thought, there's just *no end.*" The second time was when she was accused of acting as she delivered a tear-drenched eulogy for her ex-husband Sonny Bono, live on CNN. She says the media sniping afterward left her ready to finally roll up her tents. "I thought, okay, *fine.* You've always wanted me. You *got* me. It's over."

Yet here she is.

"But here I am," she says in a small voice. As I get up to leave, she has an afterthought:

"I'll stay as long as I'm wanted."

In the middle of the Diva Zone, a Japanese restaurant deliveryman is shouting at a security guard.

"*ED-A-MAH-MAY!*"

"*Say what, chump?*"

"ED-A-*MAH*-MAY."

Before things get ugly, a diva gofer appears to pay for the two large sacks full of salted soybeans in the pod—edamame. Another delivery man is juggling a hot bag of Virgil's jerk chicken. The guard is tracking its intended trajectory on his walkie-talkie. Says the chicken guy:

"*These ladies gonna eat you alive, man.*"

Is it possible to satisfy a diva's extravagant desires? The most delicious aspects of her lore are often in the details. If Hollywood fans clucked over the gossip items that had Myrna Loy protecting a peach tree from frost by draping it in a mink coat overnight, there is sizable interest in the 500 pairs of shoes that line Celine Dion's mammoth closet, her 105-member entourage, the personal putting green that led David Letterman to yowl, "Oh, stop! When I go bowling, I've got to rent shoes."

Conducting my own admittedly unscientific study of some artists' backstage-perks requirements did yield some surprises. Yes, Tina Turner prefers only white flowers in her dressing room; Janet Jackson's backstage area must be draped in black and fitted with a black leather massage chair. But on closer look, comparing male and female artists lists compiled by Behind the Scenes, Inc., a Los Angeles catering company, the men are by far the more finicky and outrageous. Aerosmith's hospitality list is miles long, everything from a live flat of wheatgrass to large packs of Dubble Bubble gum. The metal group Jackyl required Fat Free Newtons, Chips Ahoy, a wooden bar stool ("To be destroyed by artist") and "1 shaved gerbil (rodent)."

By comparison, the diva lists are short and tame: herbal teas, Snapple, bottled water, broiled chicken breasts. But woe to the backstage provider who doesn't understand *presentation.* At a Whitney Museum benefit, hip hop siren Foxy Brown requested that her dressing room towels be Versace—to match her gown. Whitney Houston's advance team once brought catering up short upon discovering that the dressing room fruit basket arrived naked. The walkie-talkie crackled with increasingly urgent dispatches and indignation: "We need plastic wrap in Whitney's room now! Is anyone listening to me?" Twenty minutes of frantic calls culminated in: *"Catering, come in, are you understanding that this plastic wrap is a priority?"*

There's no doubt that diva deputations are prone to a certain self-importance as well as battle fatigue; some staffers adopt an air of gravitas more appropriate to a PLO security detail. Houston says that she has cut her entourage in half. But she could not be without a fierce cadre of front-liners. "*They're* the real divas," she says, pointing to a clutch of hair-and-makeup types hovering nearby. "They're all divas. That's my hair girl, my assistant and my makeup. They have a diva attitude. When they're doing my face it's like . . ." Here she makes exaggerated painterly strokes, steps back as if to scrutinize a canvas. "They'll say, now SIT! This liner has to make a *point!* A diva should be like *this*. They have *their* concept of what a diva should look like. And they make it work for me."

As she says this, the decade's most accomplished Diva Duster is lop-
ing down the aisle. Makeup artist Kevyn Aucoin, here to enhance Tina
Turner's Alpine cheekbones, is at the top of an elite but wildly profitable cadre of stylists, shoppers and devoted to meeting our Divine
expectations—and topping them whenever possible. Some sought-after
stylists and makeup artists can command up to $10,000 a day. The
diva industry—from CDs to cable specials, from stylists to lathered
seamstresses and bellowing paparazzi—shows every sign of continued
growth.

A frail, sickly-looking young man is leaning against the brick wall outside
Tina Turner's trailer. He has been here for over an hour, chanting quietly. Inside, Ms. T is rehydrating after rehearsal, snacking on grapes. I am
telling her about a conversation I overheard waiting in line outside the
Radio City Music Hall ladies' room during her last tour: "I told my husband," one fortyish woman said to another, "'Before die I wanna see the
Pacific Ocean and Tina Turner.'"

Tina erupts into her deep *Thunderdome* laugh. I wonder aloud if she's
aware that fans—especially women—regard her as somewhat of an Eighth
Wonder, that even in the cool professional appraisal of her body I heard
between two veteran PR women during rehearsal when Tina tossed off
her jacket was amazingly free of cattiness. Is she that wondrous creature,
the truly Teflon Diva?

Maybe it's respect for age, Tina ventures, reminding me that she will
be sixty in October of '99. Maybe it's because during these last most successful years of her divahood, she's given them little to snipe about, living
abroad, chanting and meditating—and having more closets built. "Someone said to me, 'Why isn't there ever any stuff about you in the papers?'"
Tina says. "And I said, 'Well, I haven't done anything.' My life is not very
public. After *I, Tina*, everybody found out how my life had been. I think
they were shocked. But I'm very private now. I enjoy it. And I haven't
stopped meditating, because I know that's the way you keep it plain, so
that I *don't* have to go through all that stuff again."

She has spotted the shivering man outside. "Oh, he looks sick. What's
up with him? Please, somebody find out . . ."

We talk at length about what's next. Tina makes a few noises about finding some new way to perform—something not so wild and exhausting. She is not, she's told me more than once, one of those showbiz mules who intends to die in harness. Despite her flight from Ike, her world wanderings over so many years, she insists she is a natural homebody.

"When I travel, I am absolutely miserable," she says. "I talked to an astrologist about it, 'cause I was really suffering. And he said that, astrologically, I am a home person. I try to make the hotels homey. I immediately walk into a room and get security to change the room the way I want it. I miss being at home very much."

Tina would not officially announce her year 2000 "retirement tour" until some months later. But this day she is very clear about her unsentimental view of the rock and roll life and the diva's obligation to serve:

"I enjoy it once I'm right there onstage. But every night, for over two hundred days, to think that you've got to go onstage and have a party . . . well, since I'm not a party person, I see it as a party without drink for me. It's having a party with the people. And I don't crave it, no! I'm fine when I'm there, I'm on a mission—to give the people a good time, because that's what it's about. It's not about message or anything. It's about laughter and a little bit of dancing. And all kinds of intrigue. That's basically it. But I don't miss it when I'm not onstage. *At all.* It's a job out there and people always think it's fun. It's fun to a point, yes. I remember when it was more fun to put on those dresses and do the makeup and all that stuff. But when you've had nearly forty years of it, it ceases to be that kind of fun and magic. It's a job that you've got to go out there and do. And be successful at it. That's the mission."

So she has no trouble imagining the civilian life?

"Oh, I can, absolutely. I'm looking forward to it. I know I'm going somewhere else from the stage. I know that already."

Just what her diva days have meant to her fans is something she doesn't care to fret over. Her ageless smile suggests that we keep the analysis simple. Tina Turner is a fantasy, darling. And that's perfectly okay: "Sometimes I feel like I'm this little doll with the short dress on and the red lips," she says. "I know how I was when I was a little girl. I loved those women with the hair and the lips and the makeup. I do read the fan letters. They say, 'I love your high-heel shoes with the red soles. I love your red lips. I'm eight years old.'"

Outside, the chanting has grown feebler, and Tina is on her feet, looking alarmed. "Please, bring that man in here *right now*. Let's just see what he needs."

Showtime for *Divas Live*. Tina has come offstage radiant and glistening. Behind a flying wedge of security, she is making her way through the backstage alley. Suddenly the entourage is stopped and an elderly gentleman is ushered out the stage door. He is Sumner Redstone, chairman and CEO of the huge media conglomerate Viacom, which owns MTV, VH1, this event and all its merchandising tie-ins. Soon he will be co-architect of the biggest media merger in history, between his Viacom and CBS.

Redstone is in his mid-seventies, but his raptor vision has zeroed in on the Day of the Diva and her global appeal. He will declare bluntly at a trade forum in China, "There are three billion people in Asia and two billion of them are in the MTV generation. That's who we're after." Redstone and today's huge communications conglomerates represent an evolved species of boardroom Barnums, showmen in bespoke suits who still risk much but make more by banking on our desires to watch and to know, to broadcast passion in the form of a loud, lovely woman.

"Where is she?" Redstone can be heard to ask his entourage. A frigid spring wind roaring through the alleyway has brought tears to his blue eyes. VH1's Wayne Isaak gently propels the boss toward the molten center of all this cable and broadcast frenzy, and the old man smiles.

"Ah," Redstone says. "It's *Tina*."

Through the crush, Tina's trademark streaked mane appears; her face is still wet; the black knit dress clings damply in the right places. Redstone reaches for her. And facing the wall of glaring lenses, he has himself photographed, smiling, by her side.

THE ANTI-DIVAS

po-mo mamas and

heaven-sent bitches

I've recently started to understand that you have to love yourself equally, if not more. That's not something every young girl learns overnight. Maybe it's only after a couple of bad experiences when you say, "You know what? I gotta be happy."

—*Lauryn Hill, 1998*

Yo, are you trying to play me? Trust me, honey, you don't wanna go there.
—*Queen Latifah, admonishing a guest on her TV talk show, 1999*

I n many art forms, there is no creature quite like a Woman on the Brink, be she Medea, Sarah Bernhardt—or a fire-breathing MC. Whether she was pushed or has climbed to her particular cusp, she is a lodestar for imagination, speculation, adoration and investment opportunities. How she handles herself—she is, after all, a *girl*—is a subject for intense scrutiny and odds making. She is wise to be frightened, and wiser still to act as though she's not.

Given the late 20th-century girl boom, the pop universe is teeming with alleged Next Hot Things, photographed moodily before raging wind machines, heralded by pierced-tongued publicists who lard their pitches with murmured allusions to "the next Janis," "Aretha's true heir," or "a po-mo Debbie Harry but with Chrissie Hynde's guitar chops." My small home office cannot contain the aggregate of their ambitions; periodically, I must purge the towers of promotional CDs that arrive, unbidden, in attention-craving press kits: tucked into bandannas, cutesie fake boarding passes, velvet pouches, pop-up greeting cards.

The hype has reached such gale force that, as a rule, I don't venture out into it hunting for trendsetters. But, wanting to look a bit harder at just where a woman's compulsion to be heard can take her in this contemporary, female-friendly marketplace, I stopped and listened to the whisperings, the glossy blandishments, the expert prognosticators and, of course, the music itself. I wanted to find and spend time with women on the verge who seemed to have the right stuff, and the single-mindedness to get it across.

There was certainly no joy of discovery amid a clutch of post-pubescent Instant Divas. Candied, packaged and artificially flavored product such as Britney Spears, Jennifer Lopez and Christina Aguilera skew young and sell well; as the concurrent wave of boy bands underscores, teen throbs are a pop tradition harking back to Frankie Lymon and Brenda Lee. Though they're all empty calories, like Coke and Pepsi, they're here to stay—if only for a year or two each.

Amid all the pigtails, pouts and sexed-up school uniforms, there rose a stalwart cadre of what I'd call Ingenues Renewed. Women who had been singing and playing for a decade or more were managing long-deferred breakthroughs. At forty-six, Lucinda Williams had danced all around the brink for over a decade in lead shoes—record company horror stories, bad luck, her own implacable standards. Listen to her *writing* and you know that she wasn't off watching *The Jetsons* when Flannery O'Connor and Charles Bukowski came to the family home to visit her poet/professor father Miller Williams. Her mood indigo Southern Gothic is more Flannery O'Connor than Eudora Welty, her twangy tone poems are peopled with drunken angels and dark old souls driving gold El Caminos. In terms of perfectionism and, as some would have it, outright neurosis, Williams may be as "difficult" as Laura Nyro was; also like Nyro, she has seen others score bigger hits with her compositions (notably Mary Chapin Carpenter with "Passionate Kisses"). Long a critics' darling, Williams finally won bigger airplay and glossy magazine stories on the strength of her 1998 album, *Car Wheels on a Gravel Road*. But ever the good old girl, she also opted for decidely anti-diva venues like the 1999 summer concerts series NASCAR Rocks!

Williams is a witty and reverent arranger; she sings over Cajun fiddles, pedal steel, scorching blues licks. There is an appealing country patina to her sound that cozies up to her dreamers, lovers and losers like a bourbon-stained quilt. And, unlike the pre-fab shabby chic fluttering from home-furnishing catalogs and Garth Brooks these days, it works. The same can be said for gutsy, tireless up-and-comer Susan Tedeschi; when I met up with B. B. King's tour in Texas in late 1998, Tedeschi was opening with lambent, full-bore sets that made an ancient mode of discourse—the blues—sound like this year's model. As one of B.B.'s horn players put it, "sounds like that little girl been on this earth a *long* time."

Mercifully, some girls just wanna have fun. In the lusty tradition of rock's women of appetite comes an antic tag team, Cibo Matto. The first foodie rockers—complete with menu-like website and titles like "Sci-Fi Wasabi," "Beef Jerky," and "Know Your Chicken"— named themselves after an Italian saying meaning "crazy for food." Their choruses are carotid-blockers: "Extra sugar Extra salt Extra oil and MSG!" Cibo Matto's aesthetic may be as deep as those trays of plastic tekka maki displayed in sushi bars. And when I first saw and heard this Japanese duo (who sing in English, having lived in Manhattan for over a decade), I kept thinking of the miniature twin maidens in the *Godzilla* movies who magically summon the avenging gypsy moth Mothra with their shrill, unintelligible keening.

But, like certain junk foods, they grow on you. And their second album, *Stereo Type A,* was a concerted effort to distance themselves somewhat from the original tasty gimmick. Post-war Japanese kids have proved themselves intrepid cultural ominvores, trekking to gospel brunches in Harlem, importing low-rider Impalas customed by L.A.'s Latino car clubs. Singer Miho Hatori and keyboardist Yuka Honda turn out wry global pop, part hip-hop, part bossa nova kitsch, with bassline supplied by an admiring rock scion (Sean Lennon) and occasional guest walk-ons by his mother, Yoko Ono, and Sonic Youth guitarist Thurston Moore. While some divas are writing liposuction into their record deals, Cibo Matto moans cheerfully about gaining ten pounds on a European tour. Their favored mantra could have come from a punked-out Yiddish mama: *Shut up and eat!*

While Cibo Matto is enjoying the attentions of the art-appreciation crowd—notably a coveted appearance on PBS's series *Sessions at West 54th*— other girl bands are working toward a longevity that groups like the Supremes and Ronettes never enjoyed. To say some punk is maturing would be downright oxymoronic. But as their chops deepen, some founding riot grrls are learning to lighten up a bit. Most likely this is because, like Hole, they've learned to write and play better—well enough to explore and enjoy the notion of *range*. I confess to having found the so-called "angry girl" scene tediously self-limiting much of the time. Untempered rage, male or female, can be as numbing and one-dimensional as some knee-jerk gangsta rap; too often, posture is the only message, and that can slip easily into self-parody.

No one would ever accuse punk veterans Sleater-Kinney of going soft; the Pacific Northwest trio made ears bleed with their aptly titled howl of an album, *Call the Doctor*, in 1996. But since then, they have been admittedly spooking themselves with songs that skitter toward audible tenderness and pleasure; "Get Up" (from *The Hot Rock*) is actually happy. They're flirting with humor, parodying the whole rock-star persona in a mocking video "You're No Rock 'n' Roll Fun," for their spring 2000 release *All Hands on the Bad One*. In re-enacting those stark, lip-synching on a white backdrop eighties MTV pretensions, the band admitted they were making fun of themselves as well. Love, laughter, parody—it's all another kind of brinkmanship: "It was kind of scary at first to have songs that actually sound pretty," guitarist Carrie Brownstein admitted in an Internet chat. "That is not a place we've very comfortable in."

Discomfort is a long-standing rock essential; true romance can renew and startle punk in the way sexual terrors inform the blues. And tough sexual politics needn't disappear; on another cut called "The Professional," Brownstein carps smartly about the stubborn male hold on the music industry, delivers notice that all that's about to change. And the band backs the complaint with a half-minute segment rock writer Michael Goldberg called "the purest of rock moments . . . messy and loud and fast and confusing and truly thrilling." How to explain the neural punch of such a plunge—in this case, a duet of speed-babble over kinked, cramped and stuttered power chords? It's the long term catch-22 in writing about punk; try and pin a specimen to the printed page and it can dissolve before your eyes. The best I can come up with is a voluntary amusement park near-death— say, the thirteen-story free fall in Mariah Carey's beloved Disney ride, Tower of Terror. *Something* flashes before you. Is it your life? Just pure adrenal chemistry? Are we having . . . fun?

Such is the power—albeit spotty—of the hard-charging, reinvigorated anti-diva. And at Sleater-Kinney's record label, that rudely heroic northwest indie outfit, Kill Rock Stars, there is another sign that things have indeed come full circle: KRS has also released some cuts by original tough grrl Ronnie Spector. Knowing Ronnie, I'm sure she was delighted to find a berth amid the queercore bands and pierced Stratocaster abusers. One of her cuts was a remake of the Beach Boys' tender dragster ballad "Don't Worry Baby," first sung so sweetly by Brian Wilson in 1964. This time Ronnie was recast as the hard-drivin' competitor gently reassuring her lover on the eve of the big showdown. Maybe she shouldna bragged about her car. . . . Listening to the downloaded cut rasp and purr from the Kill Rock Stars site, I marveled at an odd but touching synchronicity I'd just stumbled into.

In April 2000, an assignment took me to Los Angeles for a talk with Brian Wilson. The third of a series of TV movies and docudramas on Wilson's troubled life—the parental abuse, the drugs, the bouts with depression—had just aired. Wilson said he paid that stuff no mind; he was working again, about to record a live album at L.A.'s Roxy. But he said the last year and his solo tour had been very hard for him. He told me he is still suffering from terrifying auditory hallucinations. "I feel like I'm hanging on for dear life," he said, then dropped his voice by way of illustration: "I'm gonna KILL you. I'm gonna kill you." That's what the voices say to him in the worst times, over and over. He says he talks back: "I'm saying 'Please, don't say that. *Please.*' That's a big word in my vocabulary. Please." When it all gets too scary, he explained, he retreats into some music. His own. But mostly Phil Spector's. There is one magic bullet, one perfect song. When he was young, it shot him through the heart:

Auto epiphany, 1961. Brian Wilson, twenty-one, is driving his 1957 Ford Fairlane around his hometown of Hawthorne, California; Judy Bowles, his first true love, is beside him on the seat. They are just cruising, silent and companionable, when suddenly, something huge, a thing that will change Brian's life forever, leaps out of the tinny dash speakers and hits him square in the collarbone, pins him to the seat. He can't drive, he can barely breathe, but somehow he manages to pull over as the Ronettes' classic "Be My Baby" —with its chimes, its strings, its achy wha-uh-ohs—fills the car and his suddenly roaring brain.

"I was just so scared of that sound I couldn't move. That *big* wall of sound. It's just very scary," Wilson explained. He has always insisted that he could not have crafted the Beach Boys' lush, layered records if he hadn't been thunderstruck by Phil Spector's productions, "Be My Baby" among them. And he told me there was a moment on his own tour last summer that he counts as one of the greatest in his life. Ronnie Spector walked into his dressing room in New York. Wilson was smiling as he told the story; his voice was softer than a prayer: "She sings, 'Be my little baby, Br-iannnnn.' And I said, WHAT? She said, 'I'm sorry but I *love* you, Brian. *Be my little Brian...*'"

For the briefest moment, it flared again, that Fairlane radiance. And the boy in the car?

"I came undone."

Brian fights on and frets for his life; Ronnie sings fearlessly for an outfit called Kill Rock Stars. The rock tides do toss up heartbreaking survivors. And just as easily as the music can close over their heads, it can buoy them back up.

But what is the strongest, the surest current now? By the late nineties, something interesting was happening, something far more radical, in its way, than the three-year run of Sarah McLaughlan's Lilith Fair, the rise of the female singer/songwriter, and all that diva fever. Headline copy has settled on "neo soul" in an attempt to contextualize this music—black women's music—that is both deeply personal and emotive. Like sixties soul, it pulls few punches; its directness is well suited to these confessional days. But it is shot with enough anger and irony to keep it far from cloying self-help cant and tiresome "empowerment" cliches.

Love wars are still the main topic; reports from the front, particularly in the relations between black women and black men, are not particularly encouraging, except in the women's willingness to confront age-old problems. Male rappers' jaw-dropping bitch and ho misogyny gets withering scrutiny. In many songs—notably Missy Elliott's "She's a Bitch" and Lauryn Hill's "Ex Factor," the strong black woman ascending finds herself in a dangerous no-fly zone, dodging plenty of flak. Writing in *The New York Times*, critic Ann Powers called these soul queens—Mary J. Blige, Destiny's Child, TLC, Macy Gray and Angie Stone among them—"the new conscience of pop music."

This is certainly true, but they also constitute a new economic power elite. Riding the strength of their art, they walk into boardrooms with demands Supremes, Go-Go's, even She, Tina wouldn't have dreamed of at such tender ages. They want their own record labels, production deals . . . Better educated in the arts of their deals, they've learned to hedge their bets in a notoriously fickle market. Macy Gray may be a talented anomaly—Hendrix-like outfits, a hennaed Don King 'do, a wacky, infectious little voice that can conjure Eartha Kitt channeling Toni Morrison. And she arrived on the charts full-blown—with a jeans endorsement. Having broadened her career to film (in *The Blues Brothers Two* and *The Cider House Rules*), Erykah Badu took the stage as an Oscar presenter in a towering acid-green turban and ensemble that finally took the heat off a surprisingly understated Cher.

Two of these soulful newcomers who most intrigued me—Lauryn Hill and Missy Elliott—are both singer/songwriters, but decidedly not given to the sort of Prozac-infused navel gazing of a Morissette or Apple. Their girl talk is wise, womanly and laced with incendiary wit. They can versify and diversify, making themselves at home behind the mike, or seated at the soundboard as writer/producers. They are primarily hip-hop artists and they are hitting that market at its phattest, big-money, crossover peak. Lauryn Hill would forge a now-mighty empire from the tiny kitchen of her parents' home in South Orange, New Jersey. Missy "Misdemeanor" Elliott knew she had to venture far from her home in Portsmouth, Virginia, to find her way.

Theirs are among the most direct, influential voices in this new century's popular music. Their journeys are just begun, their stars still ascending, the endorsements falling like logoed manna from nervous multinationals seeking to hitch their stars to an edgy, thinking 21st-century fox. And while Hill and Elliott may seem to have arrived at the speed of light—or a very high baud rate—their funky, post-modern fables have the same mandate that sent so many of their forebears bumping down that scary lonesome road: Trust your own voice. *Sing.* And go where you must to do it.

Hill and Elliott are *forward* in their mien, and in their songs. There is not—nor has there ever been—anything coy or simpering about them. They are women of appetite *and* intellect, one a maddeningly svelte young mother of two, the other an antic video Trickster who until recently did most of her shopping in the plus-size department. If Hill has been accused of piety, Elliott's rhymed diatribes can make ample, parent advisory–level use of the profane. Yet both are strongly, deeply religious. Their voices, while very different, speak toward the bold future of loud-mouthed, amped-up, beat-busting women.

Not surprisingly, they proved themselves world-class *talkers* as well. Listen to them tell their own stories and it's clear that their noisy urgencies were apparent at a very early age. All along, they were self-propelled; neither depended on the wiles of Svengalis and A&R smoothies. Their art enjoys no leisure of composition or production; it's breathlessly over-scheduled, assistant-ridden and cell-phone dependent. One must run to keep up with them. Bookings are frantic for studio time, photo shoots, manicures, trainers. The support teams—managers, lawyers, personal assistants, security, stylists, nannies, publicists, video directors and webmasters—would never fit in Bessie Smith's lush private railcar. (And it was big enough to stash a revival-sized tent pole.) And, like Joni Mitchell, Aretha Franklin and Madonna, Hill and Elliott are very much creatures of their times.

They came of age as very American girls, alternately confused, dreamy, delighted and mad as hell—girls who knew they had to leave home in order to find their way back. Born after the sixties' epic social clashes and assassinations, both enjoy the fruits—bitter and sweet—of the civil rights and the women's movements. They had working mothers and never doubted brilliant careers for themselves. Martin Luther King, Jr.'s, birthday was a holiday before they left grade school; by the time they reached twenty-one, the video age—ubiquitous enough to give them *America's Funniest*, MTV's most excessive and the uncensored police beating of Rodney King—helped show them just how far things still have to go.

Their album titles—*The Miseducation of Lauryn Hill* and *Da Real World*—speak directly to the maddening, and some say widening, gap between perception and reality, especially in matters of race and of the heart. Their takes on love and sexual politics surely reflect the differences in their upbringing (Hill in a stable, middle-class family, Elliott raised by a single mother after years of tough economic times and domestic abuse). They offer no pat solutions, but their conjugations of the problems are very . . . *advanced*.

Theirs, then, is cusp music. It is well suited to the Information Age, deft at dissecting the cargo cult worship of images it has engendered, rhyming its inconsistencies and celebrating its freedoms in bold, original videos. Lyrically, they are provocateurs; they suspect that despite all the data available, we may know less than ever when it comes to l-o-v-e. They also know the market value of their toothsome reality bites and have no qualms about commanding it. Never have I met artists so young with such bear-trap grasps of the business and their worth within it. And more than any artists I've encountered along these congested pop byways, they have always been in a tremendous hurry.

"BREAKER ONE-NINE . . . DO Y'ALL COPY?"

There she goes again—Lauryn, you slow down!—*leaning back on her banana-seat bike, popping wheelies and churning up divots in the small neat lawns as she leads a howling pack of kids screaming dialogue from that southern-cracker sitcom,* The Dukes of Hazzard. *Thwuck-thwuckkkkkk—they have pinned baseball cards to the spokes with clothespins pinched from Mama's wash lines; their little legs pump hard to get that delicious motor sound. Lauryn rides fastest, brakes last, scares her mother—and herself—to death. So many patches of ebony skin she's thoughtlessly left on these sidewalks in South Orange, New Jersey. So heedless, the skinny girl, doing backflips—over and over—in the junky, glass-and mattress-strewn DMZ that separates her middle-class neighborhood from the serious nabe.* Lauryn baby, use your head . . .

"Little black kids digging a show with Confederate flags all over the cars. Now what was *that* about?" Lauryn Hill is laughing about her *Dukes* obsession. She releases a boingy bloom of dreads from their ponytail as we settle on the front stoop of the small brick house she grew up in. "It started out on that concrete," she says, waving a manicured hand at the sidewalk bordering a neat front yard the size of the living room. She believes that all of her double-dare tendencies—extending right to the solo album that she is trying to complete—were nurtured here, along with what she calls her "off-the-wall" gymnastics. "I was a renegade child," Hill says. "I was always flippin' off fences."

She was—is—a mad showoff, she admits. And she was an impressionable child, even if the pop/cult icons du jour that thrilled her didn't exactly match the Hill family demographic. She loved *Charlie's Angels* and that fab Farah Fawcett 'do: "I was this black girl with thick kinky hair and I always wanted to feather it. And I couldn't, it wasn't even *possible*. I needed grease to keep it down. I was just *not* fly. I also loved the *Flashdance* era. But my mother wouldn't let me go outside with anything hanging off my shoulder." Laughing all the way, this true child of the MTV age takes us through her Madonna and Prince eras, "lace from head to toe . . . the rubber bracelets . . . ridiculous!"

Likewise, falling in thrall with the *Dukes* may have been a bit . . . perverse. But it was just one of the countless deeply infused American ironies that have made her such a witty, literate rapper with the Fugees—a versifier who can toss off lines on sushi, Bertolucci and manifest destiny with ease and savoir funk. Lauryn read; her mother, Valerie, was an English teacher. Lauryn watched; the projects were just blocks away. Lauryn had a *mouth;* she started rapping and singing at fourteen with a pair of older Haitian guys from the area.

Wyclef Jean and Prakazrel (Pras) Michel were seven and four years older, respectively. *They* had . . . ambitions. She was in it for fun. Between them, play and purpose found a workable synergy in a primitive studio nearby now known as the Booga Basement. The Fugees (short for refugees, honoring their Haitian and African roots) crossed musical checkpoints at will, playing *guitar* in front of hip-hop audiences, breaking into actual *melody*, referencing Bob Marley and Duran Duran—the Eagles!—and declaring in their music and their interviews: NO BORDERS.

It was genius for the then-dawning Information Age; the Fugees mixed operating systems (hip-hop percussion, rock guitar) and cultural icons with the speed and sly wit that also pushed Beck into the edgiest pop frontiers. Their approach—like Hill's solo work—was stubbornly full-circle, convinced a future is unthinkable unless it references and honors the past. And their sound offered blessed relief from the more tedious forms of rap orthodoxy dominating the charts. The Fugees took their appealing mess out live, toured with the speed and quick-hit cunning of a guerilla cadre, 45-gigs-straight in a "wack smelly old bus," rapping, back-flipping, riffing until Lauryn scared herself—again.

"I prefer the bus because we were all together," she says. "But it wasn't good for me. I did a lot of hurtful things to myself. I never took drugs or indulged in alcohol, nothing like that. Just overworking. I would work until I fell. Literally, I would pass out."

The Fugees' first album, *Blunted on Reality*, in January of 1994, caught the wild improv of their live shows but did not make much of a ripple. In 1996, their more cohesive second release, *The Score*, flew into 18 million homes and brought them a pair of Grammys. Now, in the late spring of 1998, as Hill is about to release her first solo album—much of it written and recorded while she was pregnant with her first child—she is the first to admit that hers has been a wild, bumpy ride—not unlike the bruising Batman roller coasters she rode at Great Adventure last night to celebrate her twenty-third birthday. On this sunny afternoon, she is telling me that the ferocious motion of her dirt-bike daze, a childhood both "sweet and tough" gave her the agility for all her cross-cultural street poems—and the stamina for the road.

"But then," she says, "it was time to come home."

These warm, greening days, Hill is busy spooking herself here in the cellar, which houses a newly completed recording studio. She is just weeks away from releasing her album. She wrote, produced and sang it in a mode so personal you can wring the DNA from the tracks. Listen to the few nearly finished cuts she's selected and meet Lauryn, a.k.a. L, a.k.a. L-Boogie, a.k.a. Mama (to son Zion, ten months). The Voice that flared out of the Fugees' remake of Roberta Flack's "Killing Me Softly with His Song"— a single that had even non-rap fans asking "Who is *that* singing?"—is on full display here. The timbre is alternately tender, tough, swaggering and celebratory, much like Hill's young life.

There is a passionate, churchy tribute to Zion that makes no bones of the fact that having a child out of wedlock, at a crucial arc in her career, was something plenty of folks advised Hill against. She did not identify his father publicly until recently: He is Rohan Marley, former University of Miami football star and son of reggae legend Bob Marley— and yes, he is still her boyfriend. He has moved from Jamaica to be with her in New Jersey. And in the interests of investigating that "deep manwoman dynamic," Hill is not above dissecting their skirmishes in a bittersweet love lament ("Ex Factor") that hies to the finest Marvin and Tammi traditions of soulful give-and-go. Much of her cant advances the agenda Aretha Franklin tossed forth with her 1968 "Respect." Hill's update? She wants "reciprocity."

Hill's tough, well-intentioned scrutinies are not restricted to male behavior. In "Doo Wop," she takes her sisters to task for sexual missteps and lewd video-ho displays. L-Boogie reasons aloud: Why flash your ass, and obscure the shining gem within?

To all the tender young girls out there in hard, non-African hair weaves and Korean manicures—babies trying to be Foxy Brown or Lil' Kim in the seventh grade—she warns, "Lookit what you bein'."

By turns reverent, sassy, street-tough and blue, Hill flashes the kind of flexibility that augurs a long career. But spinning out such an idiosyncratic piece so early is a risk: It's not the Fugees. It's not straight hip hop. It's not easily binned into any of the market's current shrink-wrapped categories. At the project's outset, Hill heard the familiar mantra of today's shaky, don't-rock-the-boat music biz: Follow the monster hit with another in exactly the same groove.

"The record industry reminds me so much of high school," she says, shaking her head. "You got the cool group of kids from this class. Then everyone else is categorized in relation to that cool group . . ." There is a certain safety in running with those hard-rapping, Chanel-logoed herds—at least for the moment. But, says the renegade child, she's had enough of the in crowd for now. "I never stood out on a limb by myself. It's really scary. But it's the dopest."

The album's title was never in doubt.

"I'm calling it *The Miseducation of Lauryn Hill*."

There is something you should know about the rough schooling of all these young rappers, Hill says—something curled deep beneath the windshield-shattering boom-beat and the swagger, something that belies the gangsta-tuff Gucci-coochie burlesque. Sure, hip-hop is by nature a very competitive sport—Hill has never been above drawing a little verbal blood herself. But take a closer look at the gladiators. They're killing onstage, but they're not shaving yet.

"There's a lot of youth, a lot of youth in hip hop, man," Hill says. "And naïveté."

Does she mean that they're shipped out unprepared?

"YOW! WHAT? You're talking about kids who come from Yonkers, the projects. Then all of a sudden they're at the *Mondrian*."

Trying to manage a morning nosh at the stark, edgy "community table" in that minimalist/chic L.A. hotel might flummox the preternaturally hip David Bowie. And there's a lot of zip codes between a wake-up YooHoo and a part-skim double latte. In the sixties, the Motown "charm school" known as Artist Development drew giggles from its Detroit housing-project Supremes and Marvelettes as they struggled to parse salad and fish forks. But at least Motown founder Berry Gordy acknowledged that he was propelling his young black hitmakers into foreign and often hostile territory. Early on, the Fugees boarded their bus with some of the same trepidation.

"It's like being completely and totally out of your element and pretending as if you fit," Hill says. "As if you belong. You're right, there's no Motown charm school. There's no A&Rs really who develop artists anymore. No caretakers. They don't nurture artists. They nurture hits."

And so it is that over the years, Hill has seen so many young ones disappear from the scene. They used to barnstorm the black college campuses together, "planting your stickers everyplace, doing all these shows, being at Howard [University] homecoming. And then you're not seeing these kids anymore."

She might have disappeared as easily, she figures: "I was a little smart-ass. I thought that I could avoid some of the traps and the pitfalls, but we're dealing with a monster. It's hard enough just to grow up, period. But to grow up in the music business? I always had my parents to fall back on, to guide me and keep me humble."

Thus Lauryn Hill has landed, only slightly bruised, in the land of *Vogue* and visibility. She poses comfortably in Dolce & Gabbana, in Versace; she takes meetings with the likes of director Joel Schumacher and regretfully turned down a role in Jonathan Demme's production of Toni Morrison's *Beloved* due to pregnancy. Teenage acting gigs (on the soap *As the World Turns*, in Whoopi Goldberg's *Sister Act 2)* have given her an appetite for tastier roles and a good ear for the slick jive of those who control them. But she prefers to take their calls from the comforts and security of home. South Orange is on the FedEx map, and fat packages of demos and scripts mound the hallway.

"I see a lot of people who use the road to keep things away," she says. "It's almost like running. And it's hard to stay connected [to home]. I remember the first time I left. When I came back, everything in my house seemed smaller. Yo, what is this, a dollhouse? Because I'd been in hotels with big couches, and big TVs."

Wisely, she has created a halfway house here in the ancestral home.
It's big enough to contain the phalanx of family and assistants, and too small
for any seriously inflated ego to balloon. Hill bought her parents a lovely,
larger house down the street and lives, with Zion and his dad, between the
two. This much-lived-in home is now part office, part hangout and definitely a work in progress. Woodwork has been stripped, new dentil mold-
ing hammered up, but an old NFL banner remains. Melted candles from
family Kwanzas past share mantel space with computer disks. In the back-
yard, Hill's Dalmatian cocks its head quizzically at the hum of a big new
generator. The whole house has been rewired and retrofitted with surge
suppressors.

Hill's current operation takes power—a kind of girl power that would
melt the Spice Girls' vinyl fringe. Power is good, Hill thinks, as long as
you're careful how you reveal it. She has a good girlfriend who, when she
sees a young woman hanging too far out there over the top of that fly leather
bustier, will say, "Girl, she's just showin' too much *power.*"

Hill's Book of Revelation is definitely more conservative. We've
begun to discuss just what *is* sexy these days when Hill's mother, Valerie,
arrives with a sleepy Zion draped on her shoulder. His curled lashes flut-
ter; baby dreads-to-be are caught and bunched with maternal fastidious-
ness. Zion inflicts a world of hurt on silk and suede; Mommy says she can't
get too attached to those pristine Gucci jeans now that there's always peanut butter on the gearshift knob.

As Zion heads in to continue his nap, his mother and I plunge deeper
into the issue of cleavage-as-signifier. Given her lyrics in "Doo Wop," I want
to know what Hill thinks about what I call the new Simper-Sex. It's practiced by that breed of Contemporary Female artist prone to making videos
in short, wet, boff-me shmattes, who moan and squirm their lyrics amid a
circle of dudes panting like Dobermans in heat. I'm fussing about the throw-
back, Pet-of-the-Month aspect—those onanistic Mariah Carey mouth exercises, the mile-long ooohaahhoooohs that would make Barry White reach
for the Viagra, the astounding, exploding Janet Jackson boob-a-thon.

Having suffered my tirade, Ms. L-Boogie grins her assent. She prefers not to name names and she will not judge her sisters. Except . . . "I *like*
feeling sexy, but I think my whole perception of sexy is different," she says.
"There's sexy and there's cheap. I think a lot of young women don't understand the power of mystery."

Worse off, she fears, are the tender things who haven't taken the time to understand the deeper mysteries of who *they* are: "They are the culmination of some *man's* fantasy. Instead of doing what they think would be appropriate, somebody says, 'Well that looks HOT on you, yo.'"

She thinks it can come back at you when the next sizzlin'-est young thang answers the booty call with a steamier video and triple-D sales figures: "After they make a certain image popular, they're victim to their own insecurity," Hill says. Pack yourself too tightly, too long in that red vinyl Versace bondage frock and you are a prisoner of s-e-x and mistress of no one, including yourself. Hill, who started off on equal footing with her male bandmates, who laid down her drive-by disses in both baggy jeans and thigh-skimming minis, says she's always taken a hard look in the the mirror before taking the stage.

"I think people took me seriously. I think people were also like, yo, she's cute. But I don't have any problem with being feminine. As a matter of fact, I like going from fatigue pants to a short skirt. I just think that there's a threshold and you have to be very careful. I've always wanted to be presented and treated with a certain level of respect and esteem. So I would never put myself in a position where people could deny me that—because you're receiving signals from my cleavage."

Today, as every day, Hill is showing understated girl power in black stovepipe pants, a denim shirt and high, high-heeled wooden sandals secured by the thinnest leather whipcord. Childbirth has not thickened the slim waist and long legs. Her appetite, as we head into the kitchen for some Italian takeout, is plenty robusto. Seated at the table where she, her brother and mom enjoyed her dad's countless culinary experiments, she tucks into an order of pasta, buttered chunks of bread—with a hot fudge sundae holding in the freezer.

"I was well fed in this kitchen," she says, "in more ways than one."

As an artist, Hill's greatest strength—besides the voice—is her flexibility. Writing and producing Aretha Franklin's single "A Rose Is Still a Rose" earlier this year, Hill led the Queen of Soul gently, gloriously into hip-hop idioms. She saw no reason to fear their age or genre differences. Aretha was just twenty-six in 1967—and the mother of two—when she sat down at the piano in a Muscle Shoals, Alabama, studio and worked out the matchless chords for "I Never Loved a Man," her first huge hit. ("Tell me!" Hill hollers parenthetically, "WHAT WAS SHE DOING—that woman at the piano—if not producing herself? She didn't get the credit, but you better believe those are *her* arrangments." It's a complaint Aretha also makes in her 1999 autobiography about her fabled early Atlantic Records sessions: "one point was deceptive and unfair: I was not listed as co-producer.")

They were very close in age—Aretha twenty-six and Hill twenty-four when *Time* magazine saw fit to run cover stories on "The Queen of Soul" and "Neo Soul on a Roll," respectively, hailing each woman as the avatar of a strong new music that spoke for an age and a people. Arista's Clive Davis put the two women together for that single ("A Rose"), which he hoped would continue the mandate Aretha charged him with long ago: "I am a working woman and mother and therefore I need hits."

Hill's plan was simple: "Working with Aretha, I wanted her to be infused in hip-hop, but also infused in the music of her past." From what she's seen, Hill believes that the most common pitfall in trying to work with a truly great voice like Aretha's is a tendency to gild the lily with nineties studio sophistications: "Even gospel in the late sixties, the blues scales, the chords they used," Hill says. "Everything was a little bit simpler than what it is now." And the production process itself was far less fragmented. "Now in music we don't treat it with the same synergy because people don't really go in a room and play together. So what you have is a piano player who's doing everything that they can possibly do. A bass line that's doing everything it could possibly do—these are the over producers. There's overplaying and outplaying because no one is together. Then Aretha has to come and sing over top of all of that. And it tends to not allow her to shine the way she should. She is just a pure shine."

What of the dynamic? I ask Hill. Who was zoomin' who when the queen and the avowed anti-diva jumped to it? "It smelled like church in that booth," says Hill, smiling broadly. "Like paper fans with sticks."

Hill had turned her attentions to another gospel queen just months earlier. Producing a song she wrote ("On This Day") for CeCe Winans, Hill went for a sound that was church and contemporary—and gave birth hours after leaving the soundboard.

Writing for herself, Hill knows just when to relieve sharp rap staccato with gusting melodic hooks and choruses. She is capable of clunkers (notably the regrettable rhyming of Al Capone, Nina Simone and "defecate on your microphone" on *The Source*). But on a mammoth subject (those sex wars) she can make her case with a pointillist's attention to detail and a facile knack for summing up: *How you gonna win when you ain't right within?*

Hill credits her catholic worldview largely to her father, Mal, a computer consultant who commuted to work in Manhattan. He would bring back shiny bits of street-vendor magic for the children—Chinese yo-yos, swimming frogs, battery-powered birds. And often he hauled his family back on evenings and weekends to Chinatown, Harlem, Brooklyn: "My father was very strange—in the best possible way. He exposed me and my brother to a whole lot of different cultural things. Like I was going to dim sum parlors when I was six. And I was saying, 'Yo, why can't we go to IHOP, Daddy?' I was having Chinese dumplings for breakfast, upset because it wasn't sweet or cold. There was a huge West Indian community around here. We met some African people, had friends from all over—Korea, Ghana, Haiti. It *raises* you. You have this real eclectic vision."

I saw a pristine copy of Creedence Clearwater Revival's 1971 *Creedence Country* on Hill's studio turntable. Lenny Kravitz was on the boom box upstairs; beginning the interview, Hill quizzed me with a mysterious few bars of doo-wop culled from her mom's righteous collection. Given her upbringing as a musical ominvore, she has always bristled when habitual classifiers call the Fugees alternative rappers.

"Where I came from," she snorts, "alternative rap was like no-skills rap."

Buy a Rottweiler, practice snarling in the mirror and mo-fo your mad self into a gig.

"I think we've always been experimental, we've been inventing," she says. We have emptied all the takeout tins with the help of her older brother (and website designer) Malaney. Hill's uncle Mike is on the phone trying to book studio time in Manhattan; Raquiba Sealy is frowning over the computer that oversees the Fugees' Refugee Project charitable work. And through it all shoots Tajh, a three-year-old cyclone with a world-beating fade. He is the son of Miriam Farrakhan, Hill's personal assistant.

"Miriam and I have been friends since eighth grade," Hill explains. "We had these boyfriends who were like ghetto superstars. They had a singing group and we were their girls." As the consorts of such royalty, the girls were expected to attend the guys' gigs. But there was no . . . reciprocity . . . "I was across town doing my little thing with the Fugees and they would discourage me," says Hill. "My gosh, WHAT ARE YOU DOING? Lauryn, you can SING. What are you doing? I went to all their gigs, but they didn't give me the same support. They were a little more cool and I was a little more . . . ethnic."

Valerie Hill is at the wheel of the family car—again—ferrying her teenage girl to another alleged gig with these wild but polite Haitian boys, one the son of a preacher man. Wyclef is in the backseat, finishing a full plate of rice and fish that his mama pushed at him as he ran out the door. Crash! Mrs. Hill hits the brakes. Whassat? Lauryn is screaming, "Clef! Whatchu doin'?" It seems he's finished supper and tossed his mother's china plate out the window.

"You CRAZY, man?"

They pull up to the place—another high school/community hall/church basement. There is Pras and oh, what a sight. Everybody else in cornrows, the man blows his head up into a monster Afro, grows springy muttonchop sideburns like some disco Earth Wind and Fire freakazoid. And oh mercy, no—tonight Pras is in a skirt . . .

"I called 'em ghetto kilts," says Hill, laughing at the vision. Miriam Farrakhan chimes in: "Pras wore a cape to the prom. With a *cane.*" Stylewise, this Fugee was a man without a country, says Hill: "He'd come in, all hip-hop on top, the big logoed shirts, alla that—then bell-bottoms. Like who—what *decade* you in?"

"Those skirts were wack," Farrakhan says. "Wonder he didn't get himself killed."

The girlfriends trade recollections of Pras couture until they are laughing too hard to speak; Hill is leaning on the kitchen counter, wiping her eyes. It has gotten rackety in L-Boogie HQ: Tajh is roaring like a lion now, phones trill, computers click and buzz. We retreat downstairs to the studio. The recording booth is dark and cool; we are sitting by the soundboard where Hill has been learning every button and toggle switch.

She wants to do more as a producer. But she has found that the respect she's enjoyed in the studio as an artist is somewhat diminished when she sits at the control board.

"Men don't do very well taking directions from women," she explains. "I think my biggest conflict is that I'm in a position where I give orders to men. And they have a difficult time taking them. For the sake of who I am, they want to do it, because they respect what I do. Something else is scratching beneath the surface. It has nothing to do with the music, or me as a writer or producer. It's testosterone versus estrogen."

We have come to the inevitable, bottom-line topic down here: *men.* I ask her: What's the deepest 411 from the heart of the battlefield? What do women want?

She does not hesitate: "*Tell the truth, man.*"

And do not *ever* assume we women know what you're thinking.

"See, perception is as good as real for some people. A lot of guys don't make verbal promises, but they allow women to *perceive* certain things. And then later it's like well, I never *told* you that."

She is on her feet, leaning forward in the shoulders-first hip-hop stance. Lauryn is breaking it down for you at my whirring Sony:

"Deal in honesty, man! And deal in truth. And those things will always come back to you."

Play those games, they'll come back at you, too.

"Karma's *real*, you know what I'm sayin'?"

Even when the love is clear, there's static on the line.

"My boyfriend tries so very hard," she says. "He really wants me to know how much he loves and appreciates me. He said to me, 'I think this is the first relationship in the history of relationships where the man has not hurt the girl.'"

She rolls her eyes heavenward.

"And I thought, 'Am I supposed to applaud now?' What is *wrong* with men that they always have to be in a position to hurt? Like it's a controlling position. I know I'm in control when I know that I can wreck her world . . ." She's laughing again. "Or bring her to HEAVEN!"

Don't get her cranked again on the man/woman thing in the Music Business. *Please.* Even Aretha wanted to know why she got into this producing thing when, baby girl, you *know* how they play you. Too right, says

Hill: "I used to do interviews with the guys, and they would ask Clef or Pras all these questions about music, and then they would ask me what color lipstick I was wearing. WHAAAAT? There is *nothing* in any song I've ever performed or written that constitutes this type of treatment, I've never sung a song that was like [she's simper-singing]: *and I wear blue eyeshadow and I love my legs* . . . NEVER! All my songs have something political just by virtue of who I am. There are *concepts!*"

The words have long been backed up with political and charitable works: camps for inner-city children, concerts to benefit Haitian refugees, relief projects in Africa. So far, the life and the lyrics match up. "People are always saying, oh, Lauryn, you're so idealistic," she says. In a day when many female MCs are turning the air blue with the frankest girl talk, Hill has publicly deplored cursing. Though her wardrobe has gone uptown, she has stuck to her dreads—albeit with the aid of ever-hovering hairdressers. She never does a show without invoking the Almighty, without leaning out toward the audience and exhorting them, "Stay strong!" She says she's got no problems with being branded a hip-hop Pollyanna. It's not nearly as annoying as the retro condescension—some of it unwitting—that she still encounters. There was the (now ex-) manager she asked to quit calling her "baby." "And he said, 'I'm sorry, baby.'"

So much to undo, so little time. No road maps.

"I may very well just go someplace for some time by myself," she muses aloud. "And raise my son. With his father. Just because that's the way it's supposed to be."

Retreat hardly seems likely, though, for a woman whose first pregnancy also incubated her best and most successful work to date. "I didn't stop at all," she says of those epic nine months. "I was on tour until about six, seven months—when I was big as a house, I was *out* there. That was such a creative point for me. They say your hair and nails grow. My mind and my spirit just thrived. The ability to write . . . everything came out like water 'cause all my emotions were right on my tongue. I was so in tune with everything that I was feeling. I was in Africa when I was like five months, working with some refugees from Zaire and Kenya. Working on projects with women, it was an incredible experience."

Writing may come easier at a time when your emotions are as engorged as your body. But the songs are not all doves and cooing babies—far from it. This is a woman who has also loved and lost, wrestled with disillusions of the heart and the business. She says she sees no reason to be coy about the autobiographical aspects of her songs. "I'm very intimate in my music-making process. I want people to know that shit HURT me. When x, y and z happened, I was in pain—*here's the song.* I've never ever tried to displace myself from the public, not at all."

She is at an age when time and options can seem limitless. There will be another Fugees album, she's sure. There will be movies. There will be more tussles with the big, loving West Indian man who is so different from Hill that her mother laughs just looking at them. "We always spar," Hill says of her life with Marley. "It's so funny because he's very attracted— and I think so were the Fugees—to my chutzpah. But they want to control. You can't put a lid on it. You can't tell me to speak only in one context. If I'm vocal, I'm VOCAL. This is who I am."

"HEY! It's ME! I'm just LAURYN! STILL ME, YO!"

Here is Lauryn Hill, not even a year past our talk, onstage in Manhattan, and on top of the music world. She is yelling into the sold-out crowd, fluttering against the dark stage perimeter like a caged raptor, hands flapping.

"STAY STRONG, y'all!"

Two fists up, dreads bouncing.

"STAY STRONG!"

She is. Lauryn and Rohan now have a daughter, Sela. She has power-lifted every award—Grammy, MTV, Soul Train, Essence—the industry has invented. Her five Grammys for *Miseducation* set a record for women artists. Within the industry, Lauryn would acquire the low-intoned, first-name-only currency of a Tina, a Barbra, a Whitney— though, as Houston herself reminded me, "My girlfriend Lauryn does not like that term diva. She's the anti-diva."

Despite Hill's vast support troops, the fashion spreads, the hot-and-cold-running "dread technicians" who maintain her natural élan, Houston has a point. On tour, Hill travels with Marley, their children, her mother, a nanny and an assistant. Hill's big endorsement contract is with Levi's, not Calvin. She is, by all accounts, hands-on with her charity for children at risk, Refugee Camp. And if, in contrast to some of the potty-mouthed female MCs, her anti-cursing statements come off a trifle schoolmarmish, if her dismissive comments on the messy, pandering sexuality of some of her hip-hop sisters has ruffled some maribou and engendered some catty backlash, she does not seem to mind. Having begun in a refugee stance, she cannot abide—or afford—to adopt a regal diva pose.

Staying palpably "real" is just as important to those other anti-divas, the self-styled "queen bitches." Three of them, Mary J. Blige, Lil' Kim and Missy Elliott, are best friends; they talk almost daily, cheer one another on and, as Missy says, "drop the 411 on men, money and *da business.*" For company—it can get lonely out there—Kim gave Missy a Pekingese puppy for Christmas. They have an idea that will make Lilith Fair look like a Campfire Girl roast: "We're talking like yo—let's do a *Bitch* Tour!" Missy told me. They are thinking small venues, big concept—a few select shows with the likes of Missy, Kim, Mary, maybe TLC—"even Whitney!" These bitches mean business, Missy Elliott says. They don't talk trash, they read royalty statements: "We realized that we're in a male-dominated field, and instead of being angry with each other, let's enhance each other."

With tongues firmly in cheek, they position themselves as ghetto fabulous anti-divas, girls who came up hard enough to know the score, and mad enough to try and change it. Street credibility is the root of their appeal and the genesis of their tough, been-there R&B and rap. Having found a way out, they are comfortable *out there*—and beyond. Of the three, there is no more anti-diva than Missy, dark and dangerous in her solo work and, in an age of video sylphs in vacuum-sealed dresses, totally against type.

Disco may be raging in America's cities, but not in hot, dusty Jacksonville, North Carolina, circa 1976. There's a Big Wheel trike in front of the Elliott unit in the mobile home community, but it's seeing little use. Missy—only child, military brat whose dad is attached to the nearby Marine base—has climbed up on the trash-can holder again; this raised platform that sits out by the road has become her stage. It's so hot the perspiration is rolling down through her tight black curls, past her ears, but Missy is dancing and singing hard. She's been out there for hours. Mama's worried.

Come on in, Punkin. Get some lunch. It's HOT. *In the child rockets, grabs some white bread, spreads some mayo on it and rushes back out to where the people slow down their cars, crane sweaty necks out the windows and call to her.*

Now ain't that a pretty child ... *When cars roll to a stop, Missy sings louder for the live bodies in the dusty Buicks.* One two three, easy as ABC ... *Then those cars creep on.*

Hey ... where you goin? Hey!

"I was the little chocolate girl with the curls," Missy tells me. "Everybody wanted to take me home." Twenty-three years later, in the relentlessly anticipatory, pre-millennial spring of 1999, Missy is a hot pink presence on street posters plastered all over Manhattan and L.A. "SHE'S A BITCH," they scream, and then, MISSY ELLIOTT. To her astonishment and delight, everyone wants to take Missy to heart—and to market. *Vogue* wants Missy; so does *Rolling Stone, Harpers, Vibe, The New York Times.* Today, she's more heavily scheduled than a Mideast peace envoy, and nearly hoarse with her efforts.

Alas, I am the day's final appointment. We have planned to chat on the ride out to her house, and then some. Missy picks me up in lower Manhattan in a car-service Lincoln; she has just come from the auto show at the Javits Convention Center, and she is positively bubbly as she describes a prototype computer-navigated Cadillac "which I was prepared to purchase RIGHT THEN AND THERE but is—unfortunately—still in the distant FEW-CHAH."

Moments later, she is asleep. Despite the honk of rush-hour Manhattan, mindless of the rap crashing from the dashboard speakers, Missy dozes on in the backseat—through Harlem, over the George Washington Bridge, past the tatty strip malls that announce suburban New Jersey. It is only 6 P.M., but she has been going full-tilt-Missy since 6 A.M., owing to the burdens of being hip-hop's It Girl. Missy stirs when the car rolls to a stop in the impeccaby trimmed drive of her rented mansionette. As her security guard punches in the alarm code, she looks momentarily surprised to find herself in this Tudor-y, custom-château-y nabe of moneyed orthodontists and fund managers. "A lot of the time," she says, "I don't feel like I really live here."

Missy is wide awake now and smiling—a trifle lopsidedly, due to this morning's root canal work—as we walk into the dark, echoing house. "You want to get to the heart of the mess?" she says. "Well, come on—if you think you can stand it." Missy leads the way up the grand front staircase, down the hall, through her master suite with the huge black-and-white deco-style bed and its yin-yang motif, past a marble bath that could float Cleopatra's barge. She turns us toward "the Matrix"—her closet.

Understand, this is no ordinary clotheshorse. This is Missy "Misdemeanor" Elliott who first blew a crater in clichéd hip-hop video in 1997 by becoming Supa Dupa Fly in an inflatable vinyl suit and goo-goo glasses —an effect so eye-popping the suit has already been boxed and sent to the Rock and Roll Hall of Fame. And then there's her latest video incarnation for the debut single of her new album, *Da Real World*. Meet Missy "She's a Bitch" Elliott, two sizes and six waistline inches leaner and meaner now, spray-painted blacker, bald, stomping, snarling and vacuum-packed into a bodysuit accessorized with a spiked G-string that signifies this: Any unauthorized entry will leave male intruders fit to replace Bob Dole in those erectile dysfunction ads. This is mondo Missy, a video mannequin so fearless she shares a stylist with Busta "Watch My Freakin' Face Melt" Rhymes, so resolutely *not* off-the-rack that she had to get Marilyn Manson's tailor-of-terror to whipstitch the "Bitch" dominatrix togs. Two sets of custom tailors on each coast are kept in a lather by Missy's mad morphs.

"You sure you wanna do this?" Missy says. The big door creaks, and finally we're in. Missy's closet is neat as a drill sergeant's, double-hung with racks of leather, suede, satin and nylon shirts, jackets and pants that have nothing scary about them except for the credit-card bills. No dresses. And against every wall , in quadruple rows, is evidence of Missy's deepest and most anti-diva addiction: sneakers. Spiderwebbed and swooshed, striped and netted, pumped, bubbled, hologrammed, iridescent, fluorescent, waffled-treaded, fancy-laced and Velcroed. Vietnamese sneakers brought back from Hong Kong by the head of Elektra records and Missy's champion, Sylvia Rhone. Prada sneakers. Missy admits to a serious Foot Locker habit; she has been known to sidle away from a photo shoot or a studio session for "a little air." As in Nike Air. "Wait a minute," she says. "I *know* I've got some hard soles. Some real shoes."

We find three pairs of clunky boots with hard soles that look virtually unscuffed. This is a woman who wore sneakers—albeit dressy white ones—to the Grammys when her debut album, *Supa Dupa Fly*, snagged three nominations. "This is just Missy," she says, waving her arm at the rows of comfy casuals. And Missy, she'll point out more than once, is "a sweet person," shy, deeply religious, a mama's girl, and, if you must know the truth, not at all crazy about performing her hallucinatory hip-hop live.

"She's a studio rat," says Sylvia Rhone, who has been trying to pry Missy out and onto the stage for a solo tour, with little success. "She *lives* in the studio. She's not a big social person. Her home is her music, her safe place is her music. That's the way she rolls." This Missy is terrified of touring, apalled by the strangeness of the road, the unfamiliar food.

"I don't go overseas much," Missy admits. "They have to tug me. The only thing I'm cool with is McDonald's over there. I get to Rotterdam, I'm thinking *Diff'rent Strokes* is on and I turn on the TV and it's ..." [Here, Missy does her glottal impression of a foreign language.] "Oh noooooo." Even in the continental U.S., she finds herself assailed by escalating Otherness. She is what friends describe as a "suspicious" eater. Out to dinner at the China Grill in Miami with Elektra label-mate Busta Rhymes and Rhone, Missy drew hoots by recoiling from the platters of Asian chews piled on the table, wondering aloud, "Where the pork chops at?"—and stopping by Wendy's afterward for a carbo fix.

So who *is* that loud, larger-than-life Missy cracking incendiary femme raps like bullwhips? (*She's a bitch!*). Who was that visionary hailed in *The New Yorker*'s 1997 Future issue as the latest, edgiest embodiment of the New Negro? How to explain the powerhouse Missy, that queen-size meteor who has so impacted the Hot 100 landscape as a writer and producer that Whitney, Janet, Mariah and even Scary Spice made her cell phone jump with urgent pleas for her infectious songs, her off-the-hook remixes? Who is this self-possessed, self-sufficient Missy, a woman so I'll-Get-My-Own that even Puffy couldn't sign her (he tried), even mighty Sony with its heaps of "mad, mad money" on the table couldn't land her? (She held out for her own label, the Gold Mind, Inc., as part of her deal with East/West Elektra.) And who, at twenty-seven, has become such an industry player that they're calling her Puff Mommy?

"Aw, that's *MISSY.*"

Even the woman at the center of the conundrum speaks her own name two different ways when she refers to herself in the third person. And she does that often. "Just Missy" is spoken in a soft, quiet voice. *MISSY,* all caps, italicized and with a slight hiss, is her handle for the inflatable character

Missy. The signifying Missy. As in hey, there goes *MISSY*. You seen *MISSY*'s latest? Whoa, that *MISSY*. *Damn.*

"That is the character Missy, the funny Missy," she says as we settle down in her large, echoing media room. "And in every one of my videos, I think every director has captured that side of Missy." Those cartoony manifestations get boxed up with the suits and archived. And just Missy stays home a lot "with my cousins" (one of whom is her assistant and trusted sounding board).

Talk to Missy—for five minutes or for hours—and the conversation never lags on her end. Like her music, her thoughts hop, leap and take odd turns but always come back to the beat. Her talk is punctuated with a deep, easy laugh and signature Missy-isms—like replacing blah, blah, blah with blasé blah. Whenever you are with her, and wherever, there is a sense of anticipation: *What's next?* There is always peripheral activity; a cousin, a pal, a publicist, a stylist stands waiting. Just now it's Missy's hairdresser Marsha, who has arrived on yet another emergency house call: Puffy party tonight! *Girl, fix this head. Pull-eze.*

Sitting beneath a framed gold record for her girlfriend Lil' Kim's "Not Tonight"—featuring one of Missy's standout guest appearances—Missy explains that the two Missys are a reasonable way of coping with her own entrenched insecurities about her size, her sexuality, her "way different" self. *MISSY* can bigfoot through scary landscapes, using humor and futuristic burlesque to get the job done. *MISSY*—big, off-the-wall and uncompromisingly black—is a genius piece of outsider art. *MISSY* was just the answer for that debut solo video "The Rain (Supa Dupa Fly)." She explains: "I felt, I'm not that skinny girl that makes guys run to the TV and be like, 'Whoa, you see her? She looks hot!' I wanted something that was going to catch their attention and be fun. But totally different."

Just Missy gets her props the old-fashioned way: She earns them. In the studio, engineers slide over and give her the controls. Acts she is producing/writing for—notably her Gold Mind protégé Nicole Ray—get the full treatment: guide tracks with vocals laid down by Missy and a personalized mix with Missy's silver-lacquered nails clicking the soundboard toggles. This Missy, says Rhone, "is really serious. She's structured her business affairs so she's not in it for floss. She's in it to provide for herself for the long run. The day we did our deal, Missy signed Nicole. Within a month she'd signed two acts; within six months we released one."

On a soundstage, the game-for-anything Missy is a video director's dream, according to Hype Williams, who did "The Rain, " "Sock It 2 Me" and "She's a Bitch." It's not your average hip-hop ingenue who will clomp to a Queens gas station in a stylized trash bag and let whooping attendants pump her up. Williams says his star was a bit edgy—until he hollered "action."

"When she got in front of the camera with all of this weird shit on, it was no problem. All of a sudden she became who she is now in everybody's hearts. I'm telling you, she's a very *advanced* person," Williams says, laughing. "You're not going to find that many young female artists that are going to go in any direction that's outside of what's typical. Typical beauty, typical fashion, style. Missy is like a Madonna for rap music, how Bjork is for alternative. She just *thinks* different."

This has not always been an asset in an industry with the mind-set of a thundering wildebeest herd. Missy says she has written contrary, quirky little "story songs" since high school, irritating and frightening her mother by scrawling them on the walls or the floor whenever something hit. The four minute tales are cobbled from scraps of overheard arguments, quiet sobbing in the girls' room, from backseat love wars. Missy's style is more wryly observational than deeply personal; like Ethel Waters composing blues for her alter-ego, Sweet Mama Stringbean, Missy decodes the runes of black American graffiti from yes, *Da Real World.*

At first, when nobody would buy her reality bites, Missy struggled to come up with what the record companies seemed to want, the quivering-thigh, do-me-in-your-Lexus crap. "I tried," she says. "The trash can would be full. Lyrically, it wasn't satisfying to me. I was telling myself, *somebody's gonna like what I do.* It was so different, yet it was so *hot.*"

Hot for Missy usually means upside down and backward, a view of modern sexuality through a mirror cracked. She has elements of Josephine Baker's playfulness and Grace Jones's sly predation, can brag about bringing a cute guy home and "turning him out" yet sound tender to the bone when she's doing it. In terms of her look and her lyrics, Missy Elliott is also a true daughter of Bessie Smith—that woman of appetites. But Missy would also have it known that she is a woman with a certain *taste.*

To wit: She loves men but has no time for their bullshit. By way of example, she offers a new favorite of hers, "We Did It." On the surface, it's a very old story: A guy beds a girl but, the morning after, won't admit it to his friends—won't be linked with her in any way. In Missy's song, that girl turns around and tells the world, pinning the chump to the wall for his hurtful hypocrisy. This reverse kiss-and-tell is a risky but just retribution. And Missy is laughing at the idea of it. "I'll say about ninety-eight percent of girls have been through this. A girl may have had sex with a guy and his friends ask him did they have sex. And he say, 'Naw, I never kissed her.'" [Here, Missy adopts a male chump voice.] "'I never even been over her house.' And when his friends are gone it's like [girl's voice now] 'You made me believe you love me and you really didn't. You can't even like me enough to admit you had some kind of feelings for me. You can't even say we did it.'"

So *this* girl will say it; she'll buy a billboard if she has to. Missy says her little story is part of a larger sea change. "Women seem strong in [my] songs because that's not just a song anymore," she says. "This is what we experience in everyday life, in business, relationships, whatever. Females are starting to be a lot stronger and have self-confidence. Like, 'I don't need you, I'm going to get my own—my own job, my own money. You want to leave, leave. You cheating on me and you think I'm going to stay here? No! I have my own stuff now, so you gotta *go*.'"

Does this sound like a ...

"Bitch! That's a bitch in a positive way to me," she says. "'Cause I think we took so much for so many years, we've been behind the males. Now you go to awards ceremonies, you see more females up for awards. Everything is just a switch. The ladies are coming *through* now."

It's been a long road to Missy's particular emancipation. The blues always stated the case clearly, but often with a degree of resignation. Female soul music was frank in its explorations of the joys of sex, in relaxing into Aretha's Natural Woman. It could demand R-E-S-P-E-C-T, could scold. But hip-hop, with its community roots, its gladiator showdowns and town-crier stance, has gone so far as to declare female independence, from Queen Latifah's "Ladies First" to the cartoony bedroom braggadocio of Lil' Kim.

Da Real World is a good deal darker and a lot raunchier than Missy's *Supa Dupa Fly*. Glock-toting, Benz-cruising Lotharios are parodied in "Hot Boyz"; treacherous, man-swiping women square off in a lewd, high-noon set-to called "You Don't Know"; a practical girl states her case clearly in

"All in My Grill": "*Will you pay my bills?*" Taken as a whole, the record has the bleak, sinister landscape of a Chester Himes novel, streetlights glinting off dark skin and blue steel, diamonds and chrome bumpers. Missy, ever the Trickster, leavens the cuts with her cowboy yips, with gusting classical strings and guest artists who pop up like rowdy wedding guests, drop a crisply rapped bomb and disappear.

Ask Missy where she's found the strength to push the envelope and she points homeward, to a petite church lady. "Just growing up, watching how my mother handled stuff. Watching my mother take a stand as far as leaving my father. Saying *This is it!* Just being that powerful woman, that single parent just made me aware."

Missy still lives with her mother; she has built a new house for them in Portsmouth, Virginia. ("Twelve thousand square feet and just this ridiculous Yorkshire terrier to watch over it.") This New Jersey house, with its soaring ceilings, its Gibraltar-sized entertainment unit with three blabbering TV screens, the mirrored animal sculptures, the sleek bar and party room, is "temporary" and not exactly a home. There's no food in the kitchen (Missy's dieting). Not even a magazine tossed about (she doesn't read them). Never a party here (she's always working). And the sweet blue Jaguar parked between the SUV and the Mercedes? She laughs. "*That's* Missy. I do love cars."

The house is beginning to fill. A passel of little boys—Marsha's sons—is playing pool with Missy's security guard, Rich Barnes. As I head for the door, Missy pulls her wallet out and extracts a color photo of a pretty smiling woman. The condition of the print indicates it's well traveled and often handled. "There she is," Missy says. "My mom."

If you want some clues to the mysteries of Missy, you must speak to her mother, Patricia, who raised her only child alone from about the time Melinda "Missy" Elliott was fourteen, and still speaks to her baby a few times a day, *no matter what.* Mrs. Elliott recently quit her job as a dispatcher for a Virginia power company after twenty-one years; now she helps management keep an eye on Missy's burgeoning empire. Every morning, she flicks on the computer in their Portsmouth home and tracks the arcs of her daughter's earnings and credit-card accounts. She is not afraid to ask aloud, with love and concern, "Punkin, how many times do you have to go to Foot Locker *in one day?*"

Pat Elliott is not a sneaker person; as a working mother, she tried on her next day's outfit every night, with her daughter staring, enthralled, on the bed. Sitting in a conference room at Missy's record company, Mrs. Elliott is the picture of considered coordination in a vibrant orange suit accessorized by an abstract print bag and shoes and diamond and platinum love tokens—brooch, bracelets—from her famous baby girl. It all feels great, but there are odd moments: "When she pulled up one day in this long stretch limousine, I'm like—is that my daughter? We rode around in these old beat-up cars, we'd patch them together. We almost *built* a car. . . . She shows me her videos, we sit in the den and watch them. I look at the video and I look over at her and I'm like '*Is this a dream? Am I going to wake up?*'"

So many times, she's asked herself where it all came from. But the more she thinks about it, the more she realizes that both Missys grew up under her roof. During an afternoon's talk, she turns up vivid Missy moments. Some you'd want to press in a scrapbook. Others, any mother might like to forget.

Missy's stories about singing on the trash cans? True, all true. Pat Elliott says her daughter was a born ham who asked for more and more dolls—only so that she could build her bedroom audience, meticulously lined up on the bed. Mrs. Elliott would peek in, expecting to see Missy doing their hair, changing them. Instead she was doing stage patter. Prekindergarten, the child had mike technique. On the long drive up to Virginia to visit her aunt and cousins, she'd mentally rearrange her material—a whole slew of songs and soul shtick that had the family begging off after a bit. Missy pitched fits. *I'm not done yet!*

"She was very smart," Mrs. Elliott says. "When she was in elementary school they took tests. Her IQ was so high they sent someone from Richmond down to give her another test. Because it was like a genius IQ. Then they skipped her two grades, from the second to the fourth." Missy, always a class clown, was devastated to find herself among older kids, all strangers. Her grades fell until her mother pleaded for her to be returned to her same-age friends, with some extra work. It wasn't the kind of school with a big budget for gifted and talented kids. And at home, there were harsher lessons. The marriage was not a good one, though it staggered along. Missy's father had left the Marines and brought his family back to Virginia with very few prospects.

The last tank of heating propane—bought with the last military paycheck—has run out. The old rented house in this damp coastal city is cold, and at night, civilian Elliott wraps his wife and daughter in military-issue sleeping bags. Missy falls asleep with him sitting sentry, mummy-like in his bag. And all night she hears him, feels him—thwack! thwack!—knocking the marauding rats off his family, rats so wily, so relentless, that Missy learns to lock the bread in the clothes dryer.

Mrs. Elliott concedes that her daughter's eating habits, which are still atrocious, probably didn't get off to the greatest start: "We'd take something like thirteen dollars and go to the grocery store, get bread, pork and beans and hot dogs. We'd butter the bread and put it in the oven for breakfast. For lunch we'd take the bread and put on some jelly. And for dinner we would take the hot dogs and beans."

As Missy hit adolescence Mrs. Elliott finally decided to leave the marriage: "The relationship I had with Missy's father, he was the one that always made the decisions. I was the one who went to work. I was a woman who believed that you go to work, you put your money in the bank, you let your husband run the show."

Neither Missy nor her mother would even divulge Mr. Elliott's first name, though Pat conceded that Missy sees him occasionally. But coinciding with the release of *Da Real World* is the debut of a new Misdemeanor lipstick, a peachy shade that Missy favors, marketed by model Iman's cosmetic company. Proceeds will benefit Break the Cycle, a nonprofit organization devoted to helping children and teenagers cope with the effects of domestic violence. "I went through the abuse between my mother and father," Missy explains in a promotional tape for the lipstick. Mrs. Elliott, without detailing the incidents, told me that Missy insisted over and over, "Mommy, we've *got* to get out." And when she finally packed Missy up and left, she says she didn't even know the basics: "how to balance a checkbook, doing your taxes, the whole thing. I kept saying I don't know if I can do it. My sister said you've gotta do it because of Missy. She saw that she was really sad."

But Missy was a dogged cheerleader. Says her mother: "Missy could feel how afraid I was. She was always behind me like, 'Ma, we can do it.' She was young, but she had an old person's mind. We'd sit on the floor and roll those penny things up." She says Missy found discount beauty supplies, the cheapest food ("Oodles of Noodles, four for a dollar, Mommy!"). Her mother laughs about some of their joint misadventures, but recalling her own panic is difficult, and a few times during our talk, she stops to compose herself. At one point—it being a few days before Mother's Day—I suggest a break and read to Mrs. Elliott from a transcript of my earlier conversations with her daughter. Within minutes of our having met for the first time, Missy had told me this:

"There's no one else like my mother. If anything would ever happen to her, I couldn't go on. That's like my heart right there [she thumped her chest]. That's my joy, my peace, my happiness besides God. If I'm going through something I can call her. I don't necessarily have to tell her what I'm going through. Just hearing her voice—it's so calming and relaxing. It's like *ahhhhhhh*. I'll just be like, 'hey, Mommy.' She'll be, 'Hey, Punkin.' She doesn't know that she's totally changed my whole mood. And I'll be like, *Now I'm okay.*"

To my astonishment, I choke up halfway through this little recitation; Mrs. Elliott is beyond help after the first sentence. All she had wanted to do, she says through a handful of tissues, was keep her girl safe. The kiddie show-business stuff, she reasoned, was Missy's little coping mechanism—a fairy dream to block out the things she'd rather not hear or see. But strangely— and a bit alarmingly—Missy's fantasies persisted long after mother and daughter were safely on their own. One day just as she was leaving work, Pat Elliott's boss chased her down in the parking lot. Missy was on the phone; it sounded urgent. "I pulled back in, ran in the door, picked up the phone and she says, 'Mom, can you get me a stamp? I want to write to Janet Jackson.'"

Having mailed countless letters to both Michael and Janet Jackson begging them, "Come get me out of school," Missy daydreamed in class, sure they'd pull up any minute and bear her away. With her mother working, Missy spent a lot of time with her aunt and cousins. It was a house with plenty of food. And whenever any one of them went into the kitchen, Missy seemed compelled to keep them company there and have a little something. At home, she'd come in at midnight, load up a plate and take it up to her room to watch TV. Scolding didn't help.

"She always thought that she wasn't pretty," says Mrs. Elliott. "She was big, she was heavy, she had the mentality that if she wasn't a real light-complexioned person or a very petite person, that she would rather stay in the background because she wasn't what people were looking for . . ." Mrs. Elliott tears up again when she recalls seeing Missy being interviewed on TV with her first girl group, Sista, hanging back and calling herself "the black sheep" with such sad bravado that the interviewer yelled back at Missy: "Don't *ever* say that. You are pretty!"

For so many years, her mother told her the same thing: You're beautiful. But she's hidden in baggy clothes, in dark recording studios. Pressed for a theory on Missy's spectacular bust-out—those neon jumpsuits, those spikes, her first solo performance ever on Letterman's *Late Show*, Mrs. Elliott sighs. "I don't know *who* pushed her out there."

It was that little girl on the trash cans who perversely refused to discard her delusions with her baby dolls, as her mother had hoped. The skirmishes began during her senior year in high school, when that awful question "What next?" jumped between them. Her mother favored college or the military. They went at it for months once Missy announced her intent to go to New York and break into showbiz. She and three girlfriends had a little group called Fay Z, which became Sista. They had a tape full of those story songs that Missy had concocted with Tim Mosley (now known as her collaborator Timbaland), a local guy who was able to conjure the quirky change-up beats that moved as fast as her thoughts.

Missy says if she closes her eyes and thinks about their first meeting—arranged by a mutual rapper pal, Magoo—she sees great big hands on a little tiny Casio keyboard. Timbaland's twitchy paws coaxed monster tracks from that discount Japanese mini-motherboard. "Hand claps," Missy remembers. "Whistles. Even with that little Casio, he'd think, well how could you get *this* sound?" Timbaland remembers groove at first sight: "Man, her songs were so beautiful to my tracks. I thought it was just a brilliant thing."

"We goin' to New York!"

Four once-giddy black girls are staring glumly at more ice and snow than they've ever seen, remembering how they screamed with joy in the hotel corridor back home the night in 1992 that singer/producer Devante, in Portsmouth with his group Jodeci, listened to them sing. Devante agreed to bring them to the city, and they went the very next week. Sista, they called themselves, all great expectations and "messed-up" hair weaves. So what are they doing now in . . . Rochester? The snow is 4 feet high; the funky rented house is stuffy with the smell of Popeye's extra-crispy, hair relaxer and unrequited ambition. What is Devante thinking? Is studio time so much cheaper up here? They've been working for months but the record hasn't come out, it's becoming clear that the record is never coming out. In the middle of the night they can hear Missy crying to Mama on the phone again, about the cold, the snow . . . "Mommy, I'm coming come."

Sista were history, and Missy was seriously depressed when she got home, her mother recalls. But she wouldn't give it up. Again, she told her mother, "Mommy, I just got to *go.*" Pat Elliott voiced her worries to her sister, who pointed out that despite coming up on such a bumpy road, Missy had proved she could resist the clichéd but persistent perils: "My sister said better let her go and find out if this is for her. She hasn't brought a baby home to you, she's not on drugs. She's not a bad kid."

So Missy lit out again and lived like a gypsy, camping out with acquaintances in New Jersey and New York, peddling songs with Timbaland on the strength of the cuts they'd placed on Jodeci's album, *Diary of a Mad Band.* They turned out make-do music, take it further than what you've got *at the moment* music. He'd hand her a track and walk off; she'd have a song in ten minutes, scrawling the lyrics on coffee cups, Wendy's wrappers, humming a melody, rushing into the booth to sing it to the track.

They began to build their effective sound collages, part subliminal life sounds—bug noises, baby cries, fatback soul samples—and part direct, staccato soliloquies that ignored the numbing clichés of rap rhythm and rhyme. Finally, the pair hooked up with Aaliyah, R. Kelly's teen protégé. They got a number-one hit for her ("If Your Girl Only Knew") and more work, with SWV, 702, Gina Thompson, Ginuwine. Missy's guest spots— notably her famous "hee hee haw haw" rap for Gina Thompson's "The Things You Do"—were pulling her closer and closer to the solo spotlight, but for a long time, she hung back.

Even when Missy signed the songwriting and Gold Mind label deal with Elektra in 1996, Rhone felt it would be a mistake to pressure her into signing as an artist as well. "I let her come to that point herself," says Rhone. "I encouraged it, I dropped hints about it. I think she realized her confidence level had grown with the success of the writing and the featured lines she was doing. I also knew that Missy didn't want to just make any kind of record. She wanted to make a statement. In order to get that vision clear, it takes some time." And when Missy said she was ready, Rhone simply said, "Let's go."

Missy was so primed that *Supa Dupa Fly* took a week to make. *Da Real World* took far longer, owing to the many obligations of *MISSY*. And now, given the mad requirements of Timbaland's solo career, it's all but impossible to corral Missy and her co-conspirator together. Sprinting down Broadway for a hastily called meeting with the pair that has been called "The Ashford and Simpson" of hip-hop, I glance up at the glassed-in MTV studio that overlooks Times Square, and there they stand, a trifle awkwardly, looking down into the street. They are here to premiere "She's a Bitch." Timbaland is in a powder blue shorts outfit with a diamond-inlaid medallion so big I can see it flash from half a block away and two stories down. Missy is in a fawn suede pants ensemble, accented with more modest ice. She has shifted her gaze north, toward Harlem, galaxies away by the look of her. Sometimes you can actually see her focus move ahead, smooth and resolute as a CD changer. *Next . . .*

The video is over by the time I get upstairs. The mood in the studio green room is celebratory, but Timbaland is a bit fretful between calls to his broker. He admits to being itchy—likes aggressive growth funds and lightning studio sessions. He says he's thinking that things have slowed for the pair as songwriters. "We had eleven number-one consecutive hits within a matter of weeks," he says. "I feel we've got to go back to that page. We've been layin' kind of low."

There's an echo of Brill Building rivalry as he voices his worries and, daily, scans the charts. If the songwriting process has gotten faster, the pace of the inevitable ripoffs has also reached warp speed. And, as is made abundantly clear on *Da Real World's* "Beat Biters," Timbaland and Missy are feeling the breath of competitors and imitators on their platinum-hung necks. Already, the partners agree, everyone else is starting to break songs down in the middle, just like in "She's a Bitch." *Beat interruptus* is a Timbaland and Missy signature; eerie change-ups midsong, sudden stops, witty reverses, hypnotic repetitions. "Beat Biters" snarls back at beat cheats: we're on to you, but fools, don't even *try* to keep up.

Timbaland says their division of labor now is much the way it was at the beginning, save for a few adjustments: "I'm moving to a different level where Missy can just sing a cappella and I can work around it. I'm trying to make our method fast . . ."

Faster than a ten-minute composition?

"I want to make it within a matter of five minutes."

In theory, speed is at the heart of popular music, especially black popular music, which has always been a jumpy, impatient form. Imbedding hooks—much the way Aretha's father, the Reverend C. L. Franklin, used his bust-a-phrase-and-repeat-it trope to implant a message—can add staying power, to a sermon or a song. And of these two collaborators, Missy is the more analytical about what she knows she must do for a hit: "I bring the realness to a song, a sexy, soulful feel—they way it's sung. My melodies are very strong in the hooks that I give them to stick out. Because if people can't remember anything in the verse, they have that hook that they can ride down the street and sing."

Or shout. "*Beep beep, who's got the keys to my Jeep. Heeheeha. Yippeeyi-ay. She's a bitch!*" . . . Infectious nonsense peppers Missy's mix. And when she writes for ingenues like Nicole or girl groups like Destiny's Child, her monster ear turns out terse girl-to-girl codes in much the way Ellie Greenwich, Cynthia Weil and Carole King did. By the dawn of 2000, Missy's stamp was instantly recognizable in the countless original songs and remixes she produced for other artists. Everyone was trying on her abrupt stops and stutters. Melody—in a fill, in a chorus—was getting stronger in her brand of hip-hop, and I asked Missy about it.

"I do think melody feels new again, " she said. "Lauryn brings that to me. We've got two different styles. Mine is more a futuristic style, and hers is more of the back in the day. And that's the good thing. When I listen to her, and I hear that back in the day, it makes me feel the songs I liked, the songs that make me happy, the songs that have feeling to them. And that's what she brings to the table. We've got different ways of handling our melodies, but they both work."

When I ask Timbaland where they are headed next, he smiles broadly and begins singing, adding the sound effects of a record skipping.

Yo bod—kkkkkkk
Yo bod—kkkdttttkkkk.
Yo bo-dyyyyy.

"That's my next style," he says. He likes the twist: Take an old familiar sound—a damaged LP, a sound now so rare you might make people jump with recognition; call it a recovered rock memory. And use it to short-circuit the normal pop expectations. Missy says they'll probably try it out on Aaliyah first; "She's like, our prototype."

Nokias are clapping shut as the greenroom party begins to break up. "Yo, don't go nowhere," Timbaland calls to Missy. Separate limos are waiting for them. But for a few minutes, they huddle, plotting the future and what it will sound like.

Kkkkkkkkk. Ktkkt . . .

Ms. Elliott reports that she's learning to feel good looking *bad*. The first time she climbed into her spiked Bitch suit, Missy looked in a mirror and startled herself. She had been watching her diet, had cut out smoking weed and started hitting the treadmill. "It was amazing," she says. "Like oh, my goodness. This is so hot. I was like oh, man, you look *good*. I'm still at it. Went to the gym yesterday and the day before that."

But this does not mean that Missy is adopting any Calista Flockheart body images. She has been losing weight at her doctor's request; there is a family history of high blood pressure and hypertension. "I'm not trying to get down to a size five or six," she says. "Just down to a size where I could be onstage and I'm not out of breath. Just a healthy size."

Beside the spike-suited *MISSY*, just Missy also makes a cameo appearance in "She's a Bitch," as a pretty woman driving a car through a tunnel, then as a rapping fox in fur. On the new album cover, Missy wears a man's dress shirt and tie—underneath a black bustier. Are we getting close to a Missy meld, where the cartoony and the fleshly can coexist on the same screen? I put the question to the only person who has seen both Missys near naked.

"Missy's come a *long* way. Now she's touching herself [when she dances onscreen]." This from stylist June Ambrose. As a matter of busi-

ness, Ambrose must inquire into a star's deepest insecurities at first meeting; it's a process she calls "total body irrigation." By now, she says she
knows Missy's limits very well. No skirts. Ever. No open toes, "though she
has beautiful feet." Then Ambrose laughs, pulling out the terrifying first
sketches for "Bitch," the ones that had Missy howling, "I ain't wearin' no
DEVIL clothes!"

She came around. Over the last three years, Ambrose has seen changes
that go beyond Missy's determined weight loss: "She'll wear undergarments
that make her feel sexier. We can now see a waist, whereas before we just
kept everything billowed out. We want to do some high fashion. I've been
giving her the collection magazines." Designer houses—this week Versace's
Versus line—have been calling to invite Missy to their runway shows. She
seems ambivalent; much of their stuff is decidedly *not* for her. And she has
her own ideas. Ambrose says that unlike so many other fashion-victim ingenues she's seen, Missy needs no day-to-day help. The powder-blue jog-
ging suits accessorized with stunning diamonds work. "I think she looks
really cute like that," says Ambrose. "*That's* Missy Elliott."

Some might argue that the "Bitch" video would have been stronger,
darker, more of an art piece without the short bursts of the new glam Missy.
But the artist disagrees. "People pretty much see me all the time on a character level," Missy says. "A lot of times when people see me in the street
they're like 'Oh, you're so pretty.' I feel like I *had* to have that shot in there.
This shows the beauty side. Just Missy in general." For the near future,
possibly a third single, she can even see "something romantic, see Missy
with the fellow in there . . ."

Ambrose just rolls her eyes and cracks, "She'll lose her mind *ten* times
before that."

Occasionally now, Missy will lose her cool, most often when confronted with boneheaded corporate glitches. "I can be the sweetest person," she says, "but I see that you're taking me lightly, it's like—
rrrrrrRRRRAAAAOOOWWW—like Linda Blair, turn that head
around!" If things get out of hand, if there are too many diva moments,
she knows she can rely on her mother to exorcise the dark side of *MISSY*
and tell her hey, do the dishes while you're at it. And when she comes
home from one of those high-floss parties—a night where the Fendi and
Fubu-clad beauties part and whisper, "There's MISSY!" and the star

crawls into bed sometime before dawn. "I go to sleep and it's like, 'Wait a minute, Missy. You can go the party and you can do your photo shoots and your interviews, but you can't make yourself stay up five minutes to say your prayers?' *He's* the one that wakes me up. *He's* the one that takes me through the day."

She says as much in the spoken religious final cut on *Da Real World*. What Sister Rosetta did on *Gospel Train* with phrasing and guitar, Missy has wrought with stinging, sexually explicit raps followed by a plea to He who knows what's really *Next*. And remembering that, no matter what the hour, Ms. Future Shock drops her knees to the floor and tells herself:

"Slow your roll, Missy."

Missy came blasting out of the box with *Da Real World*, which reached number two the week it was released, then slid disappointingly. This has disturbed her, but not overmuch. A third single, "Hot Boyz," was a mammoth hit that stayed at number one on the R&B charts for over two months; the album went platinum after all. But as summer turned to fall, then winter, there was still no tour. She just won't go. Missy's defense: She has been busy in the studio with other acts and remixes, working on her own videos. She is still completing the new home in Portsmouth, but she has no idea when she can find the time to move in.

Today we are sitting in one of the industrial-chic photo studios that honeycomb Manhattan's Chelsea Piers as Herb Ritts prepares to photograph Missy for *Vogue*; there is about a half million's worth of fur—sheared beaver, mink, chinchilla—hanging on a rack. And at this moment, there are at least half a dozen Missy compositions/productions dominating the R&B charts for delighted artists like Da Brat, Lil' Kim, Nicole, Brandy, Mariah. With all this studio work, Missy has hedged her bets against the fickleness of the market—and the surprisingly entrenched notions of female allure that can rebuff her rather advanced "manifestations." She is not surprised that people preferred the funny, cute Supa Dupa Missy to the ferocious Bitch.

"She just thinks people totally didn't get it," June Ambrose tells me as we watch the *Vogue* editor fluff a Gucci fur collar. "People loved the Missy glamour shots in that video, though. They are more susceptible to her being pretty. Puffy said to me, 'You took it too far, Money.' Like what

was *that?* He said she looked pretty, though, with her hair up. He was probably the voice of mainstream inner-city America, saying that's too Marilyn
Manson, too *out* there. For me and Missy and Hype, I loved it. I think that's
what the art form needed. I was proud of what she did."

This being the morning after the much-publicized MTV awards,
there is much to say, here amid the voluble hair-and-makeup troops. The
fine, ever-shifting line between soigné wit and crass provocateur is being
debated over cigarettes and catered lentil salad, as it was over much Cristal
at last night's after-parties. Everyone is talking about the Moment, when
Lil' Kim ascended the podium in a purple wig and gown with one perky
breast bouncing naked in the breeze, save for a sequined pastie.

Like the good style witch Glinda, Diana Ross—a woman who has
worn enough sequins to armor the USS *Intrepid*—materialized behind her
and gently flicked Kim's free-range orb with one hand and a *do-you-believe-
this?* moue. Hip-hop suffers no style police but it will respect a dyed-in-
the-mohair godmama. So Miss Ross's gesture served as a very public
Lesson: "The diva said it to Kim so eloquently," says Ambrose. "She said,
'Little one, what are you *doing?*'"

Unfazed, Kim posed a month later for the cover of *Interview* wearing
nothing but a leather helmet and stenciled-on Louis Vuitton logos. Missy
just shakes her head and smiles at her friend's antics. But she herself is no
fan dancer. Tossing aside a pair of sandals, the disgruntled *Vogue* stylista
on duty hisses, "*Well,* she won't even show her *feet.*" As Ritts finishes the
last sequence of the artist in black, fur-trimmed Gucci, Missy jumps behind the dressing-room screen and back into her bright yellow sweats. She
is in a hurry to get downstairs. "You've *got* to see my new truck," she says.

We wind our way through the river-scented parking garage in the
company of June Ambrose, who is full of car questions one might address
to a trusted mechanic. These are modern women who can discuss tire specs
and option packages with the same keen appraisal they apply to a Prada
silhouette. Style is a *total* commitment, honey. We climb into a champagne-
colored Cadillac Escalade SUV, and as Missy's fingernails—lacquered the
yellow of highway caution signs—locate an overhead switch, a voice booms
out: "Yes, Ms. Elliott. How may we assist you?" Ambrose jumps.

"Child, who and WHERE is that man?"

This is a Caddy-with-a-concierge. He has located us via satellite
tracking but he has a starched, Jeeves-ian voice. Grinning broadly, Missy

asks him for a 4-star hotel within thirty blocks and he complies—does she wish a reservation? She points to another button that summons emergency help. Having all this service at one's fingertips was a comfort at first, Missy says. She likes to drive herself, but after the first 200 miles on this buggy, she began to wonder about the implications of the leather-lined, mega-horsepower cocoon she's put herself in.

"Me and Mary J. Blige were drivin' around the other night," she says. "Mary had had a couple of drinks and we were LOUD. I mean, just being the girls, you know. Yeah, the queen bitches. This *voice* comes on."

Was Ms. Elliott in any difficulty? Did she wish some roadside assistance? A startled Missy told him no thank you, everything was cool. But soon a police cruiser appeared behind the two mouthy African-American women in the mammoth Cadillac. They were pulled over. It turned out fine—Missy, the driver, was quite sober, thank you. Still, Ambrose is squeaky with indignation: "Is this not almost the year 2000? ARE WE NOT FREE?"

"Missy," I ask, "can't you turn that thing off?"

"I thought I had. It's kinda like Big Brother, huh?"

As we have been gabbing, playing with the car's fancy options—the liquid, CD-thin TV screen that lowers for the backseat passengers, the seismic speakers—Missy's posse of *Next!* has been waiting patiently outside the car: cousins, security, a publicist. A big man toting a clutch of small, impressively logoed shopping bags shifts his weight and sighs.

"I don't know if I can turn this all off," Missy says quietly. "But I do know Missy is the *driver. MISSY!*" She twists the key and the behemoth purrs to life.

"And right now, this girl has got to *go*."

ACKNOWLEDGMENTS

I must begin with profound thanks to the women whose voices—on record, CD and interview tapes—give this book its subject matter and its life. They have endured me and my persistent inquisitions with grace and generosity. Happily, many of them can tell their stories with the same verve that sparks their music. So as much as possible, I've tried to stand back and give them the floor.

For nearly twenty years, Jann Wenner has taken fiendish delight in shipping me out on missions impossible for *Rolling Stone* ("Hey, let's see if you can get Michael Jackson to talk!"). Within that very guy-heavy enclave, Jann has always treated my work with respect, and taken the enlightened if fiscally unsound step of approving business-class flights when I was pregnant and living large. He has also given me two things in ever shorter supply these days: plenty of space for words and some of the best editors in the business to shepherd them. My thanks to them all: to Carolyn White, for helping me find and listen to my own voice; to Bob Wallace, for encouraging my mouthy forays into essay; to Robert Vare, for helping me poke around "beyond the music;" to Sid Holt for talking me off hiatus and back onto the bus; to Joe Levy for helping me negotiate the dizzying new etiquettes of hip-hop. Bob Love oversaw the special women's issue that hatched this book. He got us through that months-long marathon with a rare consideration—for the writer and the thousands of words—and a keen, unsparing eye. This book simply would not have happened without him.

I would also like to thank simpatico editors elsewhere who have paired me with some rockin' adventuresses—foremost Lisa Henricksson at *GQ* and Susan Murko at *Details*. Roberta Myers and Michael Solomon are guilty of encouraging my cranky pop philosophizing in the smart and—alas—departed *Mirabella*. Morgan Entrekin, one of publishing's remaining gentlemen, talked me into this endeavor; I deeply appreciate his act of faith. Amy Hundley, my editor at Grove/Atlantic, came late to this project but proved to be the perfect match: deft with a blue pencil and knowledgable, passionate enough about the music to nudge me into some lively girl band debates—and significant improvements. Allison Grochowski, librarian for Wenner Media, has long been the soul of patience and generosity with my research quandaries, large and small.

I know it's not politic to mention publicists; indeed, many of my worst moments have been at the hands of some self-important Gorgons of the Gate. But a small and valued minority in that profession do understand and accommodate the needs of writers seeking to actually talk to their cossetted clients. They are the rare ones who really want you to get it right. So thank you Miguel Baguer. And Kathy Schenker and her able lieutenant Luke Burland. Stacey Sanner at VH-1 managed amazing grace—and access—during Diva Days. Should Liz Rosenberg ever retire from the rigors of representing Madonna, she could kill as a standup comic—or a Mideast peace envoy.

I am grateful for some male perspectives: B. B. King helped me understand the difficulties faced by blueswomen; Clive Davis, diva enabler extraordinaire, talked long past the appointed hour about his amazing roster; the late congressman Sonny Bono volunteered a pithy tutorial on Phil Spector's glory years, Spector's girl groups and of course, Cher.

As to sweet inspiration: For years, Greil Marcus and Peter Guralnick have set a high bar for those of us given to parsing the sense and sensibility of popular music. Reading them, I became convinced that "rock journalism" could really be literature; as colleagues, I've found them encouraging and most kind. I am also beholden to two women I know only by their impeccable taste in music. I was unacquainted with deejays Rita Houston and Meg Griffin until I moved outside Manhattan a few years back and began to spend too many hours piloting the mom-mobile through the southern Connecticut hills. Their very distinct voices enlivened National Public

Radio station WFUV (at Fordham University); listening to them, I have recognized kindred spirits hopelessly mad for the music. Plainly put, on soccer and swim team days, their commentary and wonderful playlists have kept me from going nuts. Better still, I have been introduced to artists' voices—many of them female—that I might never have found. I have the same wish for Meg and Rita as I do for many other standout women in rock: Could somebody please amp up their signal? I hate to lose them in the hills.

A day just doesn't set up right unless I check in with my dear friend Flip Brophy, who is also my agent at Sterling Lord Literistic. You want Flip in your pilot house during the perfect storm, personal or professional. I can't remember life without her; I wouldn't want to try.

Good friends and relations often bear the greatest burdens during the messy birthing of a book. And so, for patience, advice, a laugh, a sympathetic ear, all blessings on Barbara and Robert Denninger, Don Kukuc and the late Moon Wallace, Jeanie and Gary Zwonitzer, soul survivors Sam and Joyce Moore, Sally Boyd and Wayne Watkins, pep girls Lisa and Marne Henricksson, Russ Shorto, David and Michaelyn Mitchell, Richard Ben Cramer, Mark Jacobson, Nancy Cardozo, Gil Schwartz, Sue Mittenthal, Harry Jaffe, Peter McQuaid, Alan Richman, Lettie Teague, Richard and Rosalind Baronio, Jane Leavy and Peter Isakoff, and, here in the Weston woods, my stalwart girlfriends Lucia Morgin and Ellen Weyrauch. For covered dishes, kid care, and sympathy, thanks to good neighbors Britt and Steve Pendergast.

Family music hours—with my husband, Mark Zwonitzer, and our children, Sam and Lila—are freewheeling, frequent and essential. We listen to everything from the Louvin Brothers to Queen Latifah, Sam & Dave and Lucinda Williams; sometimes we dance. Our intimate and absolute joy in those moments shows me, again and again, the redemptive powers of song. And of love, of course. I think the home team may soon forgive me for all those inconvenient road trips and I thank them for their sweet forbearance. Trying to properly thank Mark would probably get as overwrought as a bad country song, so I'll just stick with the title of his Kansas grandpa's favorite: "Most of All I Love You 'Cause You're You."

This book is dedicated to the memory of my father, John Kukuc, who died as it was being written. Years ago, when I first started in this unladylike line of work, he used to keep a photo of me with James Brown in his locker at work "because the guys just don't believe me." He was not a talkative man, but it was his way of saying he was proud of his little girl's rock and roll career—if a tad puzzled. He and my mother, Rose, now managing a brave solo, have shown me the sustenance of true harmony (they were married for over a half a century). I honor and thank them both.

BIBLIOGRAPHY

Albertson, Chris. *Bessie*. New York: Stein and Day, 1972.

Barnum, P. T. "The Jenny Lind Enterprise," in *Barnum's Own Story*. New York: The Viking Press, 1927.

Betrock, Alan. *Girl Groups, The Story of a Sound*. New York: Delilah, 1982.

Bono, Sonny. *The Beat Goes On*. New York: Pocket Books, 1991.

Cantor, Norman F., and Michael S. Werthman, eds. *The History of Popular Culture, Vols. 1 and 2*. New York: Macmillan, 1968.

Carr, Ian, Digby Fairweather, and Brian Priestly. *Jazz-The Rough Guide*. London: Rough Guides, 1995.

Cash, Johnny, with Patrick Carr. *Johnny Cash, the Autobiography*. New York: HarperCollins, 1997.

Cheatham, Kitty. "The Saga of the Immortal Jenny Lind." *Bridgeport Life*, 29 April 1933.

Cromelin, Richard. "The Go-Go's Again." *L.A. Times*, 25 March 1990.

Crowe, Cameron. "Joni Mitchell: The *Rolling Stone* Interview." *Rolling Stone*, 26 July 1979.

———. "Linda Ronstadt, Multi-Million Dollar Woman." *Rolling Stone*, 2 December 1976.

Dahl, Linda. *Stormy Weather: The Music and Lives of a Century of Jazz Women*. New York: Limelight Editions, 1989.

Dalton, David. *Piece of My Heart, The Life, Times and Legend of Janis Joplin*. New York: St. Martin's Press, 1985.

De Curtis, Anthony. "Whitney Houston: Down and Dirty. The *Rolling Stone* Interview." *Rolling Stone*, 10 June, 1993.

Fair, S. S. "Joan Jett." *New York Times Magazine*, September 26, 1999.

Faithfull, Marianne, with David Dalton. *Faithfull*. New York: Little, Brown, 1994.

Flippo, Chet. "Janis Reunes at Jefferson High." *Rolling Stone*, 17 September 1970.

Fong-Torres, Ben. "Emmylou Harris: Whole Wheat Honky Tonk." *Rolling Stone,* 23 February 1978.

Gleason, Ralph J. "Mama Willie Mae Thornton: 'The Blues Satisfies the Ear.'" *Rolling Stone,* 22 June, 1968.

Gordon, Beverly. "American Denim: Blue Jeans and Their Multiple Layers of Meaning." In *Dress and Popular Culture,* ed. Patricia A. Cunningham and Susan Voso Lab. Bowling Green, Ohio: Bowling Green State University Popular Press, 1991.

Guccione, Bob, Jr. "The Real Madonna: Live to Tell," January 1996.

Gutterman, Jimmy. "Honky Tonk Girl," liner notes for *The Loretta Lynn Collection,* MCA Records.

Harris, Neil. *Humbug: The Art of P. T. Barnum.* New York: Little Brown, 1973.

Henke, James. "Bonnie Raitt: The *Rolling Stone* Interview." *Rolling Stone,* 3 May 1990.

Hirschberg, Lynn. "Cher Wants To Be Taken Seriously." *Rolling Stone,* 29 March 1984.

Houston, Cissy, with Jonathan Silverman. *How Sweet the Sound.* New York: Doubleday, 1998.

Kundhardt, Philip B., Philip B. Kundhardt III, and Peter W. Kunhardt. *P. T. Barnum, America's Greatest Showman.* New York: Knopf, 1995.

Lind, Jenny. *Jenny Lind, the Artist, 1820–1851,* ed. Henry Scott Holland and W. S. Rockstro. London: John Murray, 1893.

Loder, Kurt. "Eurythmics: Sweet Dreams Come True." *Rolling Stone,* 29 September 1983.

Marcus, Greil. *Invisible Nation, Bob Dylan's Basement Tapes.* New York: Henry Holt and Company, 1997.

McDonnell, Evelyn. Joan Jett interview. *Rolling Stone,* 13 November 1997.

McLuhan, Marshall. *Understanding Media.* New York: Graw-Hill, 1964.

Madonna. "Madonna's Private Diaries," *Vanity Fair,* November 1996,

Mailer, Norman. "Like a Lady." *Esquire,* August 1994.

Margolick, David. *Strange Fruit: Billie Holiday, Cafe Society, and the Early Cry for Civil Rights.* Running Press, 2000.

Mewborn, Brant. "Eurythmics Unmasked." *Rolling Stone,* 24 October 1985.

O'Brien, Lucy. *She Bop.* London: Penguin Books, 1995.

O'Dair, Barbara, ed. *The Rolling Stone Book of Women in Rock.* New York: Random House, 1997.

Okamoto, David. "Come and Go-Go." *Dallas Morning News,* 6 December 1994.

Palmer, Robert. "Recharging the Blues in San Francisco." *Rolling Stone,* 18 October 1979.

Panassie, Hugues. *Hot Jazz.* New York: M. Witmark & Sons, 1936.

Shindler, Merrill. "The Wilson Sisters Talk Heart and Heart." *Rolling Stone,* 28 July 1977.

Shultz, Gladys Denny. *Jenny Lind, The Swedish Nightingale.* Philadelphia: Lippincott, 1962.

Spector, Ronnie, with Vince Waldron. *Be My Baby: How I Survived Mascara, Miniskirts, and Madness.* New York: Harmony Books, 1990.

"The Swedish Nightingale," editorial in *The Christian Science Monitor,* 11 August 1955.

Turner, Tina, with Kurt Loder. *I, Tina.* New York: Avon, 1987.

Wagenknecht, Edward C. *Seven Daughters of the Theater*. University of Oklahoma Press.

Ware, W. Porter, and Thaddeus Lockhard, Jr. *P. T. Barnum Presents Jenny Lind*. Baton Rouge: Louisiana State University Press, 1980.

Waters, Ethel. *His Eye Is on the Sparrow*. New York: Doubleday & Company, 1950.

Welding, Peter, and Toby Brown, eds. *Bluesland: Portraits of Twelve Major American Blues Musicians*. New York: Dutton, 1991.

Westervelt, Leonidas. "Adventuring with Jenny Lind." *New York Historical Society's Quarterly Bulletin*, October 1942.

Wild, David. "A Conversation with Joni Mitchell." *Rolling Stone*, 30 May 1991.

Williams, Martin, ed. *Art of Jazz*. New York: DaCapo Paperbacks, 1959.

Wilson, Mary, with Ahrgus Julliard and Patricia Romanowki. *Dreamgirl, My Life as a Supreme*. New York: St. Martin's Press, 1987.

Varga, George. "For Laurie Anderson, the Message Is Multimedia." *San Diego Union-Tribune*, 3 June 1984.

Young, Charles M. "Visions of Patti." *Rolling Stone*, 27 July 1978.

Zwonitzer, Mark, and Charles Hirschberg. Unpublished interviews with Carter family members, 1996–2000.

PERMISSIONS

INDEX